Rethinking the New Left

RETHINKING THE NEW LEFT

An Interpretative History

Van Gosse

palgrave
macmillan

RETHINKING THE NEW LEFT
© Van Gosse, 2005.

First published in 2005 by
PALGRAVE MACMILLAN™
175 Fifth Avenue, New York, N.Y. 10010 and
Houndmills, Basingstoke, Hampshire, England RG21 6XS
Companies and representatives throughout the world.

PALGRAVE MACMILLAN is the global academic imprint of the Palgrave Macmillan division of St. Martin's Press, LLC and of Palgrave Macmillan Ltd. Macmillan® is a registered trademark in the United States, United Kingdom and other countries. Palgrave is a registered trademark in the European Union and other countries.

ISBN 1–4039–6694–X hardback
ISBN 1–4039–6695–8 paperback

Library of Congress Cataloging-in-Publication Data

Gosse, Van.
    Rethinking the New Left : an interpretative history / by Van Gosse.
       p. cm.
    Includes bibliographical references and index.
    ISBN 1–4039–6694–X (alk. paper)—ISBN 1–4039–6695–8 (pbk. : alk. paper)
      1. Radicalism—United States—History—20th century.
    2. New Left—United States—History—20th century. 3. Social
    movements—United States—History—20th century. 4. United
    States—History—1945– I. Title.

HN90.R3G66 2005
303.48′4′097309045—dc22   2004060109

A catalogue record for this book is available from the British Library.

Design by Newgen Imaging Systems (P) Ltd., Chennai, India.

First edition: October 2005

10 9 8 7 6 5 4 3 2 1

Printed in the United States of America.

Table of Contents

Acknowledgements

This book was made possible in large part by the Woodrow Wilson International Center for Scholars, where I enjoyed a fellowship in 2000–2001. I thank Rosemary Lyon, Kimberly Conner, and the rest of the WWIC staff for their gracious and highly professional support.

It was completed while I was teaching at Franklin and Marshall College. I thank my chairs (Ben McRee, Ted Pearson, and Abby Schrader), my department as a whole, and Provost Bruce Pipes and Dean Ann Steiner for their unstinting support. I owe a special thanks to Peggy Bender, administrator of the History Department, who makes all things possible.

Various people read parts of the manuscript over the years, or offered useful guidance, including Max Elbaum, Lise Vogel, Jeffrey Escoffier, James Miller, Ellen Schrecker, and Allen Smith. None of them are responsible in any way for its errors of fact or idiosyncrasies of interpretation.

Special thanks also go to Patricia Rossi, who suggested I bring the manuscript to Palgrave, and Brendan O'Malley, a first-class editor who made it considerably better. As always, I express my appreciation to Johanna Gosse, my brilliant daughter, and her brilliant mother, Eliza Jane Reilly.

This book is dedicated to Jack O'Dell, whose life has transcended the left in the twentieth century—old, new, and newer. From him I have learned about patience and the long view. We need more Americans like him.

Van Gosse
April 2005

Preface: Why This is not Another "Sixties Book"

Since the late 1980s, an extraordinary number of books have been published about that nebulous decade or era we call "the Sixties." Clearly there is a demand, and clearly, there is much to say. Still, I feel considerable unease about this cottage industry, even though I have contributed to it with a recent volume co-edited with Richard Moser, *The World the Sixties Made: Politics and Culture in Recent America* (Temple University Press, 2003).

My concerns are twofold, and both are reflected in this book's focus not on a period, but on the collection of movements, episodically united, that made up the New Left. First, an examination of a period in this country's history through temporal parameters is almost always a short-term solution, soon made anachronistic. Such works make the impossible claim of capturing the entirety of an era. How many books simply describing "the Twenties," "the Thirties," or "the Forties" have survived? Indeed, even this nomenclature suggests a common assumption about which century one is describing, which seems quite dated as we move into a scary new world post-2001. Of course, books about the American Revolution, Reconstruction, the Great Depression, or the Cold War will remain essential to how we interpret the past, but those topics have a certain specificity which "the Sixties" lacks. Simply put, the poor decade cannot carry the freight—it's at best a convenience, a political trope, and trying to burden it with the whole weight of social change in the post-World War II era does not work. Inevitably, the best historians feel compelled to widen their scope as they attempt to write a comprehensive general history where there is no self-evident beginning or ending, no Fort Sumter, Pearl Harbor, or Black Friday. The result is that more and more historians of the Sixties now try to balance social movements on the left with those on the right, massive change with underlying continuity, and so on. To what end? One solution would be to accept that the Sixties, however one dates them, are really a phase in the history of Cold War America, part of a period that begins approximately 1945–1947, and runs to 1989–1991. But if one does not want to write a general history, with all its difficulties of compression and generalization, the alternative is to focus on a particular dynamic of the period, and that is what I have attempted to do here.

My goal in this book is to offer a new synthesis of older and recent scholarship on all of the movements of the New Left, stretching back to the post-World

War II years, and forward into the 1970s. This brings to the fore my second concern with "Sixties" books—that they require a temporal shortening and highlighting of those events, movements, and personalities that fit neatly into the purely abstract border of 1960 at one end, and 1970 at the other. Again and again, this decadal (to coin a word) mystification has contributed to the elevation of a particular wing of the New Left, its white student vanguard, while pushing other, larger movements into the background. Since I have made this argument many times elsewhere, I will not belabor it, but it is vital to acknowledge that the New Left began earlier and lasted longer than a focus on the Kennedy and Johnson years will permit.

Any book of this sort can offer only summary accounts of major events and a compressed analysis at the level of national politics, leaving out enormous local variations. I have also chosen to examine each movement in terms of its own inner development, which at best reproduces the enormously diverse and plural character of the New Left, but also downplays how movements overlapped with each other and the creative tensions between them. However, I think chronological approaches to the New Left suffer even more, turning into lists of one thing after another, year-by-year. In fact, most activists *did* have a primary allegiance to a particular movement, and, focusing on each movement's distinctive trajectory is the clearest way to narrate what happened.

The reader will find here an argument for a longer, broader view of what constituted American radicalism at the height of the Cold War. But this argument is necessarily conditional because the scholarship upon which it relies is itself so provisional; entire movements, like gay and lesbian liberation, are vastly under-studied. What will be needed eventually, when much more research into local movements and less-celebrated organizations is at hand, is a complete, probably multivolume, history of radicalism in the Cold War era, from the roller-coaster years after World War II—the Indian summer of the old Communist and progressive left—to the steady-state movement mobilizing of the later 1970s and 1980s, framed by defeat in Vietnam, the rise of the New Right, and the so-called "culture wars." Until then, this a book for those who did not live through the Sixties, or who find current accounts insufficient. At least in compact form, it's all here, and that is perhaps something new.

Chapter 1

DEFINING THE NEW LEFT

Is this America? The land of the free and the home of the brave? Where we have to sleep with our telephones off the hook, because our lives be threatened daily?

> —Fannie Lou Hamer, Mississippi Freedom Democratic Party leader,
> Speech to the Credentials Committee,
> Democratic National Convention, August 1964

What kind of a system is it that justifies the U.S. or any country seizing the destinies of the Vietnamese people and using them callously for our own purpose? What kind of a system is it that disenfranchises people in the South, leaves millions upon millions of people throughout the country impoverished and excluded from the mainstream and promise of American society, that creates faceless and terrible bureaucracies and makes those the place where people spend their lives and do their work, that consistently puts material values before human values— and still persists in calling itself free and still persists in finding itself fit to police the world? . . . We must name that system. We must name it, describe it, analyze it, understand it, and change it.

> —Paul Potter, President of Students for a Democratic Society, speech at the
> April 1965 rally against the war in Vietnam

We define the best interests of women as the best interests of the poorest, most insulted, most despised, most abused woman on earth. Her lot, her suffering and abuse is the threat that men use against all of us to keep us in line. She is what all women fear being called, fear being treated as and yet what we really all are in the eyes of men. She is Everywoman: ugly, dumb (dumb broad, dumb cunt), bitch, nag, hag, whore, fucking and breeding machine, mother of us all. Until

Everywoman is free, no woman will be free. When her beauty and knowledge is revealed and seen, the new day will be at hand.
—Statement of Purpose, New York Radical Women, 1967

From the 1950s through the 1970s, a series of social movements surged across America, radically changing the relationship between white people and people of color, how the U.S. government conducts foreign policy, and the popular consensus regarding gender and sexuality. Together, these movements redefined the meaning of democracy in America. Indeed, a commitment to a radical form of democracy, and "power to the people," is what linked them together. They constituted a New Left, a "movement of movements" that was considerably greater than the sum of its parts.

There are many fine studies of the movements that made up the New Left and the politics of the time, as well as of "the Movement" (as it was sometimes called) in specific towns and cities. The full history of the New Left impinges upon everything significant that happened in the United States in these years—the presidencies of Eisenhower, Kennedy, Johnson, and Nixon; the Cold War and the terrible "hot war" in Vietnam; and the intimacies of family life. This book is an attempt at synthesis and interpretation, focusing on the social movements themselves. It presumes that, however constrained by circumstance, resources, and ideology, people do attempt to make their own history. The history of the New Left is an example of how they succeeded, and how their success marked a radical change in this country's direction.

WHAT THE NEW LEFT ACHIEVED:
A DEMOCRACY—IF WE CAN KEEP IT

Looking back at the legal, social, cultural, and electoral transformations that took place in barely twenty years, the New Left's achievements seem quite extraordinary—if one keeps in mind the America that existed before.

In states ranging from Maryland to Texas, a way of life based on white supremacy (the legal, economic, and physical subjugation of African Americans) was broken up by nonviolent mass protest in the decade after 1955. At the same time, black activists and their white allies in the North and West organized systematic challenges to pervasive *de facto* discrimination. Facing enormous pressure, in 1964 and 1965 Congress enacted first a Civil Rights Act making illegal any kind of racial, ethnic, religious, or gender-based discrimination in employment and all public accommodations, and then a Voting Rights Act striking at disfranchisement by race in all fifty states. By the late 1960s, blacks were voting in large numbers in the South, the walls of official segregation mandating separate-and-unequal schools were crumbling, and in the North black people had begun taking over city governments. Inspired by the black freedom movement, other movements for racial equality spread across America in the late 1960s, demanding political power and dignity for Mexican Americans (Chicanos), Puerto Ricans, Native Americans, and Asian Americans. Elected office ceased to be an exclusively white prerogative. Thousands of blacks, Latinos, and Asians entered politics. Because of new opportunities and government programs to combat discrimination in education and employment, millions of people of color achieved middle-class security. And the open racism that had always been part of American life was forced underground, though it hardly disappeared. For the first time in its history, the United States officially became color-blind.

An equally momentous change took place in how Americans perceived the actions of their government around the world. For generations, a small elite of upper-class white men controlled U.S. foreign and military policy—how the most powerful nation in history used its enormous power. After World War II, there was overwhelming public support for a military strategy to contain communism and other revolutionary upsurges anywhere on the globe. The only significant dissent came from hardline conservatives who felt the United States should risk all-out war to destroy communism in the Soviet Union and China.

In the late 1950s, the danger of a nuclear holocaust spurred a new peace movement demanding restrictions on nuclear weapons. Other Americans reacted positively to the revolution against a U.S.–backed dictatorship in Cuba, demanding "fair play" for the new government of Fidel Castro. Meanwhile, presidents Eisenhower and Kennedy quietly intervened in Vietnam's civil war between nationalist Communists and right-wing, pro-U.S. forces. In 1965, to prevent a Communist victory, President Lyndon Johnson sent a massive army to Vietnam. To Johnson's surprise, this full-scale ground war provoked a nationwide antiwar movement, which tore apart the Democratic Party and forced him from office. With its armed forces locked in a stalemate and demoralized, the United States was compelled to withdraw from Vietnam by 1973. The antiwar movement, which spread into Congress, the churches, and other important institutions, had demonstrated the impact of grassroots citizen protest on foreign policy. Ever since, what President Richard Nixon denounced as the "Vietnam syndrome" has acted as a potent brake on American interventionism.

The final challenge to established authority was twofold. Women challenged patriarchy—the right of all men to rule over women, and some men to rule over other men. Gay men and lesbians challenged the entire apparatus of normative heterosexuality that undergirded patriarchy. Earlier in the century, a powerful feminist movement had thrived, but by the 1950s feminism was mocked. It survived underground, in women's professional groups and trade unions. By the early 1960s, however, women were questioning their exclusion from "men's" jobs, higher education, and politics, and initiated a civil rights movement of their own. At the same time, young women active in the black freedom and student movements analyzed their confinement to supporting roles. Inspired by the call for Black Power, in the later 1960s they started a Women's Liberation movement through local groups emphasizing "consciousness raising." By the 1970s, the new feminist movement had grown enormously into multiple, separate feminisms of white, black, and Latina women. Within a few years, legal codes were amended to end discrimination and enforce reproductive freedom, as embodied in the Supreme Court's 1973 *Roe v. Wade* decision legalizing abortion.

Meanwhile, a related movement demanding dignity and legal protections for gay men and lesbians gathered force, bursting onto the national scene after rioting against police harassment broke out at New York's Stonewall Inn in June 1969. Gay Liberation took off nationwide, and then rapidly turned toward challenging discrimination and building political influence in the 1970s. From a stigmatized, invisible minority, gay people suddenly emerged and "came out" into the streets.

Taken together, these movements represent the essence of those years we call, somewhat inaccurately, "the 1960s." And because each sought to overturn existing structures of racial, gender, and economic privilege in favor of a radical vision of equality and democracy, they are defined as movements of the left. Collectively, they called themselves the New Left to underline their separation from the Old Left of the century's first half, based in the labor movement and focused on the struggle of workers against capitalists. And collectively, they built a new democratic order, based on the legally enforceable civil equality of all people, which has survived and extended itself since the sixties—even as the New Right born during those same years mounted its own massive "movement of movements" that surged to power in the 1980s and 1990s.[1]

WHY A *NEW* LEFT, AND WHERE DID IT COME FROM?

It is important to specify clearly at the outset what this book means by the term New Left (the original usage was by former British Communists in the late 1950s, who were seeking an alternative to the model of a hierarchical

---

[1] See my essay, "Postmodern America: A New Democratic Order in a Second Gilded Age," in Gosse and Moser, eds., *The World the Sixties Made*.

political party). In the United States, the term was used in an inclusive manner for most of the 1960s to encompass the black, student, antiwar, and other movements. Later, when historians began writing about the period in the 1980s and 1990s, many defined the New Left as just one of the movements of that time, limiting its scope to young whites in the Students for a Democratic Society (SDS). In the view of these scholars, the white-student New Left coexisted alongside all the other radical causes. However, it is highly problematic to make age, whiteness, and student status the defining characteristics of the New Left; however unintended, the consequence is to put those white youth at the center of the narrative, with other movements at the margins. Certainly, young people of all races played a central role in activism, and predominated in movements like Black Power and Women's Liberation. Often they served as the shock troops of the larger New Left, as in the 1964 Mississippi Freedom Summer and the Berkeley Free Speech movement that same year. Gripping, televised images allowed the news media to cast radicalism as a generational battle, a perception shared by many on all sides. But too many key activists from the 1950s through the 1970s were over thirty, or even fifty, to permit us to equate the New Left solely with a "youth revolt." The typical local leader of the antiwar or Civil Rights movements was a middle-aged woman or a Protestant minister, not a college student.

While recognizing that the term "New Left" was always ambiguous, this book returns to the original and more inclusive definition as a "movement of movements" encompassing all of the struggles for fundamental change from the early 1950s roughly to 1975.[2] This broader definition allows us to focus upon the connections between different forms of activism—for instance, how civil rights organizing in the South radicalized some whites, who then went on to lead the antiwar and women's movements. All of these movements overlapped, and each saw itself as part of a challenge to the established order. Therefore, it seems valid to assign them equal shares in what the New Left did and did not accomplish.

The next task is to trace the New Left's origins. First and foremost, it was a confrontation with the existing political, social, and cultural consensus in American life during the 1950s. Politically, it questioned the premises of what scholars call *Cold War liberalism*, the prevailing ideology linking a bipartisan majority of Democrats and moderate Republicans in a commitment to New Deal–style big government at home and aggressive anticommunism abroad.

[2] For a fuller discussion of how the term New Left came into usage in the United States, and how until the late 1960s it was used broadly to encompass all of the radical movements of the time, see Van Gosse, "A Movement of Movements: The Definition and Periodization of the New Left," in Roy Rosenzweig and Jean-Christophe Agnew, eds., *A Companion to Post-1945 America* (London: Blackwell, 2002), pp. 277–302.

Socially, it confronted the deep, enduring inequalities built into America's history—the second-class status of African Americans and other people of color; the economic marginality and powerlessness of women; the hatred and contempt directed at homosexual men and women; the ostracization and selective repression employed against political dissenters; and the invisibility of the poor. Finally, the New Left was also a cultural revolt, a decentralized, flamboyant upsurge against the new, affluent suburban way of life in postwar America. Whether as Beatnik folksingers, civil rights protesters, or "homophile" activists for gay rights, New Leftists refused to play by the rules, and that refusal became overtly political. Chapter 2 describes the Cold War politics and middle-class conservatism of the 1950s that, in combination with the social changes resulting from World War II, stimulated the New Left's many movements.

The assertion of a "new" left presumes that there was an "old" left preceding it. Yet many writers have discussed the so-called Old Left only to emphasize how the "newness" of the New Left discarded everything that came before. This perspective ignores the deep continuity between the movements of the New Left and the diverse Marxist, radical, and pacifist organizations that managed to survive during the Cold War, despite considerable repression. While the New Left's focus on radical democracy and its diffuse, decentralized character were genuinely new it had deep roots in the fragmented movements of the apparently outdated Old Left. As we shall see in chapter 3, these organizations influenced the development of the New Left throughout its history.

RADICAL REFORM, CULTURAL REVOLUTION, AND THE MANY COUNTERCULTURES

Two final points need to be made about this book's focus on the New Left as a constellation of overlapping but distinct movements. First, the history of the New Left cannot be neatly confined to the ten years between 1960 and 1970; I see its history as broken into two distinct phases, each roughly a decade long. This book follows that periodization, covering first 1955 to 1965, when radical dissent slowly re-emerged as a current in American life, and then 1965 to 1975, when a militant, vastly larger New Left demolished the old system of Cold War liberalism. Some historians refer to the waves of radical change spread out over parts of three decades as the "long 1960s," a useful way of defining the period.

Second, amid the extraordinary diversity of New Left movements, there is one fundamental distinction to keep in mind. Certain of these movements functioned with explicit and immediate policy goals, which may have been very radical, but could be met by specific governmental actions. To the extent those goals were met, the movements ceased to exist, or at best transformed themselves into something new. One example of this kind of movement seeking *radical reform* was the Civil Rights movement, which demanded federal action (binding legislation or judicial rulings backed up executive force where necessary) to abolish discrimination and segregation and suppress the various mechanisms used to keep black people from voting. Another example is the anti-Vietnam War movement, which for eight years reiterated its call for "Out Now!," the withdrawal of all U.S. military forces from Southeast Asia. Eventually these movements met their goals and then rapidly dissipated, although significant segments of those movements extended their dissenting activism into new areas. In both of these cases, the movement's history is defined by the trajectories of different national organizations, coalitions and campaigns seeking to force a confrontation with governmental power, so as to produce major policy changes.

Quite different were those movements aiming at longer-term and more diffuse *cultural revolutions* that would change the actual character of American society by abolishing an entire structure of oppression. These movements' goals could not be met by any specific government measures; typical examples were Black Power and Women's Liberation, which profoundly altered the consciousness of millions of Americans and instigated massive social changes, without ever defining themselves through the achievement of specific reforms, or coming together in structured national coalitions or campaigns. Highly localized, focused often on charismatic personalities (writers and orators rather than organizers), constantly expanding into new areas of life, it is much harder to say when these movements ended. However, their achievements are clear.

Finally, there is a major part of the "long 1960s" which this book only barely touches: the ongoing liberalization of American culture and society. As old standards of propriety and hierarchy were relaxed, a vastly greater array of intellectual, artistic, spiritual, and pleasurable experiences and pursuits became available, from religion to music to organic food to recreational drugs. Often, this was the environment in which radicals operated, and the countercultural search for new experiences brought many people into contact with these various movements. The mass media marketed a crude image of radicalism as synonymous with "hippies," the stereotype of alienated white youth. In fact, there were many countercultures overlapping with the many radical movements, and when one looks at Women's and Gay Liberation, or Black, Brown, Red, and Yellow Power, it is hard to say where politics ends and culture begins. Whether in a new, open understanding of sexuality, the extraordinary explosion of creativity in popular music, or the development of a distinctive Hollywood Left, culture was a vital aspect of the long wave of radicalization from the 1950s on. In this book's concluding chapter, I will discuss how the counterculture connected to the New Left at various points, and how during the 1970s—just as the movements of the left became part of a new, more democratic political order—the various countercultures merged into the mainstream of American society to create something quite new.

Chapter 2

AMERICA IN THE 1950s: "THE BEST OF ALL POSSIBLE WORLDS"

At the present moment in world history nearly every nation must choose between alternative ways of life. The choice is too often not a free one. One way of life is based upon the will of the majority, and is distinguished by free institutions . . . . The second way of life is based upon the will of a minority forcibly imposed upon the majority. It relies upon terror and oppression . . . . I believe that it must be the policy of the United States to support free peoples who are resisting attempted subjugation by armed minorities or by outside pressures.

—President Harry S Truman, Speech to Joint Session of Congress,
March 1947

[T]he State Department, which is one of the most important government departments, is thoroughly infested with Communists. I have in my hand fifty-seven cases of individuals who would appear to be either card-carrying members or certainly loyal to the Communist Party, but who nevertheless are still helping to shape our foreign policy.

—Senator Joseph McCarthy, Speech in Wheeling, West Virginia,
February 9, 1950

These have been the years of conformity and depression. A stench of fear has come out of every pore of American life, and we suffer from a collective failure of

nerve. The only courage, with rare exceptions, that we have been witness to, has
been the courage of isolated people.

—Norman Mailer, *"The White Negro,"* 1957

Two contrasting narratives sum up the paradox of the 1950s: on the one hand,
marvelous consumer abundance and the realization of the "American Dream"
for millions of families; on the other, political anxiety and enforced unity, all
under the shadow of the Cold War. Two images are often used to represent
this incongruity, that of new suburban lawns all over America being dug up
to build bomb shelters, and of happy, well-fed children learning to "duck and
cover" in their classrooms as a futile protection against Soviet nuclear attack.

To understand the radical social movements that made up the New Left,
we have to first understand the 1950s, when America seemed triumphant and
united. Much of the New Left's passionate rebelliousness was a reaction to
the authoritarian style of 1950s politics and culture. Ultimately, however, the
New Left's origins can be traced to the sweeping social changes brought about
by the wartime mobilization of 1941–1945, which penetrated into every level
and crevice of American society with profoundly disruptive effects.

COLD WAR LIBERALISM AND THE POLITICS OF
PROSPERITY AND CONSENSUS

There are a few dominant facts about life in the United States during the 1950s
that are so familiar, they have become clichés. Even now, most Americans
associate those years with great material affluence, social caution and political consensus, and aggressive anticommunism at home and abroad.

In this case, most historians are in agreement with popular opinion,
because the clichés are rooted in reality. America *was* the most prosperous
nation in the world, with no significant economic competitors. The white
majority reached a level of comfort and disposable income never seen before
in any country. From 1946 to 1964, the United States underwent the most
sustained period of economic growth in world history, effectively tripling the
average income of Americans. Any white male high-school graduate could
reasonably expect to support a family with his paycheck, to own a home, a
car, and plenty of other goods, and to send his children to college. Given that
only a few years before, Americans had faced a crippling depression in which
more than a quarter of adults were unemployed, this middle-class lifestyle
seemed miraculous. Up until World War II, the middle class had been a
distinct minority in America. Now, thanks to unprecedented government
subsidies, millions of veterans took advantage of the G.I. Bill to go to college.

The quadrupling of university enrollments in a single generation was paralleled by a boom in home construction and home ownership, mainly in vast new suburbs outside of the major cities, again subsidized by government loan guarantees.

Using government funds and policies to intervene in the economy and raise the living standards of ordinary people is the essence of what conservatives denounce as "big government liberalism," but both Republicans and Democrats knew these programs were overwhelmingly popular with voters. Only a minority of conservatives in both parties continued to rail against Social Security and government aid to education as "creeping socialism." In terms of domestic policy, therefore, this is considered a liberal era, even if this version of liberalism had conservative political consequences: the rapid consolidation of a suburban, middle-class, white electorate as the largest bloc of voters. There was no deliberate conspiracy to tame the militant working class of the Thirties and the war years, but that was the practical effect. In the words of William Levitt, the pioneer builder of new suburban housing developments, "No man who owns his own home can be a Communist."

Levitt's comment points towards the other overriding fact of postwar American society—the anticommunist imperative that ran straight through all domestic and foreign policy. During the 1930s and early 1940s, when the modern era of tax-and-spend liberal government began with Franklin Delano Roosevelt's New Deal, liberals viewed Communists and other radicals as part of the solution rather than a problem. Anticommunism remained a powerful element in U.S. political life, given the deep enmity of traditional conservatives like FBI Director J. Edgar Hoover and the southern wing of the Democratic Party, but the Great Depression created an opening for radical innovations. Leftists were welcome under the big tent of New Deal liberalism as long as they were loyal to Roosevelt, though their position was always vulnerable. Internationally, Communists in the Soviet Union and elsewhere were not seen as major threats to the United States. Not only were the Soviets relatively weak; before World War II, America had no defined international enemies, and spent little time or money on foreign affairs or military might. As late as 1939, the U.S. Army was seventeenth in the world in size.

World War II and its aftermath changed all that, leading to fundamental changes in American liberalism. Most liberals moved to the right, in terms of their willingness to contemplate structural reforms to America's political economy, and in their attitude towards activists further to their left. During the war years, liberals had seen leftists and Communists as acceptable allies for the moment in the fight against Nazi Germany. Once the Cold War heated up in 1946, with the Soviet Army occupying Eastern Europe, powerful Communist parties agitating across Western Europe, and revolutionary movements surging across Africa and Asia, Communists became the main enemy to be "contained" abroad and at home. This shift towards a resolute anticommunism was undergirded by overwhelming evidence of Soviet repression from the 1930s on. Liberals remained "liberal" in their willingness to use federal spending and tax policies to spread prosperity and correct social ills. To this traditional form of liberalism, however, they added a new commitment to a large, permanent military establishment and huge defense budgets to stimulate the economy. By the late 1950s, this militarization of the American economy and government policy led President Dwight Eisenhower to warn against the power of a "military-industrial complex" that could warp decision-making and undermine democracy. His warnings were ignored.

The dominant style of cautious, anticommunist politics was eventually dubbed *Cold War liberalism*. It was the official policy of the Democrats, the majority party from the 1930s to the 1970s. Many Republicans like Eisenhower were also Cold War liberals, favoring aggressive government spending on both the military and expensive social programs, combined with the containment of communism. Both parties still had conservative wings that opposed an activist Federal government (southern Democrats who feared civil rights legislation, Midwestern Republicans who had never accepted the New Deal), but the glue of anticommunism and prosperity cemented a powerful bipartisan consensus.

Agreement on both domestic and foreign policies meant there was little real debate about either. Eisenhower himself so perfectly represented the consensus that he could have had the nomination of either party in 1952. Throughout the 1950s, congressional Democrats like Senate Majority Leader Lyndon Johnson worked closely with Republicans like Eisenhower. In 1960 the platforms of Republican Richard Nixon and Democrat John F. Kennedy were remarkably similar in their moderation, so much so that Kennedy invented national security crises, such as a so-called "missile gap" with the Soviets, to outflank Nixon on the right. The era's leading historians, such as Richard Hofstadter and Arthur Schlesinger, Jr., maintained that the absence of political conflict was nothing new, since American politics since the Revolution had been dominated by a powerful consensus that was broken only briefly by the Civil War. Schlesinger did double-duty as a leader in the main organization of anticommunist liberals, the Americans for Democratic Action (ADA). Starting in 1949, he promoted the necessity of a pragmatic "vital center" to fight a two-front war against extremes on either right or left; he later became a prominent aide to President Kennedy. No wonder that in one of the period's most influential books, Harvard sociologist Daniel Bell argued that there had been an "end of ideology," with intellectuals giving up their historic role as critics of power.

MCCARTHYISM AND THE RED SCARE

Given the bipartisan consensus regarding most policy issues, it is surprising how much political bitterness persisted between Republicans and Democrats. The cause of this infighting was not the present, let alone the future, but settling scores from the recent past. In the name of ferreting out hidden reds plus the "pinkos" who had sheltered them, the minority Republicans smeared the Democrats, trying to discredit the New Deal and the towering figure of FDR. Their evidence derived from two sources: first, the fragmentary but accurate evidence of Soviet espionage, involving some high-level New Dealers; second, the fact that many liberal Democrats had allied themselves with radicals and Communists during the Depression and war years. This was the phenomenon dubbed McCarthyism, for the demagogic Wisconsin Republican Senator Joseph McCarthy, who attacked some of the most promi- nent men in America—including architects of the Cold War like secretaries of state George Marshall and Dean Acheson—with charges of "softness" and even treason. McCarthy's baiting of elites was especially popular with con- servative Irish and German Americans, who liked his venomously sarcastic attacks on the Ivy Leaguers controlling foreign policy. In many states, McCarthyism kept the Republicans viable as an opposition party, even though they enrolled less than a quarter of registered voters.

McCarthy's version of McCarthyism lasted only from 1950 to 1954. In 1952, he was riding high, giving the keynote speech at the Republican National Convention in which he attacked the Democrats for "twenty years of treason." But by 1954, Republican Party leaders like Eisenhower had finally had enough of McCarthy. The Senate censured him after he attacked army generals for supposed softness on communism, and by 1957 he was dead of alcoholism. By that time, however, his rampaging investigations and wild charges had left a deep imprint on American politics, encouraging self- censorship and extreme wariness among liberals. McCarthy and his allies, including senator and later vice president Richard Nixon, had repeatedly demonstrated they could wreck any career, from an obscure government office, union local, or university campus all the way up to the Senate. The result was that a whole generation of Democrats, from Harry Truman to Lyndon Johnson, felt they had to prove themselves as tough anticommunists by putting down subversion around the world and here at home. Liberal leaders like Minnesota Senator Hubert Humphrey authored bills to set up con- centration camps for leftists. In colleges, schools, workplaces, churches, and unions across the country, liberals campaigned to get rid of people who refused to answer questions in front of congressional committees or had any associations with the Communist Party USA (the CPUSA or CP).

McCarthy burst into prominence in 1950 with his accusations of secret Communists infesting the State Department, but McCarthyism's importance can easily obscure that the Cold War Red Scare had already begun years before. Deliberate repression on the basis of people's beliefs and associations was initiated not by vengeful Republicans, but by liberal leaders themselves, who genuinely believed in the Communist threat and wanted to clean house at home. More important though less dramatic than McCarthy's televised witch hunts was Truman's 1947 executive order setting up official loyalty boards to check on the political associations of all federal employees, which was followed by the creation of similar bodies at the state level. Millions of civil servants were investigated and thousands lost their jobs, without any guarantees of due process. Government loyalty investigations were followed by systematic purges of leftists in industry after industry, from the big steel and automobile plants and shipyards to Hollywood film studios, and finally to most public school systems and colleges. In 1947, Congress passed over Truman's veto the Taft-Hartley Act, which required every trade union official in the country to sign an affidavit swearing he or she was not a member or supporter of the Communist Party, if his or her union wanted recognition by the National Labor Relations Board.

The final blow to whatever power the Communists had in America came in 1949, when eleven leftwing trade unions with almost one million members were expelled from the CIO (the Congress of Industrial Organizations), the labor federation that radicals had helped establish in the Thirties. This was the decisive defeat of the Old Left, coupled with the disastrous showing of former Vice President Henry Wallace's Progressive Party in the presidential campaign of 1948. Supported by the CP and the most devoted New Dealers, Wallace had advocated seeking peace with the Soviets, an immediate end to segregation, and a wide range of liberal programs; he got 2 percent of the vote. In 1949, eleven top Communist Party leaders were convicted under the Smith Act, which made it a felony to "conspire to advocate the overthrow" of the government. Over the next five years, almost two hundred more local and state Communist leaders were prosecuted. In these trials, the main government evidence was leaflets and newspaper articles advocating the eventual abolition of capitalism. In tandem with the 1950 McCarran Act establishing a Subversive Activities Control Board to monitor and sanction "Communist-controlled" and "Communist-front" organizations, the Smith Act prosecutions established clear limits on free speech. Communism was not formally outlawed, but its supporters were tightly quarantined, and any association with "subversive activities" carried obvious risks.

The relevance of the Red Scare to the New Left is not just that it broke up the broad radical movement of the 1930s, the "Popular Front" that once had mobilized millions. Long after the CPUSA and its many allied organizations had drastically declined, the threat of war with the Soviets and the institutional apparatus of McCarthyism combined to generate a pervasive atmosphere of suspicion. Significant restrictions on political debate lasted well into the 1960s. At the height of the Civil Rights movement and the Vietnam War, congressional committees were still publicly asking people "Are you now or have you ever been a member of the Communist Party?" and demanding that they "name names." In the early 1960s, Attorney General Robert Kennedy intensified efforts to drive the now-tiny CPUSA out of existence, and supported the FBI's Counter-Intelligence Program (COINTELPRO) of systematic infiltration and sabotage of radical groups. Most important, any teacher, professor, trade unionist, civic leader, or journalist knew there were ideas that one could not voice without threatening one's job and community status. Virtually anything new or different, from rock'n'roll to sex education, might be denounced as a Communist plot to weaken America. What seems ridiculous now was quite serious then, such as conservative charges that government programs to fluoridate drinking water were Soviet-inspired. No wonder that Richard Hofstadter, trying to place McCarthyism in a larger context, underlined the importance of "the paranoid style in American politics."

THE NEW LEFT'S HIDDEN ORIGINS: WORLD WAR II AS SOCIAL REVOLUTION

While underscoring McCarthyism's profound effect on political discourse, we need to be careful not to overstate the degree of tension and repression in the 1950s. A relatively small number of people, perhaps ten thousand, suffered directly from McCarthyism, most by losing their jobs and social standing rather than actually going to jail. Though the United States suffered through a bloody three-year war in Korea, there was no home-front mobilization as in World War II. To the white, heterosexual, newly middle-class majority, it seemed that Americans were living in the best of all possible worlds. As leader of the self-proclaimed Free World, the only remaining challenge was to subdue the evil empire to the East. To the various political, racial, ethnic, sexual, and cultural minorities that emerged eventually as the New Left, American politics and society seemed frozen, unwilling to acknowledge the legitimacy of any serious dissent, blind to unresolved crises of racism and widespread poverty, hostile to the simple desire to live differently from the norm in terms of family organization, sexual life, or cultural values. The irony of the 1950s is that all of these minorities, from black activists to student intellectuals to closeted gay people to women who wanted economic independence, found themselves ready and able to express a new form of dissent because of the economic and demographic changes occasioned by World War II. In a fundamental sense, the movements of the New Left were the political descendants of that wartime upheaval, which constituted a de facto social revolution; their activism was a delayed reaction to it, only temporarily stymied by the political chill of the Red Scare.

What does it mean to call World War II a social revolution? Certainly that was not the intent of the U.S. government. It simply wanted to mobilize all possible economic and human resources efficiently and with maximum speed to overcome the powerful military machines of Germany and Japan. But the effect of this nationwide mobilization was to disrupt nearly all of America's long-established traditions and hierarchies, especially those regarding race and gender. The simplest way of understanding these disruptions is to remember that, above all, the federal government needed two things: men to serve in the huge new ground, air, and naval forces being assembled overnight from scratch; and workers to fill up the vast "arsenal of democracy," the factory complexes across America that converted en masse to tank, truck, plane, and ship construction from 1940 on. By 1945, sixteen million men had served in the military, out of a population of 133 million before Pearl Harbor. Coming from farms, small towns, and urban neighborhoods, all of these men were sent great distances, often overseas, in the company of men different from their neighbors and friends at home. They were exposed to new places, strange ideas, foreign food, and unfamiliar languages and cultures, amid the possibility of enormous danger and great responsibility. The upsetting and reorganization of life on the home front was just as great. The influx of men into the armed services created an extraordinary demand for labor, which with startling speed broke down a multitude of customs and rules about who could and could not perform heavy, well-paid factory work. Three million women took "men's jobs," encouraged by explicit government appeals featuring photos of smiling women riveters and welders in overalls. Just as important, World War II accelerated the stream of black migration from the agricultural South, as over one million African Americans left sharecropping in a semi-feudal economy for northern cities and factories.

African Americans immediately understood the radical implications of participation in the huge citizen army and the wartime economic mobilization. Black soldiers deeply resented their continued segregation within the armed forces and the open racism of many of their superiors, especially in view of U.S. propaganda that constantly held up America as fighting for equality and freedom against the Nazis and Japanese. In 1942, a leading black newspaper, the *Pittsburgh Courier*, proclaimed a "Double V" campaign, meaning victories over fascism abroad and white supremacy at home. In 1941, even before the United States officially entered the war, the black union leader

A. Philip Randolph scored the most dramatic political advance since Reconstruction. He threatened a March on Washington by 100,000 angry blacks if something was not done to open up jobs in the defense plants. In response, FDR authorized a Fair Employment Practices Committee to investigate discrimination. Membership in the National Association for the Advancement of Colored People (NAACP) boomed during the war, from 50,000 in 1941 to 450,000 in 1945. Black voting power in northern cities steadily increased with migration from the South, and it became clear that African Americans now held a potential balance of power between the historically pro-civil rights Republicans and historically segregationist Democrats. The latter had gained the majority of black votes in the late 1930s because New Deal job programs delivered tangible benefits to desperate poor people, including African Americans. Eleanor Roosevelt became a national symbol of racial equality, befriending black leaders. FDR appointed liberal justices to the Supreme Court, which began to strike down segregationist laws. Many expected a massive campaign for civil rights at the war's end, and black veterans were at the forefront of voter registration campaigns that sprang up throughout the South. Anticommunist investigations and redbaiting in the late 1940s and early 1950s temporarily blunted this political mobilization, but it is clear that World War II unleashed a demand for equal citizenship among African Americans that could not be contained.

There was no comparable political mobilization by women in 1941–1945, yet the consequences of the war were equally far-reaching. Before World War II, even at the height of the Depression, there were deep societal inhibitions against married women working outside the home (the great exception was married black women). Under wartime pressures, married women whose husbands were away in the military got wage-paying jobs in huge numbers, along with large numbers of younger single women. Equally important, these were not the low-wage, nonunion jobs to which women were traditionally restricted, in laundries and textile or candy factories. For the first time, women took high-paying men's jobs in the unionized heavy industries—the factories and shipyards converted to defense production. This breakthrough to economic independence, decades in advance of the feminist upsurge of the 1960s, was justified as a temporary aberration during wartime. When the veterans returned home, they reclaimed their old jobs from the women who held them. The universal assumption was that if men could afford to support them, women would prefer to stay home, keep house, and raise children.

However, the popular memory of family life after World War II does not square with the facts. Once married women entered the paid workforce, later research showed, they were unlikely to leave it. The percentage of married women with jobs outside the home increased sharply during World War II, declined for just one year, and then kept steadily rising. Just as important, the number of women enrolled in labor unions continued to grow steadily, from 800,000 in 1940 to three million by 1952. In the postwar decades women unionists were some of the most committed backers of feminist demands, such as equal pay for equal work and an end to defining job classifications by gender. The difference between wartime and the 1950s was that instead of high-paying factory jobs, the increasing number of women wage-workers were again restricted to low-status "women's work" as clerical and sales help. At the same time, the percentage of women earning professional degrees steadily declined after the war. The desire to earn their own money, and a quiet but deep dissatisfaction with the restrictions on women's career prospects, were central to feminism's revival in the Sixties. That fuse was lit much earlier, when husbands, fathers, and brothers were literally absent because of war, and their authority suffered an irreversible decline.

Though the catalytic effects of wartime mobilization were most evident among blacks and women, they were felt among many other groups too—Mexican Americans, Native Americans, farm and small-town residents who first saw the bright lights of the big city, middle- and upper-class Protestants who fought alongside working-class Catholics and Jews, the gay men and women who discovered each other in the anonymity of service life. Besides the Civil Rights movement, and the growth in women's employment and unionization which spawned feminism's "second wave" in the 1960s, other wings of the New Left grew out of societal shifts and policy decisions during and after the war. The tiny homosexual rights movement of the 1950s incubated in the new gay subcultures of port cities like San Francisco, which grew rapidly in the homosocial world of wartime mobilization. The key postwar organization insisting on full citizenship for Mexican Americans was the G.I. Forum, established by returning veterans. The modern effort to restore civil rights and self-determination to indigenous peoples also began at the war's close, with the forming of the National Congress of American Indians in 1944. The war years also fostered the bohemian subcultures that surged in the 1950s, creating much of the New Left's cultural ethos, whether the Beat writers, the avant-garde jazz movement called bebop, or the group of painters later dubbed Abstract Expressionists. Finally, it was during the war and postwar years that racial tensions began to escalate in Northern cities, as black people sought housing outside the old ghettos, only to be met by white mobs. These battles for space led to the growth of a new urban militancy among African Americans and the eventual demand for Black Power, not just civil rights. In uncounted ways, World War II had shaken up American life, and ultimately all of the pieces could never be put back together.

Chapter 3

THE NEW LEFT'S ORIGINS IN THE OLD LEFT

The problem of the twentieth century is the problem of the color-line,—the relation of the darker to the lighter races of men in Asia and Africa, in America and the islands of the sea.

—W.E.B. Du Bois, *The Souls of Black Folk,* 1903

While there is a lower class, I am in it; while there is a criminal element, I am of it; while there is a soul in prison, I am not free.

—Eugene V. Debs, Socialist Party leader, Speech to the Court, September 14, 1918

Communists have no interests apart from the people, no narrow selfish "axe to grind." To be a Communist is not a career. Anyone who is found to be self-seeking or egocentric, who is not capable of collective thought and action or amenable to criticism is eventually eliminated from our ranks, no matter how important a position he may occupy. "The greatest good for the greatest number" is the ethical concept of the Communists. Communists practice an enlightened self-interest in a passionate willingness to work unselfishly so that by freeing the workers from wage slavery all humanity is free from greed and tyranny.

—Elizabeth Gurley Flynn, *Meet the Communists*, 1946

Few social movements emerge spontaneously, though it often appears that way to outside observers and even participants; the New Left was no exception. In the 1950s, when African Americans in both North and South reignited the black protest tradition, there were three other existing political currents from

America's radical past that would also prove crucial to the new radicalism. This chapter focuses on these four points of origin for the New Left: the varieties of black politics that converged in the Civil Rights movement during the 1950s; the Communist Party and the remnants of its "progressive" periphery; the older Socialist Party and the rest of the "anti-Stalinist" left; finally, the church-based pacifist movement, America's oldest radical strain. This is hardly a complete rendering of the Old Left or of broader reform currents in the first half of the twentieth century, including the union movement, post-suffrage feminism, and the liberal wings of both the Democratic and Republican parties. Such a history is outside the scope of any single book, but it is worth noting that all of these relate to the development of a new radicalism during the Cold War years.

THE BLACK PROTEST TRADITION

If one adopts an inclusive definition of the New Left, seeing it as the sum of *all* the efforts at radical reform and cultural revolution in post-1945 America, then its starting point becomes evident. Scholars and activists agree that the mass movement by African Americans seeking genuine citizenship was the primary genesis of social change in Cold War America. This movement, steadily building since the late 1930s in both North and South, shot into national and global visibility in December 1955, when a group of experienced activists initiated a boycott of segregated buses in Montgomery, Alabama. They recruited as spokesman a young Baptist minister named Martin Luther King, Jr. Through his powerful oratory and visionary leadership he became the most important leader of the Civil Rights movement and the defining radical figure of the entire Cold War era.

Historians once wrote (and journalists still do write) as if the Civil Rights movement marked an extraordinary new start for black people and for America. In recent decades, however, researchers have found deep roots for the 1955-1956 Montgomery bus boycott and the subsequent wave of nation-wide protest that crested in 1964–1965 with the passage of the Civil Rights and Voting Right acts. Even the post-1965 northern-based Black Power movement had its origins in a history of outspoken black radicalism unknown to white America.

In the 1950s, for any American thinking about what was then called "race relations," the basic reference point was still the Radical Reconstruction of the post–Civil War South from 1866 to 1877, when ex-slaves exercised their newly won constitutional rights by voting hundreds of black men into offices from county sheriff to U.S. congressman. After the last Federal troops were withdrawn in 1877, it took several decades to establish the system of white supremacy known as Jim Crow. By 1910, every southern state had deprived African Americans of the vote and after 1890, lynching intensified. The last southern black Republican left Congress in 1901, signaling the eclipse of African Americans from national politics.

Not until 1929 was another African American elected to Congress, this time from Chicago. A mass migration out of the South had begun during World War I, and over time developed into a bloc of urban voters in the North who became the reserve army making civil rights demands on both parties. It was a slow process, however, and well into the twentieth century's second half, the Democratic Party continued to include a powerful wing of explicitly racist white southerners. As late as 1952, the Democrats nominated a "moderate" segregationist for vice president, Alabama senator John Sparkman, seeking to balance the ticket headed by Illinois governor Adlai Stevenson. This stark contradiction between racial reform and white supremacy in the nation's majority party is key to understanding politics from the 1930s through the 1970s. It explains the anger felt by many New Leftists in their dealings with northern Democrats like John F. Kennedy, who rarely stood up to the southern Democrats controlling key congressional committees.

Because of their exclusion from mainstream electoral and legislative politics, African Americans early on developed alternative forms of political activity, including boycotts, civil disobedience, marches, and mass protest meetings. In a real sense, the modern Civil Rights movement was born not in the 1940s and 1950s, but at the peak of Jim Crow in 1909–1910, when the great black intellectual W.E.B. Du Bois joined with white liberals and socialists to found the National Association for the Advancement of Colored People (NAACP). For decades, the NAACP pursued a legal strategy to chip away at segregation by exposing the hypocrisies of the "separate but equal" doctrine that the Supreme Court had endorsed in its 1896 *Plessy v. Ferguson* decision. This was a hard, grinding struggle through the courts. Though segregation was legally enforced in the South, it was a widespread social custom everywhere in the United States. Schools, universities, stores, restaurants, hotels, theaters, apartment buildings, labor unions, police forces—even the Marine Corps—openly excluded African Americans. Under these difficult conditions, the NAACP persevered. By the 1940s it was regularly winning important battles, such as the 1944 Supreme Court ruling in *Smith v. Allwright*, which struck down the "white primary," widely used by Democrats in the one-party South to exclude blacks from the only meaningful elections.

Meanwhile, within the separate world of black America, various nationalist leaders or "race men" came forward, critiquing white oppression more sharply than the middle-class NAACP, urging blacks to rely only on themselves.

In the late 1910s and 1920s, Marcus Garvey's Universal Negro Improvement Association galvanized vast numbers of working-class black people, especially those in the emerging northern ghettos, with a vision of African liberation and self-sustaining economic advancement. From the 1930s on, Elijah Muhammad proselytized for the separatist Nation of Islam, denouncing whites as "devils" and calling for a return to traditional cultural values and self-discipline as a means of escaping white control. Finally, during the Depression and war years, the Communist Party USA established a base in black America, from Alabama to Harlem, because of its aggressive support for racial equality and its commitment to organizing the poorest sharecroppers and workers.

However divided by class and ideology, activists from the NAACP lawyer in New York to the Communist autoworker in Detroit were united by a common awareness of their routine exclusion from power and respect, regardless of education or accomplishment. The historic white presumption that *any* black person was ultimately inferior to *any* white person had profound consequences for American politics. Under this premise, all forms of black political empowerment, no matter how moderate, implied the overturn of the existing order, leading to what segregationists menacingly called "social equality." This latent but bone-deep radicalism was the black protest tradition's most important legacy for the New Left—the awareness that America's history was still unresolved, and that fighting for basic democracy and citizenship rights was still a revolutionary act. While the NAACP and other northern leaders aligned themselves with respectable Cold War liberalism from the late 1940s on, at the grassroots level in the Jim Crow South, any kind of black activism remained genuinely subversive. In the 1950s, southern state legislatures used the mechanisms of anticommunist legislation to shut down the NAACP's southern affiliates by requiring membership lists to be turned over to authorities. The existence of segregation and open white supremacy, and the refusal by black people to accept their subjugation, proved to be the opening wedge for a radical challenge to all of the assumptions of Cold War America.

THE COMMUNIST PARTY AND THE PROGRESSIVE LEFT

To the white majority, the black protest tradition was mostly invisible until the late 1950s. More visible was the Communist Party (CP), founded in 1919 and the most dynamic force on the left from the 1920s through the 1940s. The CP enjoyed considerable success in the New Deal and World War II years, recruiting tens of thousands of members. More significantly, it had a larger base of up to a million sympathizers who read its newspapers, belonged to the many organizations the Party created, or were active in Communist-organized unions. In those decades, the Communists made two contributions to American democracy, while retaining an unbending allegiance to the Soviet Union's repressive socialist dictatorship. First, through their commitment to a multi-ethnic, multiracial labor movement, and their deployment of disciplined organizers, they helped build the huge industrial unions of the Congress of Industrial Organizations (CIO) during the 1930s, the era of the Popular Front alliance with liberals and other leftists. This empowerment of millions of workers made the United States a much more egalitarian society. Second, the CP was the only white-led political formation of the time publicly committed to confronting Jim Crow and the institutions of southern white supremacy, while promoting complete equality for black people. This stance earned Communists a level of respect in black America that they enjoyed nowhere else; the CP's most impressive political victory was the election of the black Communist Benjamin Davis, Jr., as a New York City Councilman from Harlem in 1943–1949.

While later radicals envied the CP's organizational resources, it never came close to achieving the legitimacy of Communist parties in Europe and elsewhere. At its peak, the Communist Party USA still operated on the fringes of New Deal liberalism and the mainstream labor movement. Most party members who were leaders in unions and other organizations kept their affiliation secret so as not to lose their jobs, adding to the CP's reputation for undemocratic, conspiratorial practices. After the wartime alliance with the Soviets turned into the Cold War, the Party's fragile base of influence collapsed. Its decades-long blind support of Soviet policy—including purges that killed millions—had cost it credibility. Liberal leaders like Eleanor Roosevelt quickly isolated the Communist-led left by forming the anticommunist Americans for Democratic Action (ADA) in 1947. A tide of legal repression and social ostracism began to wash over the left. Most important, the long-held suspicion of many Americans that all Communists were Soviet agents was confirmed by the high-profile trials of State department official Alger Hiss, convicted of perjury in 1949, and Julius and Ethel Rosenberg, executed in 1953 for stealing top-secret information on the atom bomb.

When McCarthyism began to recede in 1955 and 1956, with Supreme Court decisions overturning the Smith Act, the CP was reduced to 20,000 beleaguered members—a third of its strength in 1945. The worst was yet to come. In February 1956, Soviet leader Nikita Khrushchev denounced his predecessor Joseph Stalin as a paranoid criminal. Communists worldwide who had venerated Stalin were profoundly disoriented by these admissions. American Communists were no exception. A fierce debate broke out about how to restructure the Party along more democratic lines. As reformers argued with orthodox Stalinists, most of the members voted with their feet. By 1958, only 5,000 diehard Party members remained. As of 1960, therefore, the Communist Party appeared to exit from the scene. For liberals, it became the butt of jokes, like the jibe that the Party survived on the dues paid by thousands of FBI infiltrators. For many younger New Leftists the shrunken CP, many of whose middle-aged members held onto their pro-Soviet world-views but otherwise participated in liberal Democratic politics, exemplified how *not* to be radical.

It was a mistake, however, to presume that this small core of activists had no influence or significance. Among black Americans, the Communists still retained some respect. McCarthyism was less effective in isolating black radicals because of black America's separation from white America. Prominent individuals close to the CP, like the great actor-singer Paul Robeson and NAACP founder W.E.B. Du Bois, were deeply respected figures, and most African Americans refused to believe they were traitors. When numerous blacks were first elected to political office in the 1960s and 1970s, many had Communist connections in their pasts, like Detroit's Mayor Coleman Young and various members of Congress. In a few cities, such as Los Angeles, San Francisco, and New York, the Party had enough members to play a role in local politics, and retained footholds in the labor movement. Finally, the CP still had a national structure of paid organizers. These advantages were magnified by the New Left's decentralization. The party's resources, its connections with Communist parties in almost every country, and decades of experience in coalition-building meant that CPers and their allies often played key behind-the-scenes roles in major civil rights and peace campaigns.

More important than the diminished numbers of card-carrying Communists were the many thousands of self-identified "progressives" who had been part of the Communist-influenced left in the 1930s and 1940s and remained politically active into the 1960s and after. Their common denominators were pro–New Deal, pro-labor, and anti–Cold War (or pro-Soviet) sympathies. Some retained ties to the CP, but many did not. These networks of Old Left activists in suburban and city neighborhoods remained a vital element of Cold War radicalism, adding their ballast of experience to the romantic energy of the young. They are one of the primary reasons why we cannot define the New Left as a youth movement.

THE SOCIALIST PARTY AND THE ANTI-STALINIST LEFT

The Communist Party was the most important Marxist organization, but it had no monopoly on socialist ideas. On its right was the older Socialist Party (SP), formed in 1900. The SP and other small groups made up the "anti-Stalinist" alternative to the CPUSA. In the century's first two decades, the

Socialist Party was a considerable force, publishing hundreds of newspapers and magazines, and electing many members to state and local offices, even occasionally to Congress. The charismatic former union leader Eugene V. Debs ran as its presidential candidate four times, receiving 6 percent of the popular vote in 1912. After 1920, however, the Socialists played second fiddle to the more militant Communists, and by the 1940s, they were down to a few thousand members. Led for decades by the pacifist minister Norman Thomas, the SP retained support among mainstream labor leaders, many of whom, like United Auto Workers President Walter Reuther, had been Socialists in their youth. Thomas remained a respected figure among liberals, even during the Cold War. However, just as the CP was tainted by its unwavering loyalty to the Soviet Union, the SP's respectability after 1945 was contingent upon its support for U.S. foreign policy, and its willingness to denounce Communists at home or abroad. Thomas toured newly independent India and other neutral countries under U.S. government auspices, leading radicals to mock him as a "State Department socialist." There were also connections between Socialist leaders like Thomas and the Central Intelligence Agency, and Socialists helped the CIA create anticommunist labor groups in Latin America and elsewhere.

Though the largest, the SP was not the only organization on the anti-Stalinist left. In 1928, supporters of Leon Trotsky were expelled from the Communist Party; Trotsky was a top leader of the Russian Revolution who was exiled by Stalin and later assassinated by Soviet agents in Mexico in 1940. Although critical of the Soviet Union as a "deformed workers state," the Trotskyists considered themselves to be orthodox Marxist-Leninists, and more revolutionary than the Communists. By the 1950s they had divided into two main groups, the Socialist Workers Party (SWP) and the Independent Socialist League (ISL) or Shachtmanites, named for their leader, Max Shachtman, a former secretary to Trotsky. The SWP always criticized the Communists from the left, and never supported the United States in the Cold War. Despite its small numbers, it played a significant role in various New Left movements through single-minded discipline, especially the antiwar campaigns. Conversely, the Shachtmanites moved to the right during the 1950s, and in 1958 merged into the Socialist Party, where they formed its most conservative wing, deeply anticommunist and suspicious of the New Left.

One unanticipated consequence of McCarthyism was to increase the political standing of the Socialist Party in the late 1950s. With the Communists sapped by legal assaults and their associations with espionage and Stalin's despotism, the Socialists gained in prestige. In addition, Thomas and other Socialists had close ties to the various pacifist organizations, which guaranteed them influence with the emerging civil rights protests and the new peace movement opposing nuclear testing. The anti-Stalinist left of Socialists and Trotskyists had another advantage over the Communists, in their willingness to nurture new intellectual forums. After World War II, unorthodox Marxist currents developed around *Dissent* magazine, founded in 1954 by Irving Howe, and the earlier *politics* magazine edited by Dwight MacDonald. These New York-based journals promoted a "third force" politics, not committed to either the Soviet Union or the United States. Spurred by this independent thinking, much of the student New Left sprang directly from the efforts of Socialist-affiliated groups like the Young People's Socialist League (YPSL) and the Student League for Industrial Democracy, which changed its name to Students for a Democratic Society (SDS) in 1960.

Given its distinguished history, and its connections with the liberal and pacifist communities, access to trade union funding, and real intellectual diversity, the Socialist Party was the logical beneficiary of any radical resurgence after McCarthyism waned in the 1960s. Surprisingly, it squandered its early influence and rapidly became alienated from the radical movements of the 1960s. In a notorious episode, Socialist leaders tried to enforce a rigid anticommunism on the SDS leadership, provoking a bitter split in 1962. Then, while Communists, progressives, and pacifists all participated enthusiastically in the anti-Vietnam War movement, the SP was divided, with one wing supporting the U.S. war effort. Finally, many older white male Socialists were alienated by Black Power, Women's Liberation, and Gay Liberation. Identifying closely with the old guard leadership of the trade union movement, in the early 1970s they moved towards what became known as "neoconservatism." Instead of a revival, the SP became the paramount symbol of a bankrupt Old Left, and finally collapsed in 1972.

The dividing line between Communists and Socialists remained firm throughout the entire post–World War II era, as they had profoundly different perspectives on the Cold War. It is worth noting, however, how much they shared. Besides a commitment to the socialist worldview and the Marxian analysis of history, both of these small parties believed that the labor movement was central to changing American society, and both believed in working for pragmatic reforms, including the priority of supporting liberals in the Democratic Party. Both drew their members overwhelmingly from first- and second-generation immigrant families, with a strong Jewish presence. Other than diametrically opposing views on the Soviet Union, the most significant difference was their attitude towards African Americans; the CP had an activist record among black people, with significant numbers of black members and black leaders, that the SP could not match. Finally, both the Communists and the Socialists really were *parties*—hierarchical, bureaucratic structures. New Leftists of all ages and backgrounds were uncomfortable with permanent institutional structures, identifying them with the faceless power of corporations and Big Brother–style government. Casting around for alternative models of human relations and political activism, the New Left turned to examples of nonviolent, antihierarchical, antibureaucratic activism. Many found that they did not have to look far, that an alternative tradition existed close at hand in the long history of American pacifism.

THE PACIFIST LEFT

The true "third force" on the U.S. left was a constituency that received little attention in the century's first half—the pacifists. Unlike the Socialists and the Communists, they were not a political party, nor were they based in the labor movement. Instead, the pacifists comprised a loose network of churches, small local peace societies, and a handful of established religious denominations and secular organizations. Yet this tiny minority of white Protestants had deep roots; no American President has ever been a Marxist, but quite a few in the nineteenth century were Quakers and Unitarians. Pacifists drew on these roots to exert a profound influence on the New Left.

Pacifism rests on the assertion of nonviolence as an ethical creed—a refusal to engage in violence against others on any grounds, political or personal. Since the most fundamental power of government is to command its citizens in war, even passive forms of pacifism entail a potentially radical challenge to authority. The origins of pacifism stretch back before the American Revolution and are rooted in certain variations of traditional Protestant Christianity. The best-known pacifist group is the Religious Society of Friends (the Quakers), and there are other "Peace Churches" such as the Mennonites and the Brethren, as well as strong pacifist currents in denominations like the Unitarian Universalists. All of these denominations emphasize service to the poor and oppressed and abstention from war. In the 1930s, a new pacifist religious strain surfaced, the Catholic Worker movement led by Dorothy Day, which operated "houses of refuge" for the homeless that were also "intentional communities"—communal living experiments for Catholic Worker volunteers. The Catholic Workers abjured any formal structure, and were linked only by the national *Catholic Worker* newspaper and Day's charismatic vision.

In the nineteenth century, American pacifists organized the first peace movements, seeking to outlaw war; they also helped lead the Abolitionist movement against slavery. Most of the modern U.S. peace organizations began during and soon after World War I. The American Friends Service Committee (AFSC) was founded to aid foreign refugees, and remains today a major international organization, with hundreds of staff people in the United

States and abroad. The Women's International League for Peace and Freedom (WILPF) came together in 1916 to support a just and democratic peace in Europe. The Fellowship of Reconciliation (FOR) and the War Resisters League (WRL) formed to oppose conscription and denounce war itself.

All of these groups labored indefatigably through the 1920s, 1930s, and 1940s. At various points, pacifism became attractive, but in no sense did they lead the left in those decades. But just as the Cold War undermined the Communists, it proved to be a time of opportunity for pacifists. The visible consequences of nuclear weapons at Hiroshima and Nagasaki gave a new urgency to pacifist calls for disarmament and peacemaking. Their unwavering insistence on ethical behavior and open democratic forms of operation made them relatively impervious to redbaiting. As a consequence, throughout the Cold War era, pacifist organizations like AFSC, WILPF, FOR and the WRL provided much of the New Left's institutional stability and resources. Without them, the New Left would truly have been much "newer," and consequently much weaker.

The common experience for the new upsurge of American pacifism in the Cold War was resistance to the draft during World War II. This personal history marked pacifists out from everyone else, since most of the old Left saw the fight against Hitler as a just and even noble war. Several thousand conscientious objectors were assigned to Civilian Public Service (CPS) camps, where they worked long hours under military discipline. These camps bred an intimate culture of shared political convictions and a willingness to question authority. A generation of young activists who met each other in the CPS camps went on to lead the resurgence of American pacifism in the 1950s and 1960s, including organizers like Dave Dellinger, Brad Lyttle, and Jim Peck. Their egalitarian individualism and focus on "direct action" by small groups rather than building large, permanent organizations had a great influence on the New Left. Equally significant, white and black pacifists began civil disobedience campaigns to attack segregation long before any other group took up this strategy. In 1942 the Fellowship of Reconciliation sponsored the formation of the Congress of Racial Equality (CORE), a major organization of the Civil Rights movement and the New Left. In the mid-1940s, CORE pioneered sit-ins at segregated restaurants in cities like Chicago and illegal interracial bus tours of the South—tactics at the center of national attention in the early 1960s.

In the 1940s and 1950s, however, the pacifists seemed like harmless cranks to most Americans. Comfortable with both unpopularity and ridicule, pacifist organizations unequivocally opposed nuclear weapons, without bothering about which superpower was more to blame. This clarity placed pacifists at the New Left's moral and organizational center, as did their commitment to uniting and overcoming differences, rather than seeking to establish the dominance of their own organization.

To focus on the pacifists does not complete the history of peace activism prior to the Cold War. The traditional peace movement had two wings: pacifists, who tended toward radicalism, and what historians have dubbed "liberal internationalists," a range of reformers who were committed to strengthening international cooperation to avoid the sheer destruction of war. Between the two world wars, these wings of the peace movement collaborated in a powerful lobby backed by millions of voters and many members of Congress. Their influence discouraged military intervention in Latin America, the United States' traditional sphere of influence, and limited involvement in European affairs. During World War II, however, liberal internationalists became convinced of the need to defeat Hitler by military means. Though they fervently supported the United Nations' creation in 1945, their new, tougher approach towards national security carried over to confronting the Soviet Union. The success of the antinuclear peace movement of 1955–1963, and then the antiwar movement from 1965 on, rested to a significant extent on winning back these liberals, as discussed in chapter 5.

Despite the complexity of the Old Left, with its many different histories and organizations, it can be conveniently grouped into two categories: first, the Marxist political parties, which were class-oriented, based in the labor movement, and dominated the left in the first half of this century; second, political constituencies far removed from the mainstream, like African Americans and pacifists, whose radicalism derived from permanent outsider status. Obviously these two categories overlapped. African American Communists like Ben Davis Jr. and Socialist pacifists like Norman Thomas effectively bridged two traditions. But crucial to our understanding of how American radicalism changed in the Cold War era is how the Old Left's central concern for the working class was replaced by a focus on ending racial oppression, militarism, and male supremacy or patriarchy. This shift away from the politics of class to a broader, more diffuse set of ideological concerns marks the distinction between Old and New Lefts.

Chapter 4

THE BLACK FREEDOM STRUGGLE: FROM "WE SHALL OVERCOME" TO "FREEDOM NOW!"

Remember that the way to get this revolution off the ground is to forge the moral, spiritual and political pressure which the President, the nation and the world cannot ignore. . . . The only way is through a nonviolent army. Let SCLC, in concert with other groups committed to non-violence, begin to plan, recruit, organize and discipline a nonviolent corps. . . . Let us call for from 2000 to 7 or 8 thousand volunteers. . . . Let us prepare these people for mass nonviolent action in the Deep South.

—The Reverend James Lawson, "Eve of Nonviolent Revolution?", Southern Patriot, November 1961

The next time we march, we won't march on Washington, but we will march through the South, through the Heart of Dixie, the way Sherman did. We will make the action of the past few months look petty.

—John Lewis, SNCC Chairman, original text of speech at the March on Washington, August 28, 1963

Strong people don't need strong leaders.

—Ella J. Baker

The Civil Rights movement was the original motor force for the New Left and its dominant element during the years leading up to the political watershed of 1964–1965, when at last Congress acted to outlaw the major forms of discrimination based on race (or religion, or sex, or ethnicity) and to guarantee black voting rights. It was the only mass movement of the decade, the only one that received sustained media attention, and the only radical movement of those years that caused shifts in national political alignments: as the Republicans gave up their historic if nominal commitment to Black Americans as "the Party of Lincoln," the Democratic Party moved towards becoming the party of civil rights. In the wake of the thousands of black southerners who marched, sat-in, boycotted, and walked through mobs to register to vote, enduring arrests, beatings, burnings, bombings, and killings, came a host of other movements. Slowly, the "best of all possible worlds" of the 1950s began to seem like a straitjacket, as apparently separate sources of frustration, alienation, and nonconformity converged. Inspired by the stubbornness and daring of African Americans, all the excluded or belittled outsiders—students and bohemians, gays and lesbians, underground feminists, intellectuals and ethnic minorities—began to imagine themselves as part of "the Movement," as the New Left called itself in those days. But the revival of public protest had its start in the most modest fashion, through the long-festering frustration of law-abiding African Americans over their daily humiliations on the public conveyances of a minor southern state capital.

CIVIL RIGHTS IN THE COLD WAR ERA: THE ROAD TO MONTGOMERY

The story of a black seamstress named Rosa Parks refusing to give up her seat to a white man on a Montgomery, Alabama bus is taught to millions of schoolchildren as a single isolated act, a parable of human dignity. In one sense, this story is accurate. Mrs. Parks *was* arrested in December 1955, and the legendary Montgomery Bus Boycott did grow from that one courageous act of defiance. Yet this tale of an oppressed people suddenly waking up is a myth in many respects. First, Rosa Parks did not act on her own, nor was she simply a tired woman who had been pushed too far. She was a highly respected community figure and former Montgomery NAACP secretary, who had recently attended a workshop on nonviolent protest, or what was then called "passive resistance," at the interracial Highlander Folk School. Second, the mass movement in Montgomery seemed to spring into action overnight, but it would not have happened without years of planning and agitation. Key organizers included the black labor leader E.D. Nixon and the college professor

JoAnn Gibson Robinson, supported by a couple from the South's tiny community of white radicals, Clifford and Virginia Durr. This leadership group had long discussed the feasibility of a bus boycott and other measures to register growing political assertiveness of black Montgomerians. By late 1955 they felt the time was right, and that Mrs. Parks could be a viable symbol. They brought together black ministers to form the Montgomery Improvement Association, which issued a public call to stay off the buses. Seeking a spokesman with impeccable credentials from outside the city's existing black leadership, they chose the newly arrived 26-year-old Dr. Martin Luther King, Jr., pastor of the elite Dexter Avenue Baptist Church.

Rosa Parks' famous refusal to give up her seat also had deep cultural roots. Despite northern assumptions about southern passivity, in the mid-1950s Deep South states like Alabama were like pots ready to boil over. Anger over segregated buses was nothing new. During World War II, hundreds of black citizens were arrested, fined, or pistol-whipped by armed bus drivers in Birmingham, Alabama's largest city, for refusing to take the "colored seats," talking back, or just "loud talking." Black voter registration rose sharply in the South at war's end (from nearly zero), as thousands of returning veterans demanded their legal rights. In Upper South cities like Greensboro, North Carolina, a few blacks were elected to local office, but elsewhere, African American veterans were kept from voting in 1946 by armed gangs. Nor was the Civil Rights movement in any sense a strictly regional movement. In the North, blacks could vote but were excluded from restaurants, movie theaters, swimming pools, amusement parks, and public housing complexes, and routinely shunted into all-black, rundown schools. In cities like New York, Detroit, and Oakland, sophisticated protest movements had surged during and after World War II, laying the groundwork for the focus on the South in the 1950s.

In hindsight, many historians believe that without the overpowering effects of the Cold War and the resulting Red Scare, the modern Civil Rights movement would have confronted segregation immediately after World War II, instead of in the late 1950s and 1960s. But McCarthyism had profound consequences for the protest movements of the 1940s. In many cases, the most committed participants in the civil rights coalitions in northern cities were people close to the Communist Party. In both North and South, black and white leftists worked in partnership with moderates to challenge disfranchisement, lynching, police brutality, and discrimination in jobs and housing. McCarthyism broke up these coalitions, as black trade unionists and leaders like Paul Robeson and W.E.B. Du Bois came under fire for their opposition to Cold War confrontation with the Soviet Union. Under pressure to maintain its position in the liberal wing of the Democratic Party, the NAACP fired Du Bois in 1948, and started purging its ranks of the leftist taint. By the early 1950s, progress as civil rights in the North became at best incremental, and in the South it stalled completely, as segregationists insisted that support for the movement was simply part of the "International Communist Conspiracy" to undermine America.

Paradoxically, however, the Cold War also created new opportunities to press for full democracy and racial justice. The NAACP appreciated that the Jim Crow system was causing the United States intense embarrassment internationally. How could America claim to lead the Free World against the threat of Soviet dictatorship when it tolerated gross human rights abuses at home? This hypocrisy was constantly pointed out by newspapers in Western Europe and in the dozens of European colonies and former colonies across Asia and Africa. To make matters worse, whenever a lynching occurred or a "colored" Asian or African diplomat was denied restaurant service or a hotel room (as happened frequently), Soviet representatives would attack the United States in the United Nations. Northern Democrats and Republicans and President Truman all declared that Jim Crow posed a national security threat. Truman himself, needing black votes, had appointed an official Committee on Civil Rights in 1946, and then moved to desegregate the armed forces in 1948. Moderate black leaders expected that in return for their acquiescence in McCarthyism, they would reap substantial gains in civil rights. They were not disappointed. In 1954, the Supreme Court ruled segregation in public schools unconstitutional in the *Brown v. Board of Education* case brought by the NAACP's brilliant chief counsel, Thurgood Marshall. It was exactly the signal for which the Montgomery activists and many others across the South had waited.

To provide a kind of awful symmetry, just as the impact of *Brown* began to seep into national consciousness, a spectacularly gratuitous killing, a lynching of the most traditional sort, became headline news across the United States and the world. In August 1955, a fourteen-year old black Chicago teenager, Emmett Till, was visiting relatives in the town of Money, Mississippi. On a dare, he tried to flirt with a white woman while buying candy from her in a store. That same night the woman's husband and his half-brother abducted Till, beat him viciously, shot him to death, and dumped the body in the Tallahatchie River. Thousands of black men and boys had died in similar ways since the 1880s, but his mother, Mamie Till, and the NAACP would not let the case rest. 50,000 black Chicagoans filed past his open casket, and pictures of the mutilated, decomposed corpse ran in the popular black magazine *Jet*. An all-white jury acquitted the killers, who promptly sold their story of exactly how they killed the teenager to *Look*, then a major news magazine. At a time when many American liked to think incremental change would peaceably erode Jim Crow via court decisions, the murder of Emmett Till was a visceral reminder of the unyielding violence of white supremacy.

MARTIN LUTHER KING, JR. AND THE NEW AMERICAN RADICALISM

Black activists throughout the nation believed that the *Brown* decision heralded a legal revolution. The highest authority of the U.S. government had pronounced segregation morally and legally wrong. The decision had an extraordinary effect on both white and black southerners, since it promised disruption of their entire way of life. The question became: where will the first challenge come? Across the South, local protest campaigns began to mushroom, but the Montgomery Bus Boycott was the most publicized, in large part because Martin Luther King, Jr. was a new kind of black leader with an extraordinary appeal to both African Americans and many northern whites.

The Montgomery Bus Boycott lasted from December 1955 to January 1957. During that time, the city's black community, comprising tens of thousands of people from different backgrounds, organized itself with a remarkable unity and discipline. Repeatedly, hostile white officials and skeptical journalists were surprised by the strategic initiative of Montgomery's black leadership. A massive alternative transport system was devised to move thousands of people to their jobs without using the buses. Every week, month after month, huge prayer meetings and rallies took place. Bombings, threats, and the indictment of ninety-two boycott organizers only stiffened resistance and offended northern opinion. Throughout this time, Dr. King's stature grew. As he gave speeches in all parts of the country, the press was drawn to his calm, erudite, but impassioned persona, and his insistence on nonviolent resistance based on Christian love and the duty of redeeming white southerners from their own racism. But journalists ignored King's frequent comparisons between the Civil Rights movement in the American South and the anti-imperialist movements in Africa and Asia.

The Supreme Court's January 1957 decision requiring integration of Montgomery's buses was a major blow to the white South, and similar campaigns were wanted in other cities. Yet for the next three years, the only tangible result of the boycott was King's new Southern Christian Leadership Conference (SCLC), a regional network of activist black ministers. At first, SCLC accomplished little, serving mainly as an institutional vehicle for King. It was hampered by rivalry with the NAACP and the absence of a clear strategy. Its main accomplishments were two large national demonstrations held in Washington D.C.—a 1957 Prayer Pilgrimage for Peace, and a 1958 Youth Mobilization for Human Rights. The decade's other major racial crisis came in 1957 in Little Rock, Arkansas, where the NAACP had sued to force school desegregation. After a federal court ordered the admission of nine black students to a high school, Governor Orval Faubus defied the court's ruling.

Reluctantly, President Eisenhower sent in the 101st Airborne Division to enforce federal authority and protect the students from mob violence. Little Rock was a decisive step in breaking Jim Crow's back, and the first time federal troops were used to enforce civil rights since Reconstruction. However, it was seen as a contest between the state and national governments, with innocent black children needing the latter's protection.

In other respects, the late 1950s were a frustrating time for civil rights advocates. The pace of school desegregation slowed to a standstill. Immediately following the *Brown* decision, a few municipalities had voluntarily integrated their schools, but hardly any did so after 1957 as white resistance solidified. The numbers of registered African American voters in southern states declined as electoral rolls were purged. Across the South, white Citizens' Councils emerged, led by local elites who enforced a policy of "massive resistance" against any suggestion that whites should begin to move away from segregation.

Like many historic movements, the Civil Rights movement began haltingly. Deference to established rules was pervasive in the early Cold War years. Conformity was explicitly equated with patriotism, and dissenters of any sort were ridiculed as either Communist "dupes" or neurotic "true believers" (the title of a 1951 book by the philosopher Eric Hoffer, it became a popular term to disparage activists as deluded fanatics). In such a climate, the idea of protest itself, and of political leadership based in challenging immoral, oppressive structures of power, was thoroughly discredited. This climate of cynicism and doubt helps explain why the emergence of Dr. King had such enormous impact. Without his extraordinary personality, and the attention he drew in the North and worldwide, the Montgomery movement might have succeeded on its own terms but remained obscure. Dr. King's willingness to "speak truth to power" had a ripple effect, setting off sparks of insurgency for the next decade, culminating with his winning the Nobel Peace Prize in 1964. By personal example, he articulated a new definition for radicalism in Cold War America. He understood that this required a position of moral and spiritual rather than narrowly political authority, and under his call to full democracy the New Left constituted itself, piece by piece. Therefore we need to establish how King related to the left, and indeed why he was the paradigmatic New Leftist.

Rather than affiliating with any particular camp or school of thought in the existing left, King drew from all. His postgraduate studies at Boston University focused on the legacy of radical Christian activism, but he also was influenced by the German philosophers Hegel and Marx, and later on by Third World revolutionaries such as India's Mahatma Gandhi, the apostle of nonviolence, and Ghana's Kwame Nkrumah, who espoused a pan-African version of socialism. In his social and political relationships, King was equally open-minded. From the early days of the bus boycott, his advisors included key pacifist organizers, such as Glenn Smiley of the Fellowship of Reconciliation and Bayard Rustin of the War Resisters League and *Liberation*. King also worked with former Communist activists Stanley Levison and Jack O'Dell, even when those connections brought the unwelcome attention of the FBI and the Kennedy brothers. In all of these interactions, he was a synthesizer, learning from others. But King also brought to the New Left his own indispensable qualities. His spiritual vision of equality was rooted in America's history but unsparingly honest about the betrayals of its promises. His willingness to work with everyone on the left provided a model for how to transcend McCarthyism through personal integrity. Finally, his sheer popularity energized a great current of radical reform; he showed radicals how to once again "speak American," this time through the cadences of African American Protestantism.

By itself, of course, King's celebrity was hardly sufficient to overturn Jim Crow. Charismatic leaders cannot substitute for the power of a grassroots movement, however much they energize and inspire it. Early on, the veteran NAACP activist Ella Baker, hired by King as executive secretary of SCLC, warned presciently of the danger of "leader-centered groups" rather than "group-centered leadership." King's fame helped create the conditions for a renewed activism, but thousands of unsung local leaders did the hard grassroots organizing, county-by-county, that challenged the entrenched authority of the white power structure.

SNCC AND THE UPSURGE OF MASS PROTEST

As Eisenhower's second term moved to its close in 1960, it seemed as if the Civil Rights movement had stalled. Most activists could envision only slow progress. The 1957 Civil Rights Act was the first such federal legislation since the 1870s, but it only empowered the Justice Department to investigate individual cases of disfranchisement, rather than challenging the whole structure of white power. Here and there a few federal judges, usually liberal Republicans appointed by Eisenhower, issued local desegregation orders. Southern Democrats competed to prove their undying loyalty to "segregation now, segregation tomorrow, segregation forever," as Alabama Governor George Wallace proclaimed in his 1963 inaugural address. In January 1960, as the nation readied for a presidential election, no one could imagine how quickly things would change. What the movement needed as the 1960s dawned was a new constituency with new tactics to galvanize southern blacks, capture the North's imagination, and force apart the wall of segregation town by town.

Suddenly that constituency appeared—black youth, joined by a few whites, who pioneered a strategy of localized organizing that drew on black community traditions of resistance. Leading the way was SNCC, the Student Nonviolent Coordinating Committee, which became one of the New Left's most influential organizations. SNCC joined its efforts to King's Southern Christian Leadership Conference, the Congress of Racial Equality (which had a national network of interracial chapters), and the veteran NAACP; the movement's collective efforts made the next five years a rollercoaster of mass protest, violent repression, and intense pressure upon the Democrats controlling the national government. This history is littered with the names of places made famous: Greensboro, North Carolina; Albany, Georgia; Greenwood, Mississippi; Birmingham and Selma, Alabama. When the dust cleared, segregation as a legal and social system was collapsing, and both the South and the nation were profoundly changed.

SNCC's founding was unplanned. At the right time, the right thing seemed to happen. Four young men, students at all-black North Carolina Agricultural and Technical State University in Greensboro, decided on February 1, 1960 that they would ask for service at the whites-only lunch counter of a local Woolworths. They sat down, ordered coffee, and refused to leave. Shortly, they were joined by hundreds of others (even a few white students) and arrests followed. Within weeks, the "sit-ins" spread across the South, as groups of black youth jammed restaurants and stores that took black customers' money but refused them equal treatment. Thousands of arrests were made and network television crews flooded in. In town after town, store owners made concessions while authorities pleaded for restraint. The color line was beginning to crack.

It is easy to view the 1960 sit-ins as spontaneous eruptions. The Greensboro students had no organizational structure when they began. But that impression is no more accurate than the myth that Rosa Parks was just a woman with tired feet. In fact, those four young men drew on powerful local traditions of activism. Blacks in Greensboro had been voting for several decades, and in the late 1940s and 1950s began electing their own to local office. The city's reputedly progressive white leadership had seemed to welcome desegregation following the *Brown* decision, but somehow nothing really had happened as resistance hardened. By the end of the 1950s, more and more black Greensboroans, including students at North Carolina A&T, had concluded that the city's reputation for racial tolerance was a genteel fraud. A NAACP youth group had formed, to which several of the sit-in participants belonged. Word had spread of direct action protests in other cities, led by new student organizations like the Nonviolent Action Group (NAG) at Nashville's Fisk College, from which came many SNCC leaders.

On April 15, 1960, SCLC convened a regional meeting of student protest leaders at Shaw University in Raleigh, North Carolina. Ella Baker shrewdly advised the students to keep themselves separate from any adult group, including SCLC; for the next five years she acted as the young organization's senior adviser. The student organizers, many of whom later became famous, including John Lewis, Julian Bond, Diane Nash, James Bevel, and Marion Barry, agreed to form the Student Nonviolent Coordinating Committee to keep their southwide protest going. They affirmed a manifesto drafted by the Reverend James Lawson, a devout pacifist and former missionary in India, who had founded Fisk's NAG. This famous "Statement of Purpose" declared that SNCC sought "a social order of justice permeated by love" and that "Such love goes to the extreme; it remains loving and forgiving even in the midst of hostility. It matches the capacity of evil to inflict suffering with an even more enduring capacity to absorb evil, all the while persisting in love."

Quickly SNCC began to evolve into a major vehicle for regional action, aided by Baker's experience and her radical vision of community organizing, plus the administrative competence of executive secretary James Forman. Forman put organizers into the field in long-term projects intended to develop self-reliant leadership in local communities, rather than the short-term protest campaigns in which leaders like King and his lieutenants, Ralph Abernathy and Wyatt T. Walker, periodically flew in to lead marches and give press conferences. Early on, SNCC also received support from an unlikely source. John F. Kennedy had won in November 1960 in large part because of a call days before the election to Coretta Scott King, expressing his sympathy because a Georgia judge sent her husband to jail for months over an unpaid parking violation. Kennedy's campaign had flooded black churches and newspapers with leaflets proclaiming his support for the movement and Dr. King, and he won in several major states because of a shift of black votes. Once in office, disturbed by southern black militancy but hoping to build his electoral base, Kennedy and his brother Robert, the new attorney general, persuaded a northern foundation to fund voter registration throughout the South in order to neutralize both black radicalism and the southern Democrats. The Kennedys' presumption was that bringing potential black voters into local courthouses to register was less likely to spark violence than mass boycotts, sit-ins, and protest marches. The resulting Voter Education Project funneled hundreds of thousands of dollars to the various civil rights groups, with each taking responsibility for specific states or counties. But SNCC's voter registration campaigns, especially those nurtured by Robert Moses in Mississippi, led to the most intensive organizing and the worst repression in the whole history of "the Movement."

The president and his brother had good reason to fear public bloodletting. On May 4, 1961, spurred by SNCC's growth, a CORE-sponsored interracial team left Washington on a bus into the Deep South, seeking to test the legality of state laws requiring segregated transportation. The Freedom Riders were met with extreme violence, which transfixed the nation via television, and caused the Kennedys much torment. In the Upper South, the bus ride proved uneventful. Things changed when it crossed into Alabama on May 14. By this time, both SNCC and Martin Luther King were drawn in. Robert Kennedy urged state officials to provide police protection and called for a "cooling off" period, but state officials like Alabama Governor John Patterson openly defied the attorney general, legitimating mob violence. High-level representatives of the Department of Justice could not prevent Ku Klux Klan attacks, including bus burnings, beatings during which a white Freedom Rider suffered brain damage, and a mass assault on a Montgomery church where King was speaking, which required the last-minute mobilization of troops from a nearby Air Force base to block a massacre. More Freedom Rides by SNCC throughout 1961 underlined that the U.S. government lacked the political will to protect its citizens. Finally, the Interstate Commerce Commission ruled all buses and bus terminals must be desegregated—a considerable victory, though there was little compliance in southern towns.

The most hard-fought battle of 1961–1962 took place in Albany, in southwestern Georgia. It was a painful but useful defeat, involving many competing forces—SCLC, SNCC, the NAACP, and local leaders. The Albany Movement pressed for elemental progress: hiring blacks for municipal jobs; a biracial committee to discuss school integration; desegregating the local bus station. Most of the black community joined in concerted protest, including boycotts. But the city's white leadership, led by Sheriff Laurie Pritchett, knew that time was on its side and public violence would only damage its cause. Arresting hundreds of blacks, but always acting within the law, the city's authorities dragged the campaign out until divisions grew between local and outside organizers and the movement collapsed. King felt humiliated, and resolved that next time SCLC would pick its fight and the terms on which to fight, instead of being drawn into a local struggle with no clear strategy. For their part, many SNCC organizers were disillusioned by what they perceived as King's timidity and the constant competition for money with older groups like the NAACP.

By 1963, then, the South still seemed a battleground with no winner in sight. Across the region, local civil rights campaigns sprouted, many initiated by SNCC's field secretaries—students sent out with a few dollars and names of dedicated "local people" to contact. A smaller number were CORE projects, similar to SNCC. The existing NAACP chapters led by older, middle-class activists remained important, though their national leaders were jealous of the newer organizations and sometimes blocked the formation of coalitions. Finally, there were church-based SCLC campaigns headed by King, the one leader who could draw audiences and raise money all across the country; over the years, though they received much less attention than SNCC's efforts in Alabama and Mississippi's black-majority counties, SCLC affiliates did most of the practical work of registering new black voters. It had taken the two decades since World War II for this diverse, complex movement to assemble, with the capacity to move all parts of the black community, and to engage in the widest possible variety of political action and protest. In the twenty-four months from early 1963 to early 1965, it would smash segregation forever.

1963–1965: THE DESTRUCTION OF JIM CROW

In the winter and spring of 1963, SCLC forced an epic confrontation for power in Birmingham, Alabama, the most segregated of the South's major cities, known as "Bombingham" because of its tradition of Klan violence. Having learned the lessons from the defeat in Albany, King and Reverend Fred Shuttlesworth (the indomitable leader of the Alabama Christian Movement for Human Rights, SCLC's affiliate) defined a short, intense campaign with precise goals. They deliberately faced off against a notoriously repressive police commissioner, Eugene "Bull" Connor, a living symbol of white power. From the beginning, Connor used police dogs and fire hoses to break up peaceful demonstrations, leading to dramatic media coverage which was beamed across the world. At a strategic moment, SCLC organizer James Bevel unleashed crowds of neatly dressed black high school students, who were arrested in the hundreds as they sang "freedom songs." At the same time, however, poorer blacks reacted fiercely to police violence, using bottles and bricks to fight back. Dr. King went to jail to underscore his refusal to back down, and from his cell, wrote the "Letter from Birmingham Jail" that underlined his fundamentally radical stance, denouncing moderate approaches to the sustained evil of Jim Crow in ringing phrases that evoked the entire history of black struggle in America:

> We know through painful experience that freedom is never voluntarily given by the oppressor; it must be demanded by the oppressed. Frankly I have never yet engaged in a direct action movement that was "well timed," according to the timetable of those who have not suffered unduly from the disease of segregation. For years now, I have heard the word "Wait!". . . . We have waited for more than 340 years for our constitutional and God-given rights. The nations of Asia and Africa are moving with jetlike speed toward the goal of political independence, and we still creep at horse and buggy pace toward the gaining of a cup of coffee at a lunch counter.

Facing a strict black economic boycott, the disapproval of the outside world, and possible deepening racial violence, white business leaders negotiated a settlement over Connor's head—though all they granted was token black employment in downtown stores and further talks toward eventual desegregation.

Alabama was only one instance of intensifying confrontation in the Deep South. In neighboring Mississippi, a violent white insurrection broke out in October 1962 to prevent a black student, James Meredith, from entering "Ole Miss," the University of Mississippi, under a federal court order. Over two days and nights, several thousand whites traded rifle fire with hundreds of federal marshals. Meanwhile, in dozens of small Mississippi towns, SNCC-initiated mobilizations were growing in militancy, as the underground "organizing tradition" of the black poor and working class burst forth, led mainly by women, the small number of independent farmers, and high school students. Whole families came into the Movement, and were thrown off plantations, lost their jobs, and were beaten and shot at. Often they fired back too, as mothers used shotguns to chase off white hoodlums and protect their homes, ignoring SNCC's commitment to nonviolence. In most organizers' recollections, women played central roles, facing down sheriffs, white plantation overseers, and election registrars, as well as the middle-class men who typically monopolized leadership in southern black communities. Many of these middle-aged women, like Fannie Lou Hamer, Victoria Gray, and Annie Devine, became models for the youth who "went South" with SNCC, as examples of articulate, courageous leadership despite the triple burdens of class, race, and gender. They were key to the victory won in the Delta town of Greenwood, where a SNCC field secretary, Sam Block, canvassed door-to-door for months with a core of teenage organizers, just to assemble a group willing to go to the courthouse and try to register. By spring 1963 the unimaginable had happened: Block and his local allies had built a visible, militant mass movement in the citadel of white supremacy, the Mississippi Delta. Sensing an opportunity, SNCC's executive secretary James Forman brought in dozens of organizers from around the state to wage an all-out fight, and reaped a harvest of press attention and momentum as concessions began to be won.

One result of both SCLC's and SNCC's increasingly confrontational campaigns, and the grudging victories they forced, was increased repression. June 11, 1963 was an historic date in more ways than one. That morning, Alabama Governor George Wallace staged his famous "stand in the schoolhouse door" at the University of Alabama, trying to block the admission of several African American students. That evening, President Kennedy made a historic speech on national television. Speaking extemporaneously and with evident passion, for the first time he denounced segregation as an evil to be ended without delay. Using the starkest language of any President since

Lincoln, Kennedy told the nation that "We are confronted with a moral issue. It is as old as the Scriptures and is as clear as the American Constitution . . . whether all Americans are to be afforded equal rights and equal opportunities; whether we are going to treat our fellow Americans as we want to be treated." He also called for comprehensive civil rights legislation to ban all forms of segregation and discrimination. As if to validate Kennedy's urgency, only hours after his speech, Medgar Evers, the NAACP's courageous Mississippi state director, was gunned down in his driveway, provoking nationwide shock (his killer, Byron de la Beckwith, was acquitted twice by all-white juries, and was not convicted until 1994).

Evers' murder upped the ante, but before the final assault on Fortress Mississippi, a transcendent national event took place, the August 1963 March on Washington for "Jobs and Freedom." Following King's victory in Birmingham, he endorsed an idea suggested earlier by Bayard Rustin and A. Philip Randolph. Building on Randolph's 1941 March on Washington Movement, they urged a new march to press for strong civil rights legislation and to address the economic inequality faced by all African Americans. At first, the established civil rights leadership, led by the NAACP's Roy Wilkins and the Urban League's Whitney Young, refused to participate, fearing a divisive event. Over the summer, however, they agreed, and the March on Washington became a drive to support the Kennedy Administration's new civil rights bill. It received public backing from the president himself in July. Buoyed by this legitimacy and support from powerful groups like the United Auto Workers union, the march became a national cause, the first great demonstration in a generation and the largest protest rally in U.S. history up to that point.

At the last minute, as a quarter of a million people streamed into Washington in late August, a crisis threatened. Various sponsors read the text of SNCC chairman John Lewis's speech. Angry over years of public violence against civil rights organizers while the Kennedy administration refused to act, Lewis lashed out in frankly revolutionary language, damning the president and conservatives in both parties. The outraged Catholic archbishop of Washington threatened to walk off the stage if Lewis read his speech. Hours before the march's official opening, Justice Department official Burke Marshall proposed a toned-down version of the speech (although it had already been released to the press). Under protest, Lewis read Marshall's version, and the huge event went forward, capped by King's "I Have a Dream" oration.

Three months later, on November 22, Kennedy was shot dead in Dallas, Texas, leaving an uncertain legacy in civil rights. His legislation banning all forms of segregation in public facilities was stalled in Congress, and the attitude of his successor, Lyndon Johnson, remained unclear. If further proof was needed that the battle was far from over, on September 15, 1963 Klan terrorists blew up a church in Birmingham, killing four young black girls during Sunday school; not until 2001 were two of the bombers finally convicted.

In 1964, the focus shifted back to Mississippi, as SNCC's years of community organizing resulted in a massive voter registration campaign supporting the new, explicitly interracial Mississippi Freedom Democratic Party (MFDP). To support the MFDP, the Council of Federated Organizations (COFO) assembled a coalition of all the civil rights groups working in the state, though SNCC and its smaller partner CORE were responsible for the most of the organizing. It was clear that the state authorities and the Klan, working closely together, would go all-out to stop the MFDP and crush COFO. To catalyze national attention and provide the beleaguered local organizers with protection, Robert Moses and others in SNCC proposed a Mississippi Summer Project, bringing in hundreds of northern whites as foot soldiers and nonviolent shields. The ultimate goal was to stage a parallel presidential primary election, open to all races, to legitimate the Freedom Democratic Party, and give it a case for replacing the all-white Regular Democrats at the 1964 National Democratic Convention.

During spring 1964, recruiting for Mississippi spread rapidly on northern and western campuses like Yale and Stanford. The moral challenge and physical danger of Freedom Summer galvanized the emerging student vanguard. In late June, hundreds of young whites gathered at an Ohio campus for training in nonviolent resistance by Moses and Forman. But already, three CORE workers (a black Mississippian, James Chaney and two white northerners, Michael Schwerner and Andrew Goodman) were reported missing in the town of Philadelphia. Over the course of that famous summer, nearly a thousand white northerners went to Mississippi, while the FBI and the Navy searched for the bodies of Goodman, Schwerner, and Chaney at the orders of President Johnson. They were finally found buried in an earthen dam. A lynch mob including the local sheriff had shot and beaten them to death, the first of fifteen activists killed that summer. The northerners fanned out across the state, staffing Freedom Schools for black children and going door-to-door to persuade adults to try and register to vote. They lived with local black families who slept next to shotguns and buckets of water to douse gasoline bombs, and watched black churches burn. Many were driven off the highway by white toughs and threatened by mobs, knowing that only their skin color protected them from homicidal violence.

No matter what its outcome, the Freedom Summer had an extraordinary impact on many white students. It came to a disturbing conclusion at the Democratic Convention in August, in Atlantic City, New Jersey. 80,000 people had voted in the MFDP's alternative primary. Its delegation, headed by the former sharecropper Fannie Lou Hamer, went to Atlantic City expecting to be seated. Instead, Johnson used liberals like vice-presidential hopeful Senator Hubert Humphrey, and movement leaders like Rustin and King, to place intensive pressure on the Freedom Democrats to withdraw their challenge to the all-white Regulars. Johnson feared losing southern electoral votes to Republican candidate Barry Goldwater, who took a strict "states rights" stand against civil rights legislation. To Johnson's consternation, the MFDP refused to give up its principles. Mrs. Hamer argued her case with searing eloquence before the convention's Credentials Committee on live national television, prompting an unscheduled press conference by LBJ to preempt her testimony. Eventually, the Johnson forces forced a majority of the committee to deny the MFDP challenge, awarding them two symbolic seats on the convention floor; by this time, the white Regulars had already left, refusing to endorse Johnson. The Freedom Democrats went home disgusted, and SNCC organizers who put their lives at risk in Mississippi's backwoods regarded the defeat of the "Mississippi challenge" as an unforgivable betrayal. The tenuous alliance between the emerging New Left and the Cold War liberal establishment was coming apart.

It is ironic, even tragic, that during 1964–1965, as the Civil Rights movement moved to the left, the Johnson administration finally fulfilled many of Cold War liberalism's promises. In June 1964, Johnson had twisted arms to push Kennedy's comprehensive Civil Rights Act through Congress, outlawing discrimination on the basis of race in employment and all public facilities from restaurants to movie theaters. In the end, a majority of northern Republicans had joined with northern Democrats to override the filibustering of southern Democrats—the last meaningful expression of the Republican Party's historic commitment to black equality. Then in 1965, as the final great confrontation of the southern movement heated up, the administration prepared a sweeping Voting Rights Act. In both cases, the debate in Congress indicated without any question that the political mainstream acted decisively not from a suddenly discovered commitment to equality, but because of the crisis the Civil Rights movement had forced. The liberals in power followed, rather than led, but by 1964 it was too little, too late for many in "the Movement."

In early 1965, King and SCLC were again in the forefront as the focus shifted back to Alabama. The year before, King had won the Nobel Peace Prize, an unprecedented (and to many whites, unimaginable) international honor accorded to black America's struggle for human rights. SCLC hoped to repeat the success of Birmingham through a series of demonstrations that would provoke local authorities, garner national attention, and create a crisis. Selma, a county seat in the Black Belt where SNCC organizers had faced brutal repression by Sheriff Jim Clark, was chosen as the target. A march was planned from Selma to the state capitol in Montgomery. On Sunday, March 7, 1965, an orderly crowd crossed the Edmund Pettus bridge, and was charged by state troopers on horses, clubs flying. Dozens were clubbed unconscious, including SNCC chairman John Lewis, and the ABC television network interrupted its regular program (by coincidence, a Hollywood blockbuster about Nazism, *Judgment at Nuremberg*) with live coverage of the carnage.

Churchpeople from around the country flew in to join the rescheduled march on Montgomery, led by King. A white Unitarian minister from Boston, James Reeb, was beaten to death by white assailants on Selma's streets, provoking national outrage. Only days before, a black teenager, Jimmy Lee Jackson, was shot to death when he tried to protect his mother from a policeman, but his death received little attention, another cause of bitterness for movement organizers. Eight days after Selma's notorious "Bloody Sunday" at the Pettus Bridge, the President himself spoke to Congress, evoking Lincoln and his own status as a southern white man, and emphatically repeating the movement's slogan, "We shall overcome." Johnson demanded approval of a Voting Rights Act that would be the first direct federal intervention to guarantee black voting rights since Reconstruction. It passed overwhelmingly in August, banning literacy tests and providing for special government examiners empowered to register voters in any county where voting fell below a minimum level. It remains in force to this day. Though years of struggle to register black voters and enforce the laws against segregation lay ahead, by the middle of 1965 Jim Crow was clearly on the way out. With its passing the Civil Rights movement lost much of its direction, or so it seemed. In fact, having accomplished many of their goals, a significant number of black organizers refused to rest on their laurels and began moving towards the next logical step—a strategy of self-determination and autonomy, or Black Power.

THE ORIGINS OF BLACK POWER

Traditional historical narratives of the Civil Rights movement stop at this point in 1965, treating the complex, unresolved narrative of the Black Power movement as something distinct and separate—with the militancy of Black Power negatively counterposed to the nonviolence of civil rights. There is a basic problem with this approach. Often, it simply reproduces the hostile and uninformed coverage of the Black Power movement in the mainstream white media after 1965. To most whites, Black Power seemed to come out of nowhere. In fact, it had deep roots in black political traditions, and had steadily gathered force as an alternate strategy during the ten years from Montgomery to Selma. During that decade, white Americans and their political leaders had assumed three things. First, that the struggle for black equality was strictly a southern issue. Second, that its unquestioned leader was Martin Luther King, Jr., with his insistence on nonviolent integration into white society. Third, that once legal segregation was abolished and southern blacks could vote, the struggle was over. Thus, when black urban neighborhoods outside the South, the so-called "ghettos," rose up in violent rebellion in 1964 and after, and young militants began talking about Black Power "by any means necessary," in Malcolm X's words, most whites were stunned if not outraged. What their shock and anger revealed was the gulf of incomprehension separating even liberal whites from the real lives of black people. Whites did not—could not, would not—understand that African Americans in *all* parts of the United States, from Boston to Los Angeles, felt oppressed by powerful structures of economic and political exclusion. Even if they could vote and were not legally barred from eating, sitting, or living where they chose, black people outside the South were thoroughly aware of the jobs, neighborhoods, schools, clubs, restaurants, bars, bowling alleys, pools, and other public spaces closed to them. Though most supported the civil rights campaigns, the North included numerous political groups opposed to nonviolent integration and contemptuous of King. These organizations were usually called "nationalist," reflecting their emphasis on African Americans as a separate people with the rights of self-determination and self-defense.

Historically, black nationalists had focused on building economic and political independence for black people through the control of businesses and community institutions. Since Booker T. Washington, this was a powerful message for blacks who found themselves working for white employers, shopping at white-owned stores, and dealing with white salespeople, even in their own neighborhoods. In the post–World War II era, because of highly discriminatory banking policies supported by the federal government, black business people had little access to credit and would-be black homeowners found it very difficult to get mortgages, so that the mass of African Americans remained renters and consumers instead of owners and sellers. In many northern cities, while the black middle class did grow, conditions for the working-class majority steadily deteriorated after 1950. Major industries like automobile manufacturing, where black men had gained a foothold in the 1930s and 1940s, began the long process of deindustrialization, moving factories to nonunion, low-wage locations in rural areas, southern states, or overseas. Cities like Detroit, Cleveland, and Buffalo, the bustling hearts of the World War II "arsenal of democracy," were turning into a proverbial Rust Belt as early as 1960. Though effective in mobilizing southern African Americans and northern white sympathizers, King's ringing speeches about brotherhood and equality before the law had little relevance to the slum housing, systemic unemployment, rundown schools, and white business dominance afflicting the northern ghettos. This contradiction between a rights-focused movement oriented to the South, and the deepening social problems in the urban North, birthed the various nationalist and radical currents that coalesced into the Black Power movement after 1965.

The touchstone for twentieth-century black nationalism was Marcus Garvey's Universal Negro Improvement Association. It declined in the 1930s, but small Garveyite groups persevered through street-corner speaking in Harlem and other cities, keeping alive the idea of a powerful Black Nation. A new strain of nationalism surged to prominence in the 1950s—the Nation of Islam (NOI) or Black Muslims. Founded in the 1930s, the Nation of Islam was a small religious sect led by the Honorable Elijah Muhammad, who called for total withdrawal from white America and uncompromising self-reliance. He derided the Civil Rights movement and avoided politics of any sort. Among the northern black poor, the Nation of Islam quietly built a following as the only group that openly mocked whites as "blue-eyed devils," while practicing an austere and impressive self-discipline. However radical its critique of white supremacy, the NOI was extremely conservative culturally, which gave it an air of patriarchal authority. Its clean-cut male members, striking in their conservative suits and bow ties, swore off alcohol, drugs, and tobacco, and spent their time selling the newspaper *Muhammad Speaks*, working in the NOI's various businesses and drilling as the paramilitary Fruit of Islam. Women were expected to be obedient helpmeets, but were treated respectfully, and family life was emphasized. The Nation was especially successful at prison recruiting. Muslim organizations remain an established part of prison life to this day, offering emotional support, physical protection, and a political worldview to imprisoned black men. The Nation of Islam's most famous convert was Malcolm Little, introduced to its doctrines by his brother while jailed for burglary in Massachusetts in the late 1940s; their parents had been dedicated Garveyites. Upon his 1953 release, the renamed Malcolm X began a legendary career of public speaking and organizing of dozens of new mosques for Elijah Muhammad. Drawing on his hard work and riveting oratory, the Nation grew rapidly in the late 1950s, recruiting thousands of members.

More important than its own membership, however, was the Nation of Islam's influence among much larger numbers of black people. While relatively few accepted the Muslims' strict discipline, millenarian religious beliefs, and abstention from politics, many were deeply attracted to its assertion of pride in blackness. Its public meetings were the only place where a young person could go to hear an alternative view of black history and buy books by black scholars scorned by the white academy. Above all, the Nation of Islam had Malcolm X, whose slashing wit about the humiliations shared by black people in a "white man's country" endeared him to many who otherwise had little use for Elijah Muhammad's abstruse spiritual doctrines. And, despite the Nation's official contempt for politics, from the late 1950s on, Malcolm increasingly involved his Harlem mosque in street rallies for African liberation leaders like Kwame Nkrumah visiting the United States, union campaigns, and other secular causes. He also led his tough Fruit of Islam cadres to stand in disciplined formation outside police stations, demanding the release of young black men brutalized by white cops, something few African American leaders had ever attempted.

Global politics were key to the new nationalism. The post-1945 decades were an era of colonial revolution, as the vast African and Asian empires of the English, French, Dutch, Belgians, and Portuguese were broken up, and new nations appeared by the dozens. With few exceptions, the Europeans gave up their colonial possessions only under great political pressure or through outright military defeat. This process began when the British left India in 1947, and finally ended when white-ruled South Africa came under black majority rule in the early 1990s. In the 1950s, the world's attention focused on Africa. The Mau-Mau rebellion led by Jomo Kenyatta broke out in Kenya, and the National Liberation Front of Algeria began guerrilla warfare against the French. All over the continent, similar struggles erupted, leading to the 1957 independence of Ghana from British rule, the first important European colony in Africa to achieve freedom. This West African nation was led by the charismatic Kwame Nkrumah. Like many African independence leaders, he had been educated in the United States at a historically black college—in his Nkrumah's case, Lincoln University outside of Philadelphia. Nkrumah was such an important figure that both Vice President Richard Nixon and Dr. Martin Luther King, Jr. flew to Ghana to attend the independence celebrations in 1957. In subsequent years hundreds of African Americans, including Dr. W.E.B. Du Bois, immigrated to Ghana, drawn by Nkrumah's blend of nationalism and socialism. The term "Black Power" was actually coined by the novelist Richard Wright as the title of a 1954 book about Ghana on the eve of nationhood. One of the most prominent U.S. organizations that championed Africa's liberation and modernization through high-level conferences and academic exchanges was the all-black American Society for African Culture (AMSAC). Only later did it surface that AMSAC was backed by the CIA, as a way of keeping African American support for the new African nations within safely anticommunist limits.

Ghana's independence was followed by a series of dramatic events: Fidel Castro's victory in Cuba in January 1959; the massacre of sixty-nine peaceful black demonstrators by white South African police at Sharpeville on March 21, 1960; and the assassination in late 1960 of Patrice Lumumba, President of the newly independent Congo, by groups linked to the CIA. Cuba was a powerful impetus to black radicalism in the United States both because of historic connections between African Americans and Afro-Cubans, and because Castro was a scathing critic of Jim Crow. Hardcore segregationists held him personally responsible for fomenting the freedom rides and sit-ins. In 1961, Cuba gave sanctuary to North Carolina NAACP leader Robert F. Williams, whom many blacks saw as a genuine hero after he organized armed self-defense against Ku Klux Klan intimidation (see chapter 5). From Cuba, Williams broadcast calls for revolution on a "Radio Free Dixie" program beamed to the United States, and was named chairman-in-exile of the small Revolutionary Action Movement (RAM), a forerunner of the Black Panther Party. Also in 1961, the Kennedy administration indicted a prominent black journalist, William Worthy, for traveling illegally to Cuba, though most African Americans thought his crime was reporting fairly on Cuba's revolution. Events like these were closely watched in black communities, because they highlighted the hypocrisy of the U.S. government's claimed support for freedom. Black newspapers bitterly commented on the silence over Sharpeville and other instances of brutal repression by white-minority governments in Africa, versus the loud denunciations of Castro and vigorous efforts to undermine the Cuban Revolution.

In this atmosphere, local nationalist and radical groups began to proliferate. In February 1961, New York's On Guard for Freedom invaded the United Nations' Security Council chamber to protest Lumumba's murder, interrupting U.S. Delegate Adlai Stevenson and causing a riot. On Guard members were also active in the Liberation Committee for Africa, which published a magazine called *The Liberator*, covering African guerrilla struggles and debates in the Civil Rights movement, and often mocking King as a tool of white liberals. Meanwhile, young blacks around the country created organizations like the Bay Area's Afro-American Society, focused on issues of cultural identity and self-assertion. Outside the south, CORE and NAACP chapters in cities such as Philadelphia and Cleveland organized strikingly militant challenges to de facto segregation, anticipating Black Power's assailing of customary white prerogatives like control of construction industry jobs. New York CORE's widely publicized attempt to shut down the 1964 World's Fair was a harbinger of disruptions to come. On Maryland's Eastern Shore blacks were segregated and poor but had never lost the vote, unlike the rest of the South. In 1963–1964, a SNCC-affiliated movement in the city of Cambridge, led by Gloria Richardson, confronted the white power structure in protests that set off street fighting and gun battles with local whites, ended only by a yearlong National Guard occupation.

A nationalist upsurge brewed among black artists as well. Since the late 1950s, avant-garde musicians like John Coltrane and Max Roach, and numerous young writers like LeRoi Jones (active in both the Fair Play for Cuba Committee and On Guard) had worked to frame the revolutionary new aesthetic later dubbed the Black Arts Movement. The jazz singer Abbie Lincoln, Roach's spouse and collaborator, broke a social taboo in 1962 by letting her hair grow naturally into what was later called an Afro. She wrote essays in the widely read *Negro Digest* urging black people to define their own sense of beauty separate from white norms, a radical step at that time. The bestselling novelist James Baldwin lent his prestige to black protest's new direction, beyond just demanding civil rights. He warned of "the fire next time" if more was not done about black poverty and hopelessness, and sponsored magazines like *The Liberator*.

In the early 1960s, Detroit was a key incubator of proto–Black Power politics, with a plethora of new initiatives. The Group for Advanced Leadership (GOAL) organized African art exhibits, broadcast a radio show, and worked closely with Malcolm X. James and Grace Lee Boggs, veteran independent Marxists, acted as advisers and mentors to GOAL. James Boggs (a lifelong autoworker born in Alabama's Black Belt) acquired early fame with his 1963 book, *The American Revolution: Pages from a Negro Worker's Notebook*, in which he argued that African Americans had replaced the working class as the revolutionary vanguard in the United States. The Reverend Albert Cleage published a muckraking newspaper, the *Illustrated News*, which decried black subservience to the Democratic Party machine. All of these forces collaborated in the groundbreaking November 1963 Northern Negro Grassroots Leadership Conference, an early attempt to unite groups wanting to move past civil rights toward Black Power. As keynote speaker, Malcolm X gave a clarion call to revolution, "Message to the Grassroots," which was made into a record. Also in 1963, activists like William Worthy, Reverend Cleage, and the Boggses initiated the all-black Freedom Now Party. In 1964 they ran candidates in Michigan, drawing few votes, and the FNP soon collapsed. This premature attempt at independent electoral politics anticipated how many Black Power groups in the late 1960s and 1970s would use the ballot as a way of mobilizing black communities for self-determination.

Looming above all of these efforts in the early 1960s was Malcolm X's growing celebrity. His breakthrough was a five-part 1959 COS News television documentary called "The Hate That Hate Produced," anchored by Mike Wallace, later of *Sixty Minutes*. Subsequently, he gave numerous speeches at elite white universities like Harvard, and even debated at Oxford University in England. His speeches were dubbed onto records and distributed widely in the African American community. An extraordinary speaker, funny and human even when uncompromisingly confrontational (think of his famous one-liner, "We didn't land on Plymouth Rock, Plymouth Rock landed on us"), he inspired blacks and challenged whites with his razor-like logic. In early 1964, Malcolm left the Nation of Islam, denouncing what he considered Elijah Muhammad's moral transgressions—he discovered The Messenger had a series of children with various secretaries—and the Nation's refusal to participate in politics of any kind. After a tour of the Middle East and Africa, he renounced strict racial separatism, and declared his willingness to work with revolutionary whites. He initiated a new secular political organization, the Organization of Afro-American Unity (OAAU), with a program of community empowerment, self-defense when necessary, and political action—the "ballot or the bullet," as he called it. In March 1964, Malcolm gave a prophetic speech in Cleveland, warning Lyndon Johnson that "If he's for civil rights, let him go into the Senate next week and declare himself. . . . Let him go in there and denounce the Southern branch of his party. Let him go in there right now and take a moral stand—right now, not later." But by the time LBJ was finally ready to give that speech, one year later, Malcolm would be dead. In February 1965, he was assassinated by vengeful Nation of Islam members while speaking in Harlem, before the OAAU could get off the ground. His death set the stage for a nationwide turn to Black Power, as revolt began spreading in the northern ghettos.

Chapter 5

CHALLENGING THE COLD WAR BEFORE VIETNAM: "BAN THE BOMB! FAIR PLAY FOR CUBA!"

Nonviolent obstruction makes real to the construction workers the issues symbolized by the missile base. A construction worker and the public may regard the missile base as a new source of income for the locality, a glamorous toy . . . . Actually, a missile can cremate alive three million people and pulverize the largest city. The realities of death are excluded from an American city, but a nonviolent resister sitting in front of a truck raises these realities to public consciousness. The truck driver finds himself faced with the choice of running over the man and killing him or stopping and dragging him out of the way . . . . He sees a man sitting in the dust before his truck who is silently saying to him, "Kill me before you build this missile base; kill me before you help kill a million innocent people."
—Committee for Non-Violent Action leader,
Brad Lyttle, *"On Nonviolent Obstruction,"* Liberation, November, 1958.

The idea of a "revolution" had been foreign to me. It was one of those inconceivably "romantic" and/or hopeless ideas that we Norteamericanos have been taught since public school to hold up to the cold light of "reason." That reason being whatever repugnant lie our usurious "ruling class" had paid their journalists to disseminate. The reason that allows that voting, in a country where the parties are exactly the same, can be made to assume the gravity of actual moral engagement. The reason that permits a young intellectual to believe he has said something profound when he says, "I don't trust men in uniforms" . . . .

The rebels among us have become merely people like myself who grow beards and will not participate in politics. Drugs, juvenile delinquency, complete isolation from the vapid mores of the country, a few current ways out. But name an alternative here. Something not inextricably bound up in a lie . . . . There is none. It's much too late. We are an old people already. Even the vitality of art is like bright flowers growing up through a rotting carcass.

But the Cubans, and the other new peoples (in Asia, Africa, South America) don't need us, and we had better stay out of their way.

—LeRoi Jones, "Cuba Libre," 1960

While 1955 was an auspicious time for black protest, there were few positive signs for peace activists. That year marked the height of the Cold War, when public dissent over foreign policy seemed impossible. In 1953, the Korean War had ended in a truce, with no clear victor. In 1954, the United States's key European ally France was driven out of its colony in Vietnam by nationalist Communists led by Ho Chi Minh. In those same two years, the CIA overthrew democratic, mildly leftist governments in Guatemala and Iran, replacing them with right-wing dictatorships. Fighting "the International Communist Conspiracy" seemed like a holy war, where any means were justified. In this atmosphere, no one could have predicted how a drive by scientists and pacifists to de-escalate the superpowers' nuclear confrontation, and a popular revolution on an island only ninety miles from Florida, would capture much of the public's imagination.

SAVING THE WORLD: THE NEW ANTINUCLEAR ACTIVISM

To general surprise, a new antinuclear peace movement became a political force between 1955 and 1963. This movement encompassed traditional pacifists, liberals committed to international law and disarmament, women speaking out as mothers, younger radical pacifists committed to "direct action" against the warmaking machinery, a fresh generation of student activists, and former Communists seeking vehicles to oppose U.S. foreign policy. It had four key organizations: the Committee for a Sane Nuclear Policy (SANE), and the Committee for Non-Violent Action (CNVA), both founded in 1957; the Student Peace Union (SPU), founded in 1959; and Women Strike for Peace (WSP), founded in 1961. Another important institution was the magazine *Liberation*, which began publishing in 1956 and quickly became an intellectual center for the New Left as a whole.

In their tactics and organizational structures, these groups differed greatly. What they shared was horror at the possibility of "Mutual Assured Destruction," or MAD. This was the term that U.S. military strategists used to describe the standoff with the Soviet Union, where each power had the ability to incinerate the other's major population centers on half an hour's notice. At a time when many Americans declared their children would be "better dead than Red," peace activism sprouted among a growing minority who found such a choice morally unacceptable. These activists used the Cold War against itself, like those early civil rights leaders who upheld the proclaimed ideals of American democracy against Jim Crow. Since 1947, presidents, secretaries of state, congressmen, religious leaders, and intellectuals had characterized the struggle between the Free World and the Soviet bloc as a manichean contest between light and dark, good and evil. This apocalyptic language suggested Americans must save humanity by "containing" and eventually "rolling back" communism. The new peace movement insisted that the end of humankind in a nuclear holocaust was a greater threat than the Soviets, and called for U.S. leadership to avoid this catastrophe.

The global "Ban the Bomb" movement of the later 1950s began by challenging a problem caused by both superpowers: uncontrolled nuclear test explosions in the earth's atmosphere, which generated massive amounts of radioactive fallout that poisoned people, regardless of their ideology. The drive to abolish nuclear testing energized, and then eventually consumed, the new peace movement. In the eight years after 1955, these groups created the first public space within the United States for dissent from the orthodoxy of national security. The antitesting campaign began among scientists. After a brief flurry of post–World War II activism, the scientific community was largely silent about nuclear war. One exception was the eminent physicist Linus Pauling, a lonely prophet. But in 1954, a random accident changed the course of world opinion. A Japanese fishing boat came too close to an American test explosion in the Pacific, and its crew received a heavy dose of radiation. Later that year, irrefutable scientific evidence about the dangers of fallout was published in the *Bulletin of the Atomic Scientists*. The scandal spurred a global outcry by top scientists and intellectuals, led by Pauling, Albert Schweitzer, and Lord Bertrand Russell of England. This furor led to the formation of several new organizations, in particular SANE.

Though it quickly became the largest peace group, SANE's expansion was more accidental than planned. In 1957 pacifist leaders from the American Friends Service Committee and other groups brought together a committee of prominent individuals (scholars, scientists, businessmen, Socialist Party head Norman Thomas, and Norman Cousins, editor of the prestigious *Saturday Review*) to call for a nuclear test ban. On November 15,1957 this *ad hoc* group published a dramatic full-page advertisement in the *New York Times* with the headline "We Are Facing a Danger Unlike Any Danger That Has Ever Existed." To their surprise, thousands of people wrote in asking to join. By 1958 SANE was a full-blown grassroots organization, with 130 local chapters. At the top, it was a prestigious group, attracting the support of former First Lady Eleanor Roosevelt and a strong contingent from Hollywood. Norman Cousins was its main leader, chairing a top-down board of directors set up to block any infiltration by leftists. Local SANE activists were much more diverse. As the only mainstream organization opposing the militarization of U.S. foreign policy, it drew in many people who had recently left the Communist Party. While SANE prospered, holding large public rallies and conducting extensive publicity campaigns throughout 1959–1963, it remained vulnerable to McCarthyism. Periodically, individuals or whole groups were forced out or resigned in protest over the leadership's tight control. SANE continued on, somewhat wounded, as the respectable public face of the peace movement.

SANE operated as a liberal organization reaching out to the political center by lobbying Congress and public education campaigns rather than through protest. Other activists sought a more direct way to "speak truth to power." This more radical response came from the Committee for Nonviolent Action (CNVA), an outgrowth of the pacifist community born in the wartime Civilian Public Service camps. CNVA was the culmination of years of discussion about how to confront the Cold War while creating a new model for human interaction. CNVA's founders believed in active nonviolence and a way of life based on cooperation rather than competition. Long before the mass media popularized communal living and organic farming in the late 1960s, radical pacifists like Dave Dellinger pioneered these alternatives. Unlike SANE—a large, hierarchical organization—CNVA was a loose network of individuals and small groups, led by an *ad hoc* steering committee. It existed to carry out visible civil disobedience, risking arrest so as to heighten consciousness. In 1957 a small group of CNVAers began "witnessing" against nuclear war by climbing fences and blocking trucks at an Air Force base on the Great Plains where nuclear tests were conducted. They returned year after year, later adding international "walks for peace" (San Francisco to Moscow in 1961, for instance) to awaken ordinary citizens to the nuclear peril. Eventually CNVA dwindled as its leaders moved on to other forms of organizing. Its main contribution was to introduce civil disobedience to the peace movement, while popularizing a mode of decentralized, informal organization that permeated the larger New Left.

By 1957, when SANE and CNVA formed, *Liberation* was already publishing. Like CNVA (with which it overlapped considerably), it crystallized the emergence of an uncompromising, revolutionary pacifist stance. Month after month, *Liberation* offered a worldview based in nonviolent fellowship and a rigorous internationalism, through first-hand reports on the Third World that were free from pro-Soviet or pro-American blinders. Three of *Liberation*'s founders played key roles in the new radicalism: A.J. Muste, retired Executive Secretary of the Fellowship of Reconciliation, who acted as a broker in overcoming divisions between communists and anticommunist leftists throughout the New Left's first decade; Dave Dellinger, a CPS veteran and CNVA leader who chaired the major anti-Vietnam War coalitions of the later 1960s; and Bayard Rustin, a black pacifist who was a close adviser to Martin Luther King, Jr. and chief organizer of the 1963 March on Washington. Dr. King's first published article appeared in *Liberation* in 1956, a tangible sign of the partnership between pacifists and civil rights organizers that signaled the emergence of a New Left.

By the end of the 1950s, a full-blown peace movement had emerged in the activities of *Liberation*, SANE and CNVA. New groups kept forming based in specific constituencies, an indication of the movement's growing breadth. First was the Student Peace Union (SPU). Though it was the first nationwide organization of student New Leftists, SPU is largely forgotten today. It began at the University of Chicago, spreading first through the Midwest and then nationally. Within a few years, it reached a peak membership of 14,000, part of the 1959–1962 surge of northern student organizing that included actions in solidarity with the 1960 sit-ins by southern black students, and support for the Cuban Revolution. SPU's high point was a national day of lobbying in 1962, when 5,000 students converged on Washington to support a nuclear test ban; a delegation of their leaders met with President Kennedy. Soon afterward it declined, as the United States and the Soviet Union took major steps towards control of nuclear weapons and the focus of student activism shifted to civil rights.

The last major peace group to emerge in this period was Women Strike for Peace. Its origins were completely informal. In late 1961, the Soviet Union resumed above-ground nuclear tests after the United States refused to accept a voluntary mutual ban. Several friendship networks of women around the country had been discussing how to challenge the ongoing confrontation; most of these women were housewives and mothers, but they had shared backgrounds in activist politics. Almost spontaneously, they decided to call a nationwide mothers' protest. The instigator of this long-distance networking was Dagmar Wilson, an accomplished book illustrator. Wilson and her friends had accommodated themselves to the quasi-Victorian gender norms of the 1950s by identifying themselves in public as mothers rather than political activists. They took advantage of the era's intensely maternalist discourse by claiming the right to protect the world in which their children would grow up—a neat end-run around Cold War ideology.

On November 1, 1961, after only a few weeks of organizing via telephone, these mothers' networks called a one-day "strike." An estimated 50,000 women across the country attracted surprised, mostly positive press coverage as they wheeled baby carriages outside of city halls. Soon after, this *ad hoc* "dis-organization," as they called themselves, which refused to keep membership lists or establish a formal structure, named itself Women Strike for Peace (WSP). In 1962, WSP's fame increased when the House Committee on Un-American Activities (HUAC), one of the remaining institutional pillars of McCarthyism, ordered its leaders to testify about possible Communist infiltration. For years, this ritualized spectacle had humiliated individuals and destroyed organizations. This time, it turned out quite differently, in what WSP activists dubbed "Ladies' Day at the Capitol." In the face of a crowd of respectable , well-dressed housewives cheering on their leaders, completely stymied by WSP's lack of an organizational structure, the conservative congressmen looked like mean old men attacking innocent mothers. By invoking their status as "ladies," Women Strike for Peace faced down the McCarthyites, making them seem irrelevant. WSP continued on as an important group in the Vietnam War years, with a distinctive blending of traditional motherhood, decentralized decision-making, and radical politics (one of its best-known leaders was Bella Abzug, elected to Congress in 1970 from Manhattan's Upper West Side).

This outline of the new antinuclear peace movement jumps quickly over a wealth of activism from 1955 to 1963. The older organizations like AFSC, FOR, WILPF and WRL continued to play vital roles, as they would throughout subsequent decades, bringing institutional resources to the reviving movement. Disarmament became a modest part of the nation's political culture, so that even a cautious Cold War liberal like Kennedy finally embraced it. He negotiated the Limited Test Ban Treaty with the Soviets in 1963, and then forcefully lobbied the Senate to ratify it, one of his greatest accomplishments. Thousands of people were drawn into new forms of activism, and public rallying for peace became acceptable. But it should also be underlined how constrained this movement was. A still-vigorous anticommunist consensus sharply limited the possibilities for dissent. All peace activists, even the most radical pacifists, had to keep this in mind. These constraints help explain the peace movement's inability to mount effective protest during the Cuban Missile Crisis in late 1962. Kennedy and Khrushchev came close to blowing up each other's major cities, and with them much of the world. What better time for peace activists to denounce nuclear war? Instead, the scale of the crisis marginalized the movement. The few protests were cautious affairs, emphasizing both powers' responsibility rather than demanding a new U.S. policy. Not until the crippling, drawn-out war in Southeast Asia after 1965, with thousands of American casualties, would peace activists be able to rally a mass movement in direct opposition to the Cold War consensus.

CUBA AND THE APPEAL OF THIRD WORLD REVOLUTION

The antinuclear movement was not the only sign of dissent from the Cold War. In 1957–1958, the revolutionary insurgency in Cuba, and its charismatic (and still anticommunist) young leader Fidel Castro, provoked widespread support in the United States. Later, in 1959–1961, when those revolutionaries took power and refused to accept Cuba's historic subordination within America's Caribbean sphere of influence, a current of solidarity emerged. This short-lived "Fair Play for Cuba" movement prefigured the anti-imperialism of the later anti-Vietnam War movement. It also brought together the broadest array of constituencies of the early New Left, from old-fashioned liberals to early Black Nationalists.

Beginning in early 1957, Fidel Castro garnered enthusiastic approval from Americans and the mainstream news media for his guerrilla war to overthrow dictator Fulgencio Batista. The latter was a reliable American ally who welcomed the Mafia into Cuba in the 1950s, cementing the island's historic status as an offshore haven for gambling and sex tourism. Behind a thin façade of representative government, Batista ran a corrupt police state that violently repressed dissent. In the United States, the pro-Castro bandwagon was promoted by his fervent supporters in the Cuban-American community (so-called *fidelistas*), who staged spectacular protests like hunger strikes and unfurling pro-rebel banners in the stands during a game at Yankee Stadium. Prominent journalists vouched for Castro's courage and integrity. To a legion of reporters from *The New York Times*, *Time*, *Life*, the television networks, and the wire services, Castro seemed a dream come true, "a combination of Robin Hood, Gregory Peck and George Washington," as one student journalist put it. An eloquent lawyer leading a tiny force of students and peasants against great odds, he was a genuine revolutionary yet emphatically *not* a Communist.[1] Castro seemed like the perfect answer to the worldwide accusation that the Americans would back any dictator as long as he opposed the Reds. So inspiring was the news coverage that hundreds of young Americans, mostly recent veterans and college students on summer vacation, contacted pro-Castro groups in the United States, hoping to enlist in the makeshift Rebel

---

[1] Though many Americans find it difficult to believe, Castro did not use the word "socialist" to describe the Cuban Revolution until April 15, 1961, two days before the Bay of Pigs invasion. He did not describe himself as a "Marxist-Leninist" until 1962. There is ample evidence of his ambivalent if not hostile attitude to the Cuban Communist party in 1957–1958.

Army. They were inspired by three boys, "Army brats" from the United States base at Guantanamo who ran away from home to join the guerrillas, and were profiled in a May 1957 primetime CBS Special, "Cuba's Jungle Fighters: The Rebels of the Sierra Maestre."

The Cuban Revolution triumphed on January 1, 1959, when Batista fled the country and Castro's columns of *barbudos* ("bearded ones") entered the major cities to a rapturous reception. Within a year Castro's image in the United States went through a startling metamorphosis. In the first weeks, he was the man of the hour, and was given many live interviews on U.S. television. However, once the Cuban revolutionary government began trying and executing members of Batista's brutal secret police, several hundred in all, much of U.S. public opinion was alienated. Castro reignited Yankee enthusiasm with a whirlwind April 1959 tour of East Coast cities and campuses. Thousands cheered him at Harvard and Princeton and in the streets of New York and Washington D.C., but the Eisenhower administration remained extremely wary. In the next months, Cuba began a sweeping agrarian reform program, expropriating U.S. properties. By early 1960 both governments were denouncing each other, as the Cubans sought Soviet aid and the CIA initiated covert operations to overthrow Castro.

This growing hostility led to the formation of the Fair Play for Cuba Committee (FPCC), the first New Left organization to focus on U.S. relations with the Third World. Fair Play was a typical *ad hoc* organization of the 1960s, set up to deal with a particular crisis, and "radical" almost by accident. It was formed by Robert Taber and Richard Gibson, CBS News journalists who knew Castro, and a liberal New Jersey businessman, Alan Sagner. On April 6, 1960, they published an advertisement in the *New York Times* signed by prominent intellectuals (similar to SANE's initiation in 1957), with the headline "What's Really Happening in Cuba?" It received a strong write-in response, leading to the formation of a permanent organization with a few local chapters. FPCC's big boost came in the fall of 1960 when the tiny Socialist Workers Party (SWP) committed its organizational resources. The SWP had only 400 members, but they were tightly disciplined and full of zeal. Before long dozens of nascent FPCC chapters sprang up in cities and on campuses. This organizing was greatly aided by the runaway success of a paperback by the charismatic Columbia University sociologist C. Wright Mills. His *Listen, Yankee!*, a witty diatribe written in the voice of a Cuban, quickly sold 400,000 copies, an early New Left bestseller.

One of the most distinctive things about the Fair Play for Cuba Committee was its multiracial character, which reflected the considerable appeal of the Cuban Revolution to black Americans. Throughout 1959, 1960, and 1961, while the white press labeled Castro a "crackpot" and a "communist," some black journalists continued to sing his praises. In power, Castro had immediately and officially abolished all forms of segregation in Cuba, and vociferously attacked Jim Crow in the United States African Americans were prominent in FPCC's leadership, including the writer LeRoi Jones (Amiri Baraka), who traveled to Cuba in 1960 and wrote a famous essay, "Cuba Libre," for the avant-garde literary journal *Evergreen Review*, and the dissident South Carolina NAACP leader Robert F. Williams, who fled to Cuba in 1961. The connection with black America was secured when Castro came to New York in September 1960 to speak at the United Nations. He made a dramatic pilgrimage uptown to stay in Harlem's Theresa Hotel, where huge crowds cheered as he welcomed Soviet leader Nikita Khrushchev, and India's premier Jawaharlal Nehru. Castro also met privately with Malcolm X.

The high point of Fair Play's brief existence was a Christmas 1960 tour of Cuba by over 300 activists (mainly students)—soon after the Eisenhower administration announced a trade embargo and just before John F. Kennedy's inauguration. Then came the Bay of Pigs invasion on April 17, 1961. A CIA-led force of 1,100 Cuban exiles, many of them former Batista supporters, landed in Cuba. They were quickly overwhelmed by Castro's 200,000-strong popular militia and surrendered en masse, greatly embarrassing the Kennedy administration. The Bay of Pigs was a decisive event for the United States—its first major defeat in the Cold War—and was also decisive for the emerging New Left. It clarified that Cold War liberals like JFK did not share the goal of self-determination, and were as likely as Republicans to embrace military responses to perceived communist threats. Across the country, Fair Play chapters mobilized in protest. In many places, only a few dozen people rallied; in New York and San Francisco, several thousand took to the streets day after day while the invasion lasted. CNVA activists were arrested outside the CIA headquarters in downtown Washington. Even some key Establishment pundits like Walter Lippmann criticized the invasion as a shameful violation of international law. Yet public opinion polls overwhelmingly supported the president despite the humiliating U.S. defeat.

Following a single year of notoriety and success, from April 1960 through May 1961, the Fair Play movement rapidly declined. It came under intensive harassment by the FBI and congressional committees, and its leaders fled the country. By the Cuban Missile Crisis in late 1962, FPCC was a ghost organization. One year later, its historical reputation was irretrievably tarnished when a stunned nation heard that Lee Harvey Oswald, Kennedy's assassin, had led a one-man Fair Play for Cuba chapter in New Orleans. After this sensational event, FPCC vanished from memory, and subsequent decades of unbroken hostility between the United States and Cuba have effaced Castro's onetime popularity with many Americans. Combined with the more broadly based antinuclear activism, however, the brief but explosive flurry of solidarity with Cuba's revolution suggests that the conformity and lockstep nationalism of the 1950s was more fragile than it appeared at the time. Many Americans, even if only quietly among friends, did not accept the rigid bipolar view of the world demanded by official anticommunism. The logic of "defending the Free World" by threatening to end life as we know it and supporting repressive military dictatorships was deeply contradictory. What was required was an opportunity to challenge that logic frontally; Vietnam would provide it.

Chapter 6

THE NORTHERN STUDENT MOVEMENT: "FREE SPEECH" AND "PARTICIPATORY DEMOCRACY"

I have been studying, for several years now, the cultural apparatus, the intellectuals, as a possible, immediate, radical agency of change . . . . [W]ho is it that is getting fed up? Who is it that is getting disgusted with what Marx called "all the old crap?" Who is it that is thinking and acting in radical ways? All over the world . . . the answer is the same: it is the young intelligentsia.
—C. Wright Mills, "Letter to the New Left," New Left Review, September–October, 1960

There is a time when the operation of the machine becomes so odious, makes you so sick at heart, that you can't take part; you can't even passively take part, and you've got to put your bodies upon the gears and upon the wheels, upon the levers, upon all the apparatus, and you've got to make it stop. And you've got to indicate to the people who run it, to the people who own it, that unless you're free, the machine will be prevented from working at all!
—Mario Savio, Berkeley Free Speech Movement leader, outside Sproul Hall before the sit-in begins, December 2, 1964

In the late 1950s and early 1960s, while the New Left's central focus was the Civil Rights movement in the South, a parallel student movement germinated among white youth in the North. This upsurge in northern campus radicalism was not organized around a single cause, but embraced many. As we have seen, in the 1959–1962 period these included both nuclear disarmament and the Cuban Revolution; but other struggles also came to the fore, including protests against the House Committee on Un-American Activities (HUAC) and campaigns demanding free speech on campus. Student activists also opposed the racial and religious discrimination practiced by many fraternities and sororities and denounced the "parietal" rules that regulated students' social and sexual lives. Of particular importance was a new group, the Students for a Democratic Society (SDS), which offered a comprehensive critique of American society and a new theory of social change it called "participatory democracy."

Besides a dislike of established order, from HUAC to the frats, the cross-country student networks shared common cultural and intellectual influences. Starting in the 1950s, a distinctive folk music and coffeehouse subculture evolved in college towns and cities like Boston, San Francisco, and New York, exemplified by the rise to stardom of Joan Baez and Bob Dylan. Young men and women also developed a shared worldview via extremely influential books by American and European scholars who defined a new intellectual left. These included the Columbia University sociologist C. Wright Mills, whose books (such as *The Power Elite*) were bestsellers, the French existentialist philosophers Jean-Paul Sartre and Alfred Camus, who emphasized the individual's alienation from society; the expatriate German neo-Marxist Herbert Marcuse, author of *One-Dimensional Man*; and the anarchist Paul Goodman, author of *Growing Up Absurd*. Although rightwingers sneered at the stereotype of "Beatniks" with straggly beards strumming guitars or reading pretentious poetry, this was a very serious movement. Many student radicals were campus editors and student government leaders who met annually at the Liberal Caucus of the National Student Association, which the CIA had covertly created in the late 1940s to counter Communist influence.

Above all, white students in the Northeast, Midwest, and West were united in their commitment to racial equality and their disgust at the hypocrisy of claiming to lead the Free World against Soviet tyranny—while taking no action against a violent white supremacist order below the Mason-Dixon line. The battle for elemental human rights, and the heroic commitment of young black people in SNCC and CORE, dominated northern student consciousness. The first time that scattered groups of white youth began to define themselves as a "movement" was spring 1960, as sit-ins spread across the South. Thousands of students on northern campuses joined in sympathy protests outside local branches of those national chain stores, like Woolworths, that maintained whites-only lunch counters and refused to hire blacks in the South. This direct solidarity with the mass jailing of black youth was a catalyst, showing that white students could be an effective national voice. Over the next five years, the southern freedom movement was a magnet, radicalizing a whole cohort of young northerners. By 1965, when the Vietnam War suddenly escalated, campus antiwar activism was ready to burst open with amazing speed; unnerved, President Johnson insisted that the sudden appearance of widespread student opposition to the war could only be the work of Communist agents.

INCUBATORS OF REBELLION: BERKELEY, MADISON, AND ANN ARBOR

The easiest way of understanding the northern student movement is to look at key campuses that inspired students elsewhere. Though other schools were important, three large state universities were flashpoints for the rebellion of a minority of white students in the early 1960s: the University of Wisconsin at Madison, the University of California at Berkeley, and the University of Michigan at Ann Arbor. These schools had much in common. Collectively, Madison, Berkeley, and Ann Arbor embodied what Berkeley's President Clark Kerr called the "multiversity," destined to lead the nation into the postindustrial age of abundance. Each campus was a small city, with vast resources and a global reputation for scholarly excellence. Each was an economic and cultural powerhouse in its state. Their students, the first generation of undergraduates in U.S. history drawn from all social classes and ethnic groups in the white population, paid a minimal tuition for a first-class education, and understood themselves as the very "best and brightest" in America. Together, the great state universities afforded an excellent vantage point from which to project an alternative, radical perspective on the nation's direction. This generation bred many such perspectives and many charismatic figures. Not surprisingly, virtually all of them were young white men, though much of the actual organizing was done by women. Joined by like-minded students from elite private colleges like Harvard, Stanford, Swarthmore, Oberlin, and the University of Chicago, they formed a kind of counter-elite to the older Establishment dominated by Cold War liberals. With tremendous audacity, this group of young intellectual agitators indicted their universities and the entire structure of power underlying higher education. They proposed nothing less than the reorganization of American society.

Of these three schools, student radicalism at Ann Arbor has received the lion's share of attention, because of its place in SDS history. However, Ann Arbor's New Left was in part a response to earlier upsurges at Berkeley and Madison. These schools shared a key characteristic: both the campuses and the surrounding cities were historic sites for radicalism. Each was an oasis from McCarthyism, which hit academia hard in the 1950s—hundreds of professors were summarily fired and many more practiced self-censorship. At the University of Wisconsin, because of the state's longtime Progressive tradition, left-wing politics were tolerated even at the Cold War's height. No loyalty oaths were required of professors, and a campus branch of the Communist Party's Labor Youth League (LYL) functioned openly. It dissolved in 1956, but a group of former young Communists were crucial to Madison's New Left, with its strongly anti-imperialist bent. Many of these students studied with the historian William Appleman Williams, whose book *The Tragedy of American Diplomacy* (1959) was a searing indictment of America's role in the world. Around them a visible radical milieu developed in the late 1950s, including cooperative apartment buildings, a History department which bred a famous cohort of dissident scholars, and a Socialist Club which organized forums with controversial speakers barred from other campuses. Regular pickets, vigils, and marches protested everything from fraternities that barred Jews and blacks to the Bay of Pigs invasion, and an annual Anti-Military Ball mocked ROTC (the U.S. military's Reserve Officers Training Corps, then a fixture on most campuses). Besides its reputation for an open campus atmosphere, Madison activists published the journal *Studies on the Left*, the new radicalism's major theoretical magazine, which helped revive socialist debate among American intellectuals.

Berkeley became even more famous than Madison for its culture of protest, a reputation that has endured in popular memory. Student activism became a mass phenomenon early on at Berkeley, with thousands taking part in street demonstrations in the early 1960s—long before any other campus. This flourishing radical milieu was nourished by the confluence in the San Francisco Bay Area of a unique range of alternative subcultures. This was the one major urban area in the country where the older Communist-influenced labor movement of the 1930s remained a public force. The powerful International Longshoremen and Warehousemen's Union (ILWU) grew directly from San Francisco's bloody 1934 general strike led by Australian Marxist Harry Bridges, and the longshoremen stayed loyal to him despite intense red-baiting. From the 1950s through the end of the century, the ILWU remained a bastion of West Coast radicalism.

Beyond that, even in the 1950s, the Bay Area had a reputation for cultural and sexual nonconformity. It was a center of the Beat subculture, at places like the poet Lawrence Ferlinghetti's City Lights bookstore and the North Beach jazz bars. In October 1955 the great Beat poet Allen Ginsberg had given the first public reading of his epic "Howl" with its brutal first lines: "I have seen the best minds of my generation destroyed by madness, starving hysterical naked." When Ferlinghetti published *Howl and Other Poems* in 1956, he was prosecuted for obscenity (since the poem included words like "fuck" and "shit" and talked openly about the joys of sex between men). The judge ruled that it was protected by the First Amendment, one of a series of ground-breaking judicial rulings that opened up American culture in the 1950s and 1960s. *Howl* became a permanent bestseller—over the next forty years, it sold over 900,000 copies. Fired up by Ginsberg and other Beats like Jack Kerouac, whose autobiographical novel, *On the Road* (1957), was also a bestseller, young bohemians and "hipsters" were drifting into San Francisco well before the Berkeley campus began to show signs of rebellion in 1957–1958.

The Beats were important, as were their successors in the Bay Area, like Ken Kesey's Merry Pranksters, who claim a large share of credit for jump-starting the hippie counterculture in the mid-1960s. But over the long run, of even greater importance was San Francisco's identity as a place of refuge and pleasure for gay people, like Ginsberg. As will be discussed in chapter 7, since World War II it had developed an active gay and lesbian scene, as hundreds of servicemen and women discharged for their sexual preferences stayed in the port city rather than return home. As with the Beats, word of the city's tolerance spread informally, and gay people across the country moved there to enjoy a relative degree of freedom.

Amid this freewheeling milieu—a Communist longshoreman and a gay nightclub performer both received thousands of votes in San Francisco's 1961 supervisors' election—the Berkeley campus was an exception. Unlike the University of Wisconsin, all political activity on campus was banned. To take on these restrictions, as well as Greek domination of student government and male students' required participation in ROTC, Berkeley dissidents formed a campus political party called SLATE in 1957. SLATE was a diverse group with no ideological litmus tests, and included people with Communist backgrounds. It became a force on the Berkeley campus, winning student government elections in 1959 (which the administration promptly annulled) and taking control of the campus paper, the *Daily Californian*, in 1960.

National notoriety for Berkeley's radicals came by chance in spring 1960, when the House Committee on Un-American Activities (HUAC) announced it would hold local hearings on "Communist infiltration" of San Francisco's public schools. The committee's perpetual traveling roadshow, guaranteed to gain headlines and ruin careers, was unpopular in the Bay Area because earlier HUAC investigations had led to popular teachers being fired. When the hearings opened on May 13 at San Francisco's City Hall, hundreds of Berkeley students showed up to protest. Barred from attendance, the group resorted to a peaceful sit-in. The police responded by flushing them down the building's stairs with fire hoses, and arresting sixty-four. Next day, 5,000 angry demonstrators picketed the committee, while others went inside and then stood and sang "The Star-Spangled Banner" to disrupt the hearings. Foolishly, HUAC issued a badly made film, *Operation Abolition*, purporting to expose the Red plotters who had duped Berkeleyites into mass protest. It became an unintended recruiting tool, drawing would-be activists to Berkeley and the Bay Area. From then on, Berkeley was known countrywide as the site of mass student radicalism and well-organized confrontational protest, a reputation it maintained for decades.

Crucial to the New Left's base on campus was the neighborhood around the university. The city of Berkeley had its own activist movement of young liberals focused on school desegregation and open housing for black residents, while thousands of students and recent graduates moved into off-campus apartments around Telegraph Avenue, with its bookstores, coffee shops, and businesses appealing to the young and restless. So notorious was this urban radical enclave that a University of Michigan student journalist, Tom Hayden, stopped off there in summer 1960, hoping to soak up the tactics of Berkeley militants and bring them east to Ann Arbor. By the time he left California, after tutoring by SLATE leaders, Hayden defined himself as a radical. Back in Michigan, he became prominent as the crusading editor of the campus newspaper and founder of an Ann Arbor version of SLATE called VOICE. He also joined the Ann Arbor chapter of the Student League for Industrial Democracy (SLID). Founded as the Intercollegiate Socialist Society in 1905, SLID was the oldest Old Left student group. Its parent group, the League for Industrial Democracy, was an appendage of the cautious Socialist Party. Outside of Ann Arbor, SLID barely functioned in the 1950s. Ann Arbor's SLID was led by an older "permanent student" named Al Haber, who wanted to make the moribund group the center of an emerging campus movement. Taking over SLID's national leadership in 1960, he changed its name to Students for a Democratic Society (SDS) and recruited key activists at Michigan, including Hayden. This Ann Arbor nucleus focused on building student support for the Civil Rights movement through an April 1960 conference on "Human Rights in the North," to which they invited the leaders of the Greensboro sit-ins. In 1961, Hayden was named SDS's first Field Secretary. He immediately went to Mississippi to report on SNCC's voter registration work, sending back vivid first-hand accounts widely read by northern students. This visible commitment and Hayden's evident passion bolstered his and the organization's reputation. Several other SDS members joined SNCC's staff, cementing ties between the two groups and helping position SDS as the most impressive new national student group in the early 1960s.

THE RISE OF SDS

SDS's strategic vision was based in staking out a new intellectual platform for American radicalism. This concept led to a conference at a United Auto Workers summer camp in Port Huron, Michigan in June 1962, from which came *The Port Huron Statement of the Students for a Democratic Society*. The conference was quite small, with only sixty activists present from the handful of SDS chapters. It became important for two reasons. In the short-term, the presence of a teenage observer from a Communist Party youth group provoked a fierce internal battle with the anticommunist Socialists controlling the League for Industrial Democracy. Over the long term, *The Port Huron Statement*'s ambitious vision helped SDS attract a broad cross-section of white student leadership, and crystallized a sense that the student left truly offered something new.

Socialist Party leaders like Michael Harrington had attended the Port Huron conference, and were disturbed by what they saw. They had long felt that the SDS "kids" were oblivious to what Socialists saw as the overwhelming danger of Stalinism. Permitting a Communist youth to attend, even as a nonvoting observer, was a last straw. In New York, the LID board changed the locks on the SDS office and fired the staff. The rift was patched up, but Haber, Hayden, and the others were emboldened by the defiant position they had staked out against the Old Left. Over time, this drama with its generational overtones, became part of SDS's consciousness of itself as an historical force.

Even more important to SDS's sense of mission was *The Port Huron Statement* itself. Drafted by Hayden, it was long, wordy, and impassioned, bold in some places and conventional in others. Its most inspiring feature was the claim to speak for alienated youth in Cold War America, with the opening words "We are people of this generation, bred in at least modest comfort, housed now in universities, looking uncomfortably to the world we inherit." The most famous lines were the assertion that "we seek the establishment of a democracy of individual participation, governed by two central aims: that the individual share in those social decisions determining the quality and direction of his life; that society be organized to encourage independence in men and provide the media for their common participation." This was a new politics, somewhere between liberalism and radicalism, non-Marxist but open to socialist analysis, and focused on a total democratization of society—the economy, schools, and governmental institutions. For the thousands who later joined SDS, the idea of "participatory democracy" was very powerful.

For other New Leftists who were further to the left, the *The Port Huron Statement* was vague, not especially radical, and lacked clarity about white supremacy and America's informal imperialism. Much of it repeated Socialist

Party positions, such as the need to "realign" the Democratic Party by getting rid of the Southern segregationists, and it avoided controversial issues like the Cuban Revolution. Overall, however, the ambiguity of *The Port Huron Statement* and the romantic idealism of Hayden's writing were sources of strength, giving SDS a distinctive voice. In 1963–1964, the organization continued to grow steadily, and its national leadership was a notably dedicated group who stuck with the organization year after year, unlike many campus activists who jumped from issue to issue, discarding organizations in rapid succession. Their Intellectual tenacity would eventually propel SDS to national fame—which leads to a paradox. SDS was the only lasting organization of the white campus New Left, and understanding its rise is crucial; yet SDS and student radicalism were never one and the same. At many major universities, (especially on the West Coast and including Berkeley and Madison), its influence was limited. It is also important to maintain a sense of scale. While Haber and Hayden were rallying their small network through conferences, pamphlets, and manifestos, SNCC organizers like Bob Moses and Stokely Carmichael were registering voters in the poorest counties of the Deep South's Black Belt.

The events of 1964 illustrate the problem of viewing the New Left through SDS's history, as many scholars have done. At the center of that epochal year was the Mississippi Freedom Summer Project, which crystallized the emergence of a campus movement. SDS played no role in this great migration of nearly a thousand northern whites to work in voter registration projects and Freedom Schools. Instead, responding to the insistence of black organizers that whites should organize in the North, SDS began its own ambitious organizing drive in 1963. Declaring it was time to leave the campus, the Economic Research and Action Project (ERAP) sent several hundred young SDSers into the poorest neighborhoods of northeastern and midwestern cities to build an "interracial movement of the poor." ERAP was based on SNCC's practice of embedding oneself in the daily life of the oppressed, and supporting the development of indigenous local leaders. But instead of the South's legal apparatus of segregation with its clear color line, ERAP focused on the structural injustice afflicting poor people of all colors—unemployment, slum housing, poor schools, rundown streets, lack of opportunity. This difference between racial and class oppression proved to be crucial. Lacking a visible enemy like white supremacy and clear goals like registering voters and desegregating buses, restaurants, and libraries, the SDS organizers often found themselves punching the air, ignored by both local officials and community residents. Though a few ERAP projects lasted for years, they had little national impact, other than training a cadre of SDS leaders in community organizing.

THE FREE SPEECH MOVEMENT AND THE
BREAKTHROUGH AT BERKELEY

The 1960s' first full-scale campus revolt underscores the diversity of the student left and the centrality of the Civil Rights movement. In late 1964 the nation's attention was riveted by the Free Speech Movement (FSM) at Berkeley. The FSM was led by students active in CORE and a group called Friends of SNCC, many just returned from Mississippi, where they learned the value of "direct action" in challenging entrenched institutions. Growing off-campus participation by Berkeley students in campaigns to desegregate Bay Area stores and hotels had angered local elites and the regents who governed the University of California system. In September 1964, the university administration banned student fundraising tables on a street near campus that radicals had used for years. In the next weeks, deans cited five students for defying the regulations by setting up tables on Sproul Plaza, the university's central area, and then suspended eight. On October 1, police were called in to arrest a CORE activist and former grad student in mathematics, Jack Weinberg, and hundreds of students spontaneously sat down around the police car holding him. The sit-in lasted thirty-two hours, while speeches were given from the car's roof to a crowd of 2,000. Meanwhile, activists quickly formalized the Free Speech Movement as a coalition stretching from young Communists to Campus Republicans, including a philosophy student named Mario Savio, who had gone to Mississippi and became the FSM's spokesman. Their sole demand was the right of Berkeley students to engage in political activity on campus. Over the next two months, an escalating war of attrition, repression, and surprise attack was played out between an ineffectual administration led by President Clark Kerr and an experienced student leadership, many of them self-named "red diaper babies" from leftwing families. Savio became nationally famous, giving impromptu speeches of fervent eloquence. These organizers understood that if they kept a large base of student support by emphasizing free speech, a sacred American principle, they could bring the faculty over to their side and isolate Kerr. They succeeded.

The final straw was Kerr's refusal to bargain in good faith or accept the compromise proposals of the very faculty committees he had authorized, combined with attempts to punish individual student leaders. On December 2, thousands of students gathered outside the main administration building and listened to Joan Baez before approximately one thousand filed inside to occupy it peacefully. Kerr made a mistake repeated by many campus administrators in coming years. He allowed Governor Pat Brown, a liberal Democrat, and local prosecutor Edwin Meese III (later Ronald Reagan's Attorney General) to send in the police. At 3 A.M. on December 3 they started dragging out the protesters, arresting 764 over the next twelve hours. This rash action outraged the faculty, who voted overwhelmingly to accept a proposal based on student demands. In short order the regents went along, undercutting Kerr, and the Free Speech Movement won a smashing victory, drawing national attention and demonstrating that the student movement could no longer be dismissed.

1964 thus ended on a high note for campus radicals of all backgrounds. Together, the moral power of the Mississippi Freedom Summer, the massive popularity of the Free Speech Movement, and the growth of SDS as a nation-wide organization suggested that students were on the march. What seemed increasingly doubtful was whether the New Left could continue to work within the world of cautious Cold War liberalism. The anger, militancy, and exuberance of youth could not be contained much longer, as SNCC and its allies showed in Atlantic City, and Berkeley's radicals had made visible. These new forces would soon force a much greater confrontation, not with Jim Crow governors like George Wallace or university presidents like Clark Kerr, but with the U.S. government itself, and its escalating prosecution of a bloody, faroff war in Southeast Asia.

Chapter 7

UNDERGROUND FEMINISTS AND HOMOPHILES: "THE PROBLEMS THAT HAVE NO NAME"

For over forty years, since the Nineteenth Amendment to the U.S. Constitution gave American women the right to vote in national elections in 1920, political participation by women has grown in many directions. But full participation in all of the functions of a citizen is not yet a fact. . . . In the federal Congress, only two of one hundred Senators and eleven of 435 Representatives are women. Only two women have held cabinet rank in the federal government; only six have served as ambassadors or ministers. In federal judicial office, no women are on the Supreme Court or the courts of appeals. One woman judge serves on the U.S. Customs Court and one on the Tax Court of the United States. Of 307 federal district judges, only two are women. . . . In the states, as of 1962, of approximately 7,700 seats in state legislatures, 234 were held by women.

—President's Commission on the Status of Women,
The American Woman, 1963

Perhaps as dangerous as the actual Communists are the sexual perverts who have infiltrated our Government in recent years. The State Department has confessed that it has had to fire ninety-one of these. . . . The country would be more aroused over this tragic angle of the situation if it were not for the difficulties of

the newspapers and radio commentators in adequately presenting the facts, while respecting the decency of their American audiences.
—Guy Gabrielson, Republican National Chairman, April 18, 1950.

The image of 1950s America as conformist and repressive seems most accurate in terms of gender—the sexual and cultural dividing line between girls and boys, men and women, heterosexuals and homosexuals. In other areas of society there was visible ferment, from civil rights to the enthusiasm for Fidel Castro. Regarding sexuality and reproduction, however, the structures of authority in American society after 1945 seemed intent on maintaining an older way of life. A neo-Victorian moral code discouraged premarital sex and enforced the double standard, while frank depictions of sexuality were forbidden in movies, books, newspapers, magazines, and on radio and television. A purportedly traditional set of familial arrangements was promoted in all of these media, asserting women's natural and exclusive role as wives and mothers. Gone were the spunky factory girls and independent businesswomen portrayed in the popular culture of the 1930s and 1940s—the ideal woman was now either a maternal housewife or an exaggerated, voluptuous "sex bomb" like Marilyn Monroe. Left out of the housewife-and-mother ideal were the millions of women too poor or too independent to fit in.

Women's roles may have been sharply prescribed in the 1950s, but women did have the domestic authority and social status accorded those who raise children and keep house. Gay men and lesbians had no role, no legitimacy, and certainly no power. Medical, religious, legal, and scholarly authorities agreed that homosexuality was a curable mental disease, and that homosexuals were unstable neurotics who led sad, disgusting lives. The only serious scholarly or political attention given to homosexuality equated it with drug addiction or alcoholism. While World War II allowed many gay people to find companionship in wartime anonymity, the 1950s marked a sharp step backward. The McCarthyite purges targeted homosexuals as well as Communists, with right-wing politicians and a Senate investigating committee gleefully linking these two forms of "deviance." Thousands of gays were forced out of government jobs as security risks, and while it was interrogating, surveilling, and photographing suspected Communists and their "fellow travelers," the FBI also tracked reputed "queers." Dozens of cities were swept by antigay newspaper campaigns, with mass arrests in bars, city parks, and other public places where gay men and women tended to congregate.

In terms of sexuality and gender relations, then, the 1950s appears at first glance a time of reaction and containment rather than subversive possibilities. Ultimately, however, the currents of liberation born in depression and wartime proved uncontainable. In practice, it proved impossible to turn the clock back to an imagined small-town past where everyone knew their place. During World War II, women and gays had both experienced much greater freedom. In the postwar economic boom, physical and social mobility was even greater, through easy access to well-paying jobs and anonymous city life. The genie was out of the bottle. Looking backward, it seems apparent that both Women's and Gay Liberation were simply waiting to happen. Yet each of these movements faced enormous social resistance, and the decade between 1955 and 1965 saw only modest advances.

FEMINISM'S SURVIVAL IN AN ANTIFEMINIST TIME

In the 1950s, only a few women still called themselves feminists in public. The word seemed old-fashioned, suggesting a bygone era of "suffragettes," and was usually used as a joke or insult (both by men and by younger women). Many strands of feminism survived, however, in other guises, through voluntary service in women's clubs, the networks of female professionals and businesswomen, the YWCA and other mainstream religious groups, trade unions, and the political parties. Before the upsurge of "second wave feminism" in the late 1960s, the most dramatic event was Betty Friedan's 1963 book *The Feminine Mystique*, which was an immediate bestseller, and over time has sold more than one million copies. In this powerful polemic about "the problem that has no name," Friedan spoke for a generation of middle-class women whose university educations were wasted by the insistence of psychologists, politicians, and women's magazine "experts" that they stay at home to comfort husbands and rear children. Friedan's own life illustrates how much more complicated this story could be. Like many women, she was radicalized by the Depression. In *The Feminine Mystique*, she described herself as a housewife who wrote magazine articles on the side. That well-known account left out her years as a leading student radical in the late 1930s and then her career as a writer for a left-wing union newspaper until 1952. That Friedan covered up both her professional credentials *and* her close ties to the Communist Party indicates how McCarthyism led to self-censorship. To make her case for women's oppression, it was necessary to present herself solely as an overeducated housewife.

The Feminine Mystique's huge success was a delayed counterattack on the antifeminist campaign pushed by conservatives after World War II, which asserted that American women had become castrating and unfeminine. Widespread antifeminism in the 1940s and 1950s was a reaction to long-term social changes, accelerated by the war, which were steadily undermining the patriarchal family. After 1945, women did marry at a younger average age (twenty) than at any time since the nineteenth century, while the fertility rate shot up. However, this short-term return to tradition masked more basic changes. Despite television sitcoms like *Father Knows Best*, which portrayed an idyllic world of suburban nuclear families, more married women than ever before took paid jobs outside the home during the 1950s—a key measure of female autonomy. By 1960, 40 percent of women with children in school worked for wages, a remarkable shift in historical terms. As late as 1940, only one in six married women and one quarter of all women worked outside the home.

The one group who still proclaimed themselves ardent feminists were the former suffrage militants of the National Women's Party (NWP). The once-famous NWP was feminism's radical vanguard before 1920, when women won the vote. Ever since, led by the autocratic, single-minded Alice Paul, it dedicated itself to passing an Equal Rights Amendment (ERA) to the Constitution. Men found it easy to mock the aging NWPers with the disrespect often accorded opinionated older women. But for an organization with a few thousand members, it remained quite effective. During World War II, the NWP convinced mainstream women's groups and both major parties to endorse the ERA, and members of Congress respected its persistence. The other major organizations in the pro-ERA camp included the National Federation of Business and Professional Women's Clubs and the Association of American University Women. Like the NWP, they represented upper- and middle-class white women frustrated by the institutional barriers blocking female doctors, lawyers, engineers, professors, and businesspeople.

The ERA's failure to achieve a Senate majority reflected strong opposition from other women's groups, in particular the women's departments and aux-iliaries of labor unions. Female labor activists were fully committed to advancing women's status. The perennial question in this case, as throughout the history of feminism, was *which women*? The labor feminists led a broad liberal-labor coalition that asserted the ERA would invalidate protective legis-lation for women workers. Bills banning "night work" for women, or setting limits on how much they could be compelled to lift, had taken decades to pass. Now, the labor unions charged—with some justification—the Chamber of Commerce and pro-business Republicans were allied with the NWP to smash labor protections for women as part of an assault on organized labor. Labor feminists had a different agenda for women's advancement. They were part of an enormous if little-noticed expansion of women's role in organized labor—from 800,000 women belonging to trade unions in 1940 to about 3 mil-lion female union members by the mid-1950s. For this constituency, securing access to professional careers for a college-educated minority of women was a low priority. They believed that unionization and legal reforms that bene-fited the majority of workers would also benefit women. They did not challenge workplace segregation into "men's" and "women's" jobs—exactly the discrimination detested by the NWP and its allies. What they wanted was "equal pay for equal work," a deeply feminist demand first articulated by some of the more progressive unions in World War II and, which remains a major issue sixty years later. Labor feminists waged a long, quiet campaign through their unions and the Democratic Party to establish pay equity as a legal principle, and remarkably, they succeeded. Many states, and finally Congress in 1963, passed laws mandating equal pay for equal work. Even earlier, in 1954, the laborites had managed to make child-care expenses a legitimate tax deduction, a small but meaningful step toward recognizing the specific needs of women workers.

A NEW FEMINISM EMERGES, 1960–1965

The long-running clash between these two versions of feminism produced results. By 1960, there was increasing awareness of the frustration captured a few years later by Betty Friedan. John F. Kennedy avoided supporting the ERA, but as president, he felt strong pressure from prominent women in the Democratic Party to take some public action. In 1961, he appointed a President's Commission on the Status of Women, with Eleanor Roosevelt as "chairman" (it would take the rise of Women's Liberation to end the practice of assuming that only men headed organizations or ran meetings). Unrealized at the time, this commission became an opening wedge for the feminist renascence of the 1960s. Though dominated by anti-ERA liberals and labor union women, it engaged in a wide-ranging investigation of legal and social discrimination against women. The 1963 publication of its best-selling final report, *The American Woman*, was anticlimactic. The commission's real significance was bringing together hundreds of female elected officials, academics, professionals, and activists. A little-noticed proposal proved crucial—the National Federation of Business and Professional Women's Clubs was empowered to create state councils on the status of women to advise the President's Commission. These state bodies were the seedbed of the new movement, leading directly to the 1966 formation of NOW, the National Organization for Women.

The success of *The Feminine Mystique* and the high profile of the President's Commission on the Status of Women certified that the antifeminist neo-Victorianism of the postwar years was under siege. No one knew what was next, but in 1964, feminists won a major political victory when discrimination in employment on the basis of sex was outlawed under Title VII of the Civil Rights Act. How discrimination *against women*, a widely accepted practice across America, became part of this landmark bill intended to end discrimination *against African Americans* makes an odd story. The proposed legislation listed "race, color, religion or national origin" as categories of banned discrimination. The amendment to add the word "sex" was introduced by Representative Howard Smith of Virginia, a conservative segregationist Democrat. Did he add this language to derail the civil rights bill by making it ridiculous, since most congressmen considered discrimination against women a non-issue? Or was Smith expressing his support for white women who supposedly lacked the legal protections blacks were claiming? Certainly the National Women's Party had long appealed to southern congressmen to support the ERA on this basis. Its origins became irrelevant, however, when the amendment passed. This happened because the few women members of Congress, led by Democrat Martha Griffiths of Michigan (a nominal NWP member), made it a serious issue and the major women's organizations intensively lobbied for it. Since then, Title VII has changed the basic terrain of employment rights in the United States, putting women on an equal footing with men for the first time in history. It established the legal basis for hundreds of court cases overturning institutional and social barriers over the next decades.

From 1960 to 1965, a new liberal feminism coalesced, a continuation of the "equal rights" tradition stretching back to the nineteenth century. Among younger women and students, meanwhile, a more radical analysis calling for not just "rights" but "liberation" also began developing (as we shall see in chapter 11). These younger women were able to draw on other, less visible feminist traditions. Many of them were "red diaper babies" who grew up in Communist households, and were exposed to activist mothers and a Marxist version of feminism that used the language of "male supremacy" and "male chauvinism." From Europe came key intellectual texts, like Simone de Beauvoir's *The Second Sex*. Black women had a very different history—the majority of black married women had always worked for wages—and offered a powerful example of community leadership to young white women in the Civil Rights movement. From all these strands a new, hybrid mass women's movement would suddenly emerge in 1968 and after, shocking millions of oblivious men.

NAMING THE DEVIANT: HOMOSEXUALITY'S EMERGENCE IN EUROPE AND AMERICA

The movement for women's equality operated under the surface of conventional politics in the 1950s, and only haltingly reemerged in the early 1960s. There were few if any militant protests against discrimination, and the term "women's liberation" was unknown. Still, some women did call themselves feminists, and respectable organizations continued to campaign against legal discrimination and for the ERA. Most important, American women could look back upon a rich history of activism.

Gay men and lesbians had no such institutions and virtually no history of activism, but they did have a history. Homosexuality as a legal, medical, social, and finally a political category is a modern phenomenon. There have always been men who had sex with men, and women who had sex with women, but until recently this was simply an activity punished in some societies and tolerated, even celebrated, in others. Only in the late nineteenth century, with psychology's emergence as a scientific discipline, was same-sex eroticism labeled a separate and "deviant" identity. This definition of "homosexuality" was a reaction to the embryonic gay male subcultures of metropolises like Paris, Berlin, London, and New York. The purpose of this scientific labeling was to criminalize gay sexuality as a mental disease, but the scientists' definition of homosexuality as a social category also stimulated organized political activity by gays. In 1889, the world's first homosexual rights organization was founded in Germany, and similar groups existed for decades elsewhere in Europe—though not in the United States. These organizations were wiped out or collapsed before and during World War II. The Nazis targeted gays along with Jews and Romany (Gypsies) for extermination. Hundreds of thousands of homosexual men were murdered during the Holocaust, and after 1945 only fragments of the European homosexual rights movement survived. The focus of activism shifted to America.

Gay men and women in the United States came together as a small, persecuted minority in the early twentieth century. Most homosexuals were "closeted" and isolated, but there were enclaves like New York's Greenwich Village and the elite women's colleges where they could live with relative freedom. By the 1920s the largest cities had gay bars and cafes, and there were occasional homosexual characters and in-jokes in movies and plays. In 1929 a best-selling romantic novel was published about lesbian life, Radclyffe Hall's *The Well of Loneliness*. Then came World War II, which greatly expanded the scope and scale of gay life, but was followed by the draconian postwar antihomosexual reaction. The combination of all of these factors led to a remarkable political innovation: the formation of a homosexual rights movement at the Cold War's height, in the early 1950s.

THE HOMOPHILE QUEST FOR RIGHTS AND RESPECTABILITY, 1950–1965

How could this happen? Homosexuality was still seen as completely illegitimate in postwar America. Liberals and leftists were as homophobic as everyone else, as likely to use epithets like "fag," "dyke," "queer," and "pansy," so this new movement had no potential allies. Not even those civil libertarians who defended the rights of Communists would defend gays from police harassment and job discrimination. The best explanation for the self-described "homophile" movement's emergence and survival lies in its obscurity. Its main organizations, the Mattachine Society and the Daughters of Bilitis (DOB), were so small that few Americans knew of them, let alone considered them a threat. Living in the shadows protected homophile organizers, as did the postwar surge of public interest in the scientific study of sex. Alfred Kinsey's *Sexual Behavior in the Human Male* (1948) and *Sexual Behavior in the Human Female* (1953) revealed with dry but striking data the sexual voracity of ordinary Americans. Amid Kinsey's statistics on the prevalence of premarital and extramarital sex, masturbation, and other taboo subjects, nothing excited greater shock than his reporting that 37 percent of adult men had engaged in sex with other men at some point in their lives. Kinsey also wrote that women were as sexually responsive as men—then a novel idea to many—and that a significant number had had lesbian experiences. He found that gays constituted a sizable minority (with 10 percent of men primarily homosexual), and that even more people were situationally homosexual. Though scholars reviewing Kinsey's research in later decades pointed out that his sampling was highly unscientific, it scarcely mattered. At the time, his findings encouraged people to think beyond rigid categories of "normal" and "abnormal," and their impact was tremendous. In addition, 1951 saw the publication of Donald Webster Cory's *The Homosexual in America*, the first serious study by an acknowledged homosexual, which raised self-awareness among gay people—above all, that they were not alone.

Kinsey, Cory, and other writers helped straight people understand the increasingly visible urban gay subculture, while alerting individual, isolated gays and lesbians around the country that it existed at all. Even the most scandal-mongering journalistic exposés helped publicize this new reality. The gay and lesbian communities in cities like Boston, Philadelphia, and San Francisco were much larger than before the war, with dozens of gay bars (often seedy, Mafia-run places), as well as gay beaches and clubs. This social explosion was met with sporadic but sweeping repression, including police dragnets arresting hundreds in one night. In retrospect, some form of civil rights activity seems inevitable, if only to assert the right of homosexuals to socialize in peace. The central question became whether gays and lesbians would ever define themselves as a political constituency.

The first significant organization of homosexuals in American history, the Mattachine Society, was formed in Los Angeles in 1950 to resist police raids and promote what would now be called "gay pride." Its founders had all been in or close to the Communist Party. Led by Harry Hay, they developed a sophisticated theory of homosexuals as a distinct minority capable of "a highly ethical homosexual culture . . . paralleling the emerging cultures of our fellow-minorities . . . the Negro, Mexican, and Jewish peoples." At first, Mattachine was very successful amid the bars and beaches of southern California, drawing as many as 2,000 men and a few women into its discussion groups. It even created a Citizens' Committee to Outlaw Entrapment, the practice by which plainclothes Vice Squad officers invited gay men to have sex in public restrooms or parks and then arrested them; the group won acquittal for one of the society's founders. But McCarthyism caught up with Mattachine, and internal redbaiting forced the left-wing founders to resign in 1953. The new, moderate leadership repudiated the aggressive civil rights politics that had attracted young gays to the society, preferring a strategy of accommodation. Membership dropped precipitously, but chapters formed in other cities, including New York, San Francisco, Chicago, Denver, and Boston. From 1953 through the mid-1960s, these scattered Mattachine chapters sought respectability through dialogue with psychologists, clergymen, officials, and other experts. Often they denounced the "promiscuous" gay bar culture, and some in Mattachine even accepted the premise that homosexuality was a weakness or a sickness, but asked merely to be left alone.

The mostly male Mattachine Society was not the only homophile organization. The magazine *ONE* split off, taking a more confrontational approach of publicizing police raids and assaults on privacy around the country. In 1955, the lesbian Daughters of Bilitis was formed in San Francisco; like the Mattachine Society, it chose a deliberately obscure name drawn from ancient history to protect its members. The DOB was led by Del Martin and Phyllis Lyon, who almost fifty years later would finally achieve legal recognition of their lifetime partnership, becoming one of the first gay couples legally married in San Francisco in 2004. Like Mattachine, the Daughters of Bilitis took a cautious approach, operating as a self-help and social group more than a political force, and distancing itself from the lesbian bar scene. Between them, these two pioneer organizations had only a few hundred members in the entire country well into the 1960s. Besides publishing newsletters and offering mutual support, their major activity was occasional public lectures and discussions. Even these respectable forums still led in some cases to arrests, negative publicity, and loss of employment for those involved. Not surprisingly, the leaders of DOB and Mattachine thought it impossible to build a mass movement, and focused on lobbying sympathetic heterosexuals in the legal, academic, and religious communities to speak out for greater tolerance.

Gay politics entered a new phase in the early 1960s. First, the mass media greatly increased its coverage of gays and lesbians, with features in the *New York Times* and elsewhere—which inadvertently told isolated gays around the country where to find each other. While hardly approving, this coverage took seriously the existence of homosexuals as a social group. Increased attention aided the rise within the homophile organizations of a more assertive style. Instead of hiding their identity, young activists like Randy Wicker in New York began seeking interviews and publicity, modeling themselves on the Civil Rights movement. The Washington, D.C. Mattachine chapter aggressive lobbied federal officials, with support from groups like the American Civil Liberties Union, to end open discrimination against gays as "security risks." It was led by Dr. Franklin Kameny, who had lost a high-ranking civil service position after being arrested in Lafayette Park. At the same time, the first crack in the wall of legal sanctions on homosexuality appeared in 1962, when the prestigious American Law Institute endorsed the then-radical position that homosexual acts should be decriminalized, following landmark legislation in Britain. Only two states passed such laws, but a precedent had been established.

The most significant benchmarks for future gay rights organizing came in San Francisco. In this unofficial capital of gay and lesbian America, a critical mass of voters enabled a coalition of bar owners and political activists to assert themselves as an organized force. Bringing the bar scene into politics was critical, because gay and lesbian bars really were the gay community's common meeting places—and where police harassment was most directly felt. In the late 1950s and early 1960s, a series of corruption scandals in the San Francisco Police Department, involving shakedowns of bar owners, coincided with periodic crackdowns and gay-baiting political campaigns by Bay Area Republicans. The effect was to cast into disrepute the official practice of raiding bars and jailing patrons simply because the clientele was all male or all female. Angry gays, looking to defend themselves, found that the local Mattachine Society and the Daughters of Bilitis refused any involvement with the bars. As a consequence, new political initiatives began that broke the mold of cautious homophile activism.

In 1961, a popular drag performer from the famous Black Cat saloon, Jose Saravia, ran for City Supervisor as a protest candidate. He got 6,000 votes, a remarkable figure in a city of less than a million. That same year a League for Civic Education started distributing thousands of free newspapers in the bars, advising gays and lesbians of their legal rights and urging action. In 1962 a Tavern Owners Guild came together to wage a legal fight against the police, distributing a "pocket lawyer" booklet to gays and encouraging voter registration. All of these developments led to the 1964 formation of the Society for Individual Rights (SIR), a defiantly political gay rights organization. SIR published a slick magazine called *Vector*, set up a political action committee, and offered its endorsement, and a potentially large bloc vote, to politicians who supported civil liberties for everyone, including homosexuals. In a remarkably short time, it became a legitimate part of the Bay Area's political scene, courted by mainstream elected officials from the liberal wing of the Democratic Party.

The next stage in the transformation of gay San Francisco into an organized political constituency came when, at last, homosexuals found a significant ally in their struggle, a group of prominent liberal Protestant ministers. The religious mainstream underwent a quiet radicalization in the early 1960s because of the Civil Rights movement, as old, established denominations confronted their own histories of discrimination against African Americans. In a similar spirit, some religious leaders began questioning their failure to offer spiritual and temporal solace to the gay community. In June 1964, a four-day consultation between gay and religious leaders in the Bay Area led to the formation of the Council on Religion and the Homosexual. The last straw came when the police department raided a New Year's benefit dance for the council, arresting large numbers of both gays and straights. The resulting outrage from the churches and the mainstream press led to the court cases being thrown out. Clearly, gay people in San Francisco, if nowhere else, were becoming a legitimate minority, with rights worth protecting.

On the East Coast, protest, militancy, and pride also came to the fore in the first half of the 1960s, motivated by San Francisco's example. In 1965, a coalition of groups called the East Coast Homophile Organizations (ECHO) initiated the first public protests by gays in U.S. history, breaking with assumptions that to declare oneself homosexual in public was neither safe nor legal. The small, orderly pickets in several cities were called to protest the Cuban government's jailing of gays as "counter-revolutionary," while making the point that homosexuals were also mistreated in America. At the same time, the Mattachine Society and DOB were convulsed with factional fights, as militants like Frank Kameny demanded a repudiation of any admission that homosexuality was "a sickness, disturbance, or pathology." Of course, most of these developments were local and small-scale. Very few people in other social movements, let alone the larger society, paid them much attention. Police raids on bars and parks and mass arrests, followed by public humiliation and loss of employment, remained a common practice, even in liberal cities like New York. It would take several more years, and a much more radical upsurge by gays seeking not just tolerance but complete sexual liberation, before the New Left and the rest of America became conscious of the oppression of homosexual men and women.

Chapter 8

VIETNAM AND "THE WAR AT HOME"

We don't know anything about Communism, socialism, and all that, but we do know that Negroes have caught hell here under this American Democracy.
— McComb chapter, Mississippi Freedom Democratic Party, July 1965

It is said that we are fighting against North Vietnam's aggression rather than its ideology and that the "other side" has only to "stop doing what it is doing" in order to restore peace. But what are the North Vietnamese doing, except participating in a civil war, not in a foreign country but on the other side of a demarcation line between two sectors of the same country, a civil war in which Americans from ten thousand miles across the ocean are also participating?
— Senator J. William Fulbright, *The Arrogance of Power*, 1966

We wish that a merciful God could wipe away our own memories of that service as easily as this administration has wiped away their memories of us. But all that they have done and all that they can do by this denial is to make more clear than ever our own determination to undertake one last mission—to search out and destroy the last vestige of this barbaric war, to pacify our own hearts, to conquer the hate and fear that has driven this country the last ten years or more, so from when thirty years from now our brothers go down a street without a leg, without an arm, or a face, and small boys ask why, we will be able to say "Vietnam" and not mean a desert, not a filthy obscene memory, but mean instead the place where America finally turned and where soldiers like us helped it in the turning.
— Lieutenant John Kerry, Vietnam Veterans Against the War, Testimony Before the Senate Foreign Relations Committee, April 22, 1971

The scale of the Vietnam War made it an issue no one could avoid. The antiwar movement was able to link up disparate constituencies of the New Left, providing a center and a common language, because it alone could reach into every American home, neighborhood, town, city, and suburb. Though the fighting was done mostly by poor and working-class "grunts," 2.5 million young men (and several thousand young women) of every class, color, and region served in Vietnam. More than 153,000 were wounded and over 58,000 died, shipped home in bodybags that became the symbol of the war's cost. The war was fought to contain communism and revolution anywhere and everywhere, but its major impact at home was to break the Cold War's quarantine of militant radicalism. Eventually, the United States itself was no longer "contained," as the war destroyed the presidencies of the two preeminent Cold War presidents, Lyndon Johnson and Richard Nixon.

Three features distinguish antiwar activism from earlier New Left movements, and are crucial to understanding a movement so large and amorphous that until recently historians have had trouble explaining it. First is the antiwar movement's apparent disorganization, and the absence of major national organizations like those that led the Civil Rights movement—the antiwar movement had no equivalent to SNCC, SCLC, or the NAACP. Second, the movement kept spreading out into new constituencies each year, and new antiwar organizations and networks were continually forming—of ministers, mothers, draftees, diplomats, businesspeople, nuns, professionals, veterans, and others. The demand for peace kept surfacing in new guises, with different voices all sending a powerful message to policymakers that as they escalated the war, they faced ever-deepening protest. Third, as the war dragged on, large numbers of people not previously politically active came into the movement, radicalized by the death and suffering visible on their nightly television news programs, in their newspapers, and in the letters and terrible memories of their sons. Different antiwar organizations formed to meet their needs: a middle-aged businessman afraid for his son could hardly join an SDS chapter. The sheer fact of so many potential protesters was both inspiring and disorienting for peace activists used to operating on the fringes of American society. Instead of putting a few thousand people into the streets as in 1964, by 1967 the antiwar movement could mobilize hundreds of thousands, and by 1969 millions. One main reason for the movement's lack of central direction was that its popularity considerably exceeded its organizational resources in terms of money, staff, and professional skills. Truly, this was a mass movement, reliant on local upsurges by ordinary people. It is remarkable, therefore, how it began through just a few scattered efforts in 1964–1965.

INCHING INTO WAR, 1954–1964

Because the peace movement of the Eisenhower and Kennedy years had focused on banning nuclear tests, its progress was tied to superpower negotiations. Some leaders of the antinuclear movement felt that the successful ratification of the 1963 Limited Test Ban Treaty removed the movement's rationale; SANE founder Norman Cousins proposed disbanding his own organization. Others in SANE, like the famous Dr. Benjamin Spock (whose book, *Baby and Child Care*, originally published in 1946 & continually revised, has sold more copies worldwide than any book in history besides the Bible) disagreed and voted to keep the organization going. Both radical pacifists and youth active in civil rights groups pointed out that limiting nuclear weapons did not prevent conventional wars. Attention gradually shifted towards the escalating U.S. involvement in Vietnam. What had happened since Ho Chi Minh's Communists smashed the French Army's elite paratrooper battalions at the battle of Dien Bien Phu in 1954, forcing the colonial power to concede defeat?

In May 1954, an international conference that included France, Britain, the Soviet Union, and the People's Republic of China forced the victorious Vietnamese Communists to accept their country's temporary partition into north and south, in preparation for internationally supervised elections in 1956. The United States then installed an aristocratic Catholic exile, Ngo Dinh Diem, as president of a southern "Republic of Vietnam." As Diem built a fearsome police state under CIA tutelage, run largely by members of his family, the Eisenhower administration blocked the 1956 elections because the CIA reported that Ho Chi Minh, the hero of independence, would win any free contest. Two hostile governments now existed in the historic nation of Vietnam. Slowly, a civil war brewed in the south, as activists in the anti-French struggle reorganized. By 1959, Diem's repression was so fierce that northern and southern Communists decided to unite the country by overthrowing him. From that point on, the United States escalated military aid, sending more and more military advisers to keep the unpopular dictator in power.

The character of Diem's rule, and the U.S. role in 1954–1963, is crucial to the later antiwar movement. Over those ten years Americans were told a series of fictions by their government: that there existed two separate nations; that Diem was a charismatic democratic leader ("the Winston Churchill of Southeast Asia," in Lyndon Johnson's words); that the southern National Liberation Front (the NLF, called "Viet Cong" by the Americans) had little support; that the United States was helping "South Vietnam" defend itself against "Communist aggression" from "North Vietnam"; and finally, that the war's true cause was Chinese Communist expansionism. Until a few dissident professors and courageous journalists spoke out, these myths were universally accepted. Only a few thousand readers of periodicals like *Liberation* or the weekly *National Guardian* received more accurate reports. But this self-deluding approach provoked a powerful reaction in time. Waves of angry citizens flooded into the antiwar movement after 1965 as unpleasant truths trickled out and U.S. casualties piled up; their outrage was the movement's essential fuel. The first ripple came in 1963, as U.S. military personnel in South Vietnam reached 16,000. That spring, his power slipping away, Diem violently suppressed the noncommunist opposition led by Buddhists, who called for a coalition government and reconciliation with the north. To protest against Diem's repression, Buddhist priests began ritually burning themselves to death on the streets of South Vietnam's major cities, in front of the world's press. For the first time, Americans began to wonder about the kind of government they were supporting, and attention focused on how much Diem's immediate family, along with other Catholics, monopolized high government positions. As the regime tottered under increasingly well-organized NLF attacks, in October 1963 the United States decided to back a military coup, during which Diem and his brother, the chief of the National Police, were murdered.

Accustomed to hearing that we were assisting a democratic South Vietnam to defend itself, many Americans were shocked by Diem's fall, but JFK's assassination only a few weeks later, on November 22, caused liberals to close ranks behind his successor, Lyndon Johnson. With very little debate in Congress or the press, the scope of the U.S. war in Vietnam changed decisively in 1964. In August, the Johnson administration implemented a plan to justify further intervention and keep South Vietnam's weak military junta in power. Citing reports that North Vietnamese torpedo boats had attacked an American destroyer (later proved untrue), LBJ asked Congress for a blank check to expand the war. The so-called Gulf of Tonkin Resolution passed the House unanimously, and in the Senate, only Oregon's Wayne Morse and Alaska's Ernest Gruening voted no. In that fall's presidential race, Johnson declared he would seek "no wider war" in Vietnam, and successfully painted his Republican opponent, Senator Barry Goldwater, as a warmonger. At the same time, however, his aides and the Defense Department pressed forward with secret plans for a much larger military intervention after the election. From tape recordings of his conversations with Senate insiders, we now know that even as he escalated, Johnson had profound doubts as to whether the war could be won. Even so, he feared the loss of U.S. credibility in the larger Cold War if he withdrew. He also knew how Republicans would attack him and his party for any sign of "softness" on Communism, with charges of "Who Lost Vietnam?" like the earlier accusation "Who Lost China?" that was aimed at Truman.

Haltingly, a current of protest coalesced. In March 1964, 5,000 people rallied in New York, and later that year came the first public draft card burnings by young pacifists. Almost casually, SDS's National Council decided in December 1964 to call for a spring rally in Washington, D.C. Though the ERAP community organizing project remained its top priority, SDS leaders wanted to find a way to attack what they called Johnson's "corporate liberalism," as symbolized by Vietnam. They also decided to sponsor the demonstration entirely on their own, minus coalition partners, inviting all who opposed the war to join in—meaning Communists and other Marxists were welcome. With this simple declaration, SDS made an end-run around SANE and the other established peace groups, which tightly controlled all protests to prevent any "pro-Communist" chants, signs, or speakers. SDS thus provided an exceptionally well-timed opportunity for a new, broader kind of antiwar movement to come together in the streets—just as thousands of U.S. troops flooded into Vietnam.

ESCALATION, 1965–1966

Between December 1964 and the April 1965 rally, events drove the expansion of the anti–Vietnam War movement. Operation Rolling Thunder, the overwhelming air assault on North Vietnam, began in February. This saturation bombing campaign, which continued through Christmas 1972, was officially intended to destroy the warmaking capacity of the North Vietnamese Communists, but its main objective was always to punish and instill terror. Johnson believed he could bludgeon Ho Chi Minh and his comrades into submission—a great mistake. On March 16, 1965, the antiwar cause gained its first martyr when Holocaust survivor Alice Herz, horrified by graphic photos of Vietnamese children killed by American bombs, immolated herself. On March 18, the first all-night "teach-in" took place at the University of Michigan, with 3,000 people participating in intensive discussions on the war's real causes. This extraordinary example of grassroots democracy spread rapidly by word of mouth and press coverage. Thirty-five more schools had teach-ins over the following week, and 120 staged similar events by year's end, including a Berkeley "Vietnam Day" on May 21–22 that drew 20,000 people. Johnson was angry and confused by the lack of respect shown for his leadership, and the teams of diplomats dispatched by the State Department to debate with campus activists were strikingly ineffective.

The teach-ins and journalistic exposes of U.S. policies in Vietnam fed into SDS's planned rally. The April 17, 1965 Easter Sunday march brought 20,000 or more people to the nation's capital. Tiny by later standards, it was at that point one of the largest antiwar demonstrations in U.S. history, and made the antiwar movement a national force. It also made SDS famous, and signaled the end of the control exercised by anticommunist liberals and socialists over the New Left. Over the rest of 1965, the movement developed quickly in reaction to the rapidly escalating war. Every month troop levels rose, and by December, 184,000 GIs occupied huge fortified bases, venturing forth on "search and destroy" missions against the elusive NLF guerrillas. For the second time since World War II, the United States had committed itself to a ground war in Asia, and as a few dissenting senior officers and policymakers warned, Cassandra-like, getting in would be much easier than getting out.

By late 1965, the loose, decentralized character of the antiwar movement was apparent. SDS and SANE, the two organizations with the authority to lead the movement, both refused that role. SDS was committed to "multi-issue" politics, fearing absorption in a "single-issue" cause like Vietnam, though SDS veterans like Tom Hayden remained national antiwar leaders. SANE feared the younger activists' militancy and demands for immediate, unconditional withdrawal. Seeing itself as the responsible wing of the peace movement, SANE pursued a strategy of lobbying Congress in support of a negotiated solution to the war, though it also organized a November march which drew 30,000 to Washington, D.C. In August, 2,000 activists attended an Assembly of Unrepresented Peoples, where a National Coordinating Committee to End the War in Vietnam (NCCEWVN) was formed, the first of many attempts to create a single, united antiwar leadership body. The NCCEWVN was never strong, though it led International Days of Protest against the War in October 1965.

Instead, leadership came from dynamic local coalitions in several major cities, plus a handful of prominent individuals. Together, these local leaders and national figures would periodically pull together coalitions to call for national demonstrations. A complicating factor was the influence of and rivalry between the Communist Party (CP) and the Socialist Workers Party (SWP). In the antiwar movement, these two groups provided many of the most experienced organizers, but their constant jockeying for position was also disruptive. The movement's main centers in 1965–1966 were the San Francisco Bay area, with its powerful Vietnam Day Committee (VDC) led by former Berkeley activist Jerry Rubin, and New York's Fifth Avenue Peace Parade Committee, led by *Liberation* editors A.J. Muste and Dave Dellinger. In later years, several other citywide coalitions also played important roles, adding to the fractious collection of veteran pacifists, youthful draft resisters, former SDS organizers, radical scholars, Trotskyists, and traditional Communists who together steered the antiwar movement.

These generalizations cannot fully explain the antiwar movement's extreme diversity. Its greatest strength was also its major weakness—the fact that no group or even a coalition of groups could ever lead it. New forms of protest and individual action, as well as new groups, kept proliferating, from the bottom up. Most shocking was the wave of "direct action" in late 1965, not all of it nonviolent. Quaker Norman Morrison sat down outside the Pentagon on November 2 and burned himself to death. On November 6, the first mass draft-card burnings took place in New York, and three days later a Catholic Worker immolated himself. In the Bay Area, the Vietnam Day Committee repeatedly tried to block troop trains running through Berkeley to a new Oakland induction center for draftees, leading to clashes with police.

In contrast to 1965, 1966 seemed like a year of stasis. The war intensified, with proclamations of imminent victory based on "bodycounts" of dead guerrillas. Different counterinsurgency strategies came and went and troop levels increased steadily, but most U.S. journalists reported whatever army press officers said. Polls showed increasing ambivalence about the war, but protesters remained extremely unpopular. To most Americans, demonstrating in the streets at home while U.S. troops were overseas in combat was unpatriotic, and very possibly treasonous. Another problem for the movement was LBJ's record as the most pro–civil rights president since Lincoln, and the initiator of a War on Poverty. In 1965 and after, many civil rights organizers were hired by federally funded antipoverty programs, and most black leaders remained loyal to the administration. Building mainstream opposition to Johnson's war proved very difficult, which is why antiwar activists focused on protest, not legislation or electoral politics.

There were few major campaigns in 1966. Instead the antiwar movement kept growing locally, reaching into smaller cities and many more campuses. The year's most important initiatives happened at the opposite poles of respectability and radicalism. For the first time, a germ of opposition surfaced among the nation's elite—in Congress, the churches, and liberal Democratic politics. In Congress, the key figure was Arkansas Senator J. William Fulbright, who chaired the then-powerful Senate Foreign Relations Committee. Fulbright was a highly respected figure, an independent intellectual who had long distrusted the imperatives of the Cold War. In February 1966 he opened unprecedented hearings on Vietnam with experts from all points of view, and later that year he published a book, *The Arrogance of Power*, which acknowledged the legitimacy of Vietnam's Communist-led revolution, and suggested that the United States had made a grave mistake in trying to impose its will. Religious leaders began voicing a collective dissent through Clergy and Laymen Concerned About Vietnam (CALCAV), an ecumenical organization of Protestants, Catholics, and Jews, including prominent figures like Martin Luther King, Jr. It quickly spawned local chapters throughout the country under the direction of its executive secretary, the Reverend

William Sloane Coffin, chaplain of Yale University, another eminent figure who, like Dr. Spock, would become famous for his wartime dissent. As with Fulbright's hearings, CALCAV's visibility and elite membership legitimized speaking out against the war. Most dramatically, conventional politics was roiled when a Vietnam Day Committee leader, Robert Scheer, opposed Berkeley's liberal congressman, Representative Jerry Cohelan, in the June 1966 Democratic primary. Scheer lost but ran a very strong race, suggesting that liberals might actually be vulnerable to challenges from the left—a strange concept in 1966.

Among radicals, new forms of protest percolated. In summer 1966, three enlisted men at Texas' Fort Hood refused to go to Vietnam. The Socialist Workers Party and pacifists rallied to their defense, foreshadowing the later servicemen's movement against the war. Equally threatening was a decentralized antidraft movement, which eventually named itself The Resistance. On December 4, 1966, a "We Won't Go" conference drew 500 to the University of Chicago, and from here on the antidraft campaign grew rapidly. Popularized by the embarrassingly sexist SDS slogan, "Girls Say Yes to Boys Who Say No," the campaign to undermine the Selective Service system was legally risky, and many organizers were prosecuted. Ultimately, 60,000 young men, either draft resisters or deserters, fled to Canada and Sweden. Much larger numbers from the privileged classes evaded the draft legally through the automatic deferment granted any full-time college student, getting into stateside National Guard or Reserve units through political connections, or convincing sympathetic doctors to certify them unfit.

By January 1967, a sprawling antiwar movement had diffused across the country. Well-established in the biggest urban areas and on many campuses, it was just beginning to effect politics, the churches, and the professions. After two years of protests, the protesters remained a small minority, though public anxiety about the war was growing. Over the next two years all that would change. By January 1969, the Cold War consensus was broken into pieces by battlefield defeat, the moral shame of carpet-bombing a poor peasant country, U.S. atrocities against Vietnamese civilians, violent protest and the greater violence directed at protesters, and increasingly bitter recriminations on all sides. By January 1969, the Democratic Party had been shredded by these divisions, the war was deeply unpopular, and millions of people had come to identify themselves with the antiwar cause, while even larger numbers rallied to the new President, Richard Nixon, who promised "peace with honor" and called protesters "bums." 1967 and 1968 proved to be the defining years of the antiwar movement, when, out of deep conviction, it contributed to the military, political, and moral defeat that the U.S. government and armed forces suffered in Vietnam.

NO LIGHT AT THE END OF THE TUNNEL, 1967–1968

At first, 1967 looked like more of the same, a military stalemate in Vietnam and political stasis at home. U.S. ground forces reached a half-million superbly equipped men, though skeptical journalists pointed out they could show few gains against the National Liberation Front, with its deep roots among the nationalist peasantry going back to the 1940s. The U.S. commander, General William Westmoreland, proclaimed "light at the end of the tunnel" in defeating the elusive "VC," on the basis of vastly inflated claims of enemy casualties; certainly, Vietnamese men, women, and children died in huge numbers from the application of U.S. firepower to so-called "free fire zones," but only a small proportion of the dead were actual guerrillas. Elite dissenters in Congress and the media were still cautious, calling only for negotiations. At the year's beginning, the antiwar movement had no plan for ending the war, and simply kept protesting. Yet by January 1968, everything had changed. The antiwar movement, despite its diffuse impulses, generated a combination of strategies that blended grassroots public education and direct confrontations with power, at the same time that a significant antiwar wing emerged within the Democratic Party. Polls registered a sharp drop-off in support for the war, and a domestic crisis over foreign policy loomed for the first time since the years before Pearl Harbor.

For activists, 1967 was a year of steadily escalating confrontations with official authority, as SDS leader Greg Calvert's call, "From Protest to Resistance," galvanized many people to think about what it would take to stop the war, rather than just protesting it. On April 15, the largest demonstrations yet took place, with at least a quarter-million people rallying simultaneously in New York and San Francisco. These marches were called by a new coalition, the Spring Mobilization Committee (usually called "the Mobe") representing a tentative unification of the peace movement around the simple demand "Out Now!" October 1967 saw the most famous march of the Vietnam era, when 100,000 protesters crossed the Potomac to lay nonviolent siege to the Pentagon. Violence broke out during the crowd's overnight vigil, as hundreds were arrested, and many felt the movement had crossed a frontier by "putting bodies on the line" at the very center of U.S. military might. A famous photograph of a young woman placing a flower in a soldier's rifle barrel symbolized the urgency of peace. These mobilizations were part of a larger continuum of ever-intensifying protest. Draft resistance spread like a weed, and just days before the march on the Pentagon, 1,100 men burned or threw away their draft cards in planned public actions. Large-scale violent confrontations took place at universities like Berkeley and Madison, and by late 1967 President Johnson, Secretary of State Dean Rusk, and Secretary of Defense Robert

McNamara could not speak in major cities without facing thousands of angry, disrespectful protesters. Meanwhile, a campaign called Vietnam Summer sent several thousand volunteers to knock on doors and provide clear factual information to ordinary citizens.

Disruptive protests during wartime, while over 200 young GIs were dying every week (214 per week in 1967, and considerably more in 1968, the war's peak year), would normally isolate the protesters from the larger society. Indeed, the Johnson administration went to great lengths to smear the antiwar movement as being directed by foreign Communists from abroad. Johnson himself refused to believe that such a movement could develop on its own. The key development of 1967 was that the movement simultaneously became more radical *and* more mainstream, as more and more Americans saw the war as a transcendent moral issue, like slavery, that was outside of conventional politics. A powerful impetus came when Dr. King lent his enormous prestige to the movement in an April 1967 speech at New York's Riverside Church, in which he called his own government "the worst purveyor of violence in the world today." Though the liberal establishment, black and white, denounced him vociferously, King's uncompromising opposition to the war demonstrated the connections between the civil rights and antiwar movements, and encouraged many more Americans to reflect on Vietnam's ethical cost. Slowly, leaders of civil society, such as the faculty of elite universities, the heads of religious denominations, and presidents of labor unions, began to speak against the war.

Proof that antiwar sentiment was breaking the mold of conventional politics came when liberal Democratic activists, led by Allard Lowenstein, started a "Dump Johnson" movement in August 1967. Their goal was to persuade a prominent national Democrat to do the unthinkable and oppose a president's candidacy within his own party. In November, Minnesota senator Eugene McCarthy declared his intention to run against LBJ as an antiwar candidate, breaking with a generation of bipartisan loyalty to Truman's doctrine of militarily containing Communism at any cost. No longer could the Establishment press and leaders of both parties deride peace activists as naïve. By October 1967, two out of five Americans considered U.S. intervention in Vietnam a "mistake." With this array of shocking news a beleaguered Johnson entered 1968, believing there was no option but to continue what he called privately "this bitch of a war."

1968 made 1967 seem like merely a rehearsal for catastrophe. Even summarized, the cascading disasters of that year are hard to grasp as fitting within twelve months. On January 31—the Vietnamese New Year called "Tet"—the Communists launched an offensive of stunning scope, attacking inside dozens of South Vietnamese cities, and even penetrating the U.S. Embassy in

Saigon. Caught unawares, the Americans were profoundly humiliated. They pushed the National Liberation Front out of the cities at great cost to all sides, but no U.S. commander would ever again boast of "light at the end of the tunnel" and military victory. Weeks later, backed by hundreds of antiwar youth who traveled to New Hampshire to campaign for him, the ascetic and eloquent Gene McCarthy almost beat LBJ in that state's bellwether primary, an unheard-of event for a sitting president. Eyeing McCarthy's unexpected success, a second major antiwar candidate declared for the Democratic nomination: New York Senator Robert F. Kennedy, the charismatic brother of the dead president. On March 31, Johnson made an unscheduled live speech on network television, announcing that he was partially suspending the bombing of North Vietnam and initiating peace negotiations without preconditions. In a final bombshell, he declared he would not run for reelection.

After Johnson's withdrawal, the war's violence came home with a vengeance, smashing what was left of the liberal consensus. On April 5, Dr. King was murdered by white supremacist James Earl Ray in Memphis. He had gone there to support a strike by black garbagemen, part of his increasing focus on poor people's economic issues. In utter disgust and grief at the killing of a leader who stood for racial reconciliation and nonviolence, black people rose up in over 100 cities—the fires in Washington, D.C.'s black neighborhoods were visible from the Capitol, surrounded by National Guardsmen on full alert. Liberals and many antiwar activists pinned their increasingly desperate hopes on the Democratic race, imagining that either Robert Kennedy or Gene McCarthy could take the nomination and the presidency, and then lead the country back to sanity. These hopes proved illusory, as both their party and the nation proved resistant. In June, Robert Kennedy was assassinated after defeating McCarthy in the crucial California primary. Finally, at the August Democratic convention in Chicago, when antiwar protesters refused to disperse, the Chicago police attacked them in what a later grand jury termed a "police riot." Hundreds were beaten and gassed on network television, including many angry McCarthy and Kennedy delegates, who watched party bosses deliver the nomination to Vice President Hubert Humphrey (despite his avoiding the primaries). From the convention's podium, Connecticut Senator Abraham Ribicoff denounced the police's "Gestapo tactics," and cameras caught Democratic Mayor Richard Daley angrily shouting "Jew motherfucker" at him.

In November, Richard Nixon won a narrow victory over Humphrey with a 43 percent plurality. Nixon's campaign was a study in ambiguity. On the one hand, he claimed to have a secret plan to bring "peace with honor" and portrayed himself as a moderate. On the other, his constant references to "law and order," and attacks on student and black "militants," clearly tapped into right-wing and racial resentments. Meanwhile, the notorious segregationist George Wallace, Alabama's former Democratic governor, campaigned as an independent, appealing to working-class whites as an anti–civil rights, anti-liberal, anti-elite, anti-intellectual common man. He took almost 14 percent, winning five southern states. Cold War liberalism had come apart at the seams. To many, it seemed that American society itself was unraveling.

Antiwar activism's move into national politics, via the McCarthy and Kennedy campaigns, left the movement itself in a quandary. Many organizations like SANE focused on winning the battle in the Democratic Party. Otherwise, confusion reigned, and the poorly organized demonstrations at the Democratic Convention revealed that disarray. As Mobe leader Dave Dellinger tried to maintain order, younger Yippies (the so-called Youth International Party) led by Abbie Hoffman and Jerry Rubin strove for a circus atmosphere, parading a pig as their presidential candidate, promising a mass protest combined with a music festival, and attracting reporters happy to publicize the outlandish.

The Yippies' prominence highlights how the war polarized American society. To the Chicago police, Mayor Daley, and the majority of Americans who supported their draconian crackdown, the protesters were dirty, unpatriotic riffraff who opposed all that was normal and decent. To the protesters, the war revealed a nation corrupted by vast, unchecked wealth and power. By this point, many Americans equated the hippie counterculture with the antiwar movement, which did not accurately reflect the movement's multigenerational base or diverse leadership. The word "Yippie" encouraged this identification, because Hoffman and Rubin believed young people were leading a cultural revolution more important than mere politics. Though inspirational to some white youth, their vision of celebratory anarchy proved wildly unrealistic, and was rapidly coopted by the entertainment and fashion industries to sell music, clothes, movies, books, and all kinds of pop-culture paraphernalia. But it is too easy to say that the hippies and Yippies were a diversion from genuine politics.

The counterculture proved to be a vehicle by which antiwar and radical politics moved out into the heartland, via hundreds of local underground newspapers, and popular books like Rubin's *Do It!* and Hoffman's *Steal This Book*, which encouraged an identification with dissent through stylistic and cultural choices. These gestures—whether boys growing their hair long and wearing Army surplus jackets, or girls adopting peasant dresses and abandoning makeup and hairdos—were taken very seriously by parents, police, and school authorities. In countless small towns, people in power penalized transgressive physical appearance, which made explicit its connection to political dissent.

The antiwar movement at the end of 1968 seemed in disarray—defeated politically by Nixon; its most prestigious supporters, King and Robert Kennedy, killed; discredited by the violent chaos in Chicago. Activists felt little optimism, given Nixon's history of virulent anticommunism and their inability to frame a strategy for ending the war. Yet 1967–1968 also heralded new forms of activism that would undermine the war effort in ways never imagined before. From the student left to the Catholic Church to the military itself, a profound radicalism percolated that would burst forth during the Nixon years.

VETS, PRIESTS, AND STUDENTS: FROM PROTEST TO RESISTANCE

On May 17, 1968, nine Catholic activists, led by two priests, the brothers Daniel and Philip Berrigan, walked into a local Selective Service office in Catonsville, Maryland, seized hundreds of draft records, took them outside, and burned them with homemade napalm. They then waited calmly to be arrested. At the trial of the "Catonsville Nine" (the transcript of which was made into first a Broadway play and then a feature film), they asserted that their moral obligation to resist a genocidal war was a legitimate defense for property destruction, winning a surprisingly respectful hearing from both judge and jury. This simple event inspired the Catholic Left, a decentralized network that raided dozens of draft boards over the next several years, and sheltered the Berrigan brothers when they went underground, evading the FBI. The worst fantasies of the Cold War—clandestine saboteurs undermining America's ability to fight—had come true. Instead of fanatical Soviet agents, however, these brazen attacks were carried out by intensely spiritual nuns, priests, and laypeople, whose separation of their Christian faith from the imperatives of anticommunism was a new kind of subversion. Even more shocking was that juries often refused to convict Catholic radicals even when they admitted their guilt.

Like many outbreaks of radical dissent after 1965, the Catholic Left seemed to come out of nowhere, as the Catholic Church for decades had been a bulwark of monolithic anticommunism. Its cardinals and bishops lent spiritual authority to the war against "godless Communism," mobilizing millions of voters while teaching children in thousands of parochial schools to venerate the martyrs who had been killed or imprisoned by Communist governments. Yet alternative currents had quietly grown within the Church since the 1950s. Dorothy Day's *Catholic Worker* newspaper was read by tens of thousands who did not consider themselves leftists, and in 1964 a new national magazine, *Ramparts*, began publishing as an explicitly liberal

Catholic voice. Many of the early draft resisters were young Catholic men, and priests like Father James Groppi in Milwaukee led civil rights efforts for fair housing and integrated schools in northern cities. César Chávez's United Farm Workers (discussed in chapter 10) encouraged Catholic liberals like Robert Kennedy to identify with the poor; it is also notable that both challenges to Lyndon Johnson in 1968 came from deeply religious Irish Catholic senators.

Undergirding this upsurge was the fact that the Church itself, as a vast global organization, had begun a sweeping internal reform, which encouraged questioning at all levels. In 1962, Pope John XXIII declared that "I want to throw open the windows of the Church so that we can see out and the people can see in," initiating the Second Vatican Council (or Vatican II), which brought several thousand leading clergy to Rome from around the world over the next four years. The liturgy was modernized, and the Church committed itself to a vision of progressive social change. In Latin America, a new Liberation Theology spread, as the region's Catholic bishops declared a "preferential option for the poor," which some of the religious (the formal term for priests and nuns, people who have taken religious orders) interpreted as a mandate for revolution. Guerrilla movements spread throughout Latin America in the 1960s, inspired by the Cuban Revolution. The most famous of these was the attempt by the legendary Argentinean-Cuban leader Ernesto Che Guevara to spark a peasant insurgency in Bolivia, where he was killed by CIA-trained troops in 1967. In death, his body displayed with gaping wounds for the world's press, Che became a martyr of enduring significance, and his call for "two, three, many Vietnams" resonated for years to come. Both Liberation Theology and the revolutionary option filtered back to the United States through returning churchpeople. Though the Berrigans were the public face of the Catholic Left through their powerful writings, two of the Catonsville defendants, Thomas and Marjorie Melville, had been Maryknoll missionaries in Guatemala, where they became sympathizers of a Marxist guerrilla movement. Over subsequent decades Catholic radicalism became a durable part of the post-1960s left, focused on solidarity with the poor in and outside the United States.

Even more disturbing than the specter of radical Catholics was the spread of dissent and disaffection within the military. How could one stigmatize serving soldiers as unpatriotic or cowardly? Their claim to speak about the war could not be denied. 1968 saw the profusion of "G.I. coffeehouses" near military bases in the United States and overseas. Underground newspapers proliferated, published for or by disgruntled enlisted men. The antidraft organizers grouped in the loose Resistance network had moved beyond burning draft cards and offering counseling to potential draftees. Now, they reached out to servicemen themselves, encouraging them to exercise their democratic rights. The success of GI organizing was meteoric, as authority fragmented in the armed forces and casualties mounted. Antiwar rallies and marches routinely featured contingents of active-duty troops, even junior officers. Churches began operating as sanctuaries for military resisters. In Vietnam itself, some troops began wearing peace signs on their helmets. Black soldiers in particular responded to appeals from figures like Bobby Seale, the chairman of the Black Panther Party, and SNCC chairman Stokely Carmichael, insisting that they had no business fighting an oppressed people of color abroad while African Americans faced vicious racism at home.

Many soldiers hated antiwar protesters as much as they hated the war, and took out their tension and fear in systematic violence against Vietnamese civilians, with the tacit approval of their superiors. In March 1968, just after the brutal combat of the Tet Offensive, a company of the Americal Division wiped out an entire village called My Lai in one morning, machine-gunning hundreds of children, women, and old men. When the My Lai massacre broke as a story in late 1969, the casual sadism of the event added to the sense of moral crisis reaching deep into the military itself. By that point, battlefield discipline, the willingness to obey orders and risk one's life, had broken down completely in many units. Along with widespread heroin use, there were hundreds of "fragging" incidents, where noncoms and officers were killed or threatened (the term refers to dropping a fragmentation grenade into a superior's bunker while he sleeps).

All of this contributed to the growth of Vietnam Veterans Against the War (VVAW). It began very modestly when six vets decided to march under that banner during the April 1967 Spring Mobilization in New York. Over the next five years, VVAW became the movement's cutting edge, a "search and destroy" mission against the lies of policymakers. At the Winter Soldier hearings held in Detroit in 1970, hundreds of veterans catalogued the endemic savagery of a racist war—the tortures, murders, and rapes of Vietnamese civilians they had observed or committed. VVAW was especially important because of its working-class character. Its members were the young men who did not have student deferments or family clout to get them into the National Guard or Reserve. Their militant honesty broke through the stereotype of the protester as a privileged, cowardly hippie. Most famous was Ron Kovic, a blue-collar kid from Queens who was terribly wounded in Vietnam. His *Born on the Fourth of July* became the war's most famous memoir. When Kovic and other paralyzed or legless vets led marches in ragged fatigues, rolling their wheelchairs into the street, even hardened policemen stepped back in respect. In 1976, in the war's weary aftermath, Kovic was nominated for vice-president and allowed to address the Democratic Party Convention, a rueful recognition of those fighting men who kept their honor in a war that had none.

The sight of radical nuns, priests, soldiers, and veterans shocked mainstream Americans profoundly. In contrast, most people were familiar with the realities of student protest, which had spread across the country since the early 1960s. From 1967 on, however, the student left took on an explicitly revolutionary character, in solidarity with the Vietnamese Communists. Chants like "Ho, Ho, Ho Chi Minh, NLF is Gonna Win," became more and more common, and various polls showed that a significant fraction of the nation's several million students considered themselves "revolutionaries," while a larger number defined themselves as "radicals." By this time, the preeminent radical youth group was SDS. It had exploded in size and moved sharply left since 1965, drawing in tens of thousands of supporters in several hundred chapters. Backing up this grassroots base, SDS also had dozens of traveling organizers, a network of regional offices, and a national newspaper, *New Left Notes*. At its peak, over a thousand chapter delegates attended its annual conventions. One catalyst for SDS's growth was the enormous attention it received from journalists, both friendly and hostile. The press was fascinated by the self-confidence of its leaders, their flair for the dramatic. Tom Hayden, author of *The Port Huron Statement*, was only one of various nationally known figures who came out of SDS, speaking, lecturing, and organizing across the country.

Yet SDS's status as the dominant force on the student left proved to be very brief. In plain terms, it was swamped by its own growth. Like many student groups, lack of experience and constant turnover among activists made it difficult to maintain cohesive leadership or a coherent strategy. The fluidity of student organizing also left SDS wide open to ideological factionalism, which contributed greatly to its sudden collapse. The Progressive Labor Party, a small Maoist splinter from the Communist Party USA, sent its younger members into SDS in 1966. Operating inside, the "PL'ers" (as they were known) pushed a dogmatic brand of Marxism emphasizing the historic vanguard role of the industrial working class. They took over many local SDS chapters and set their sights on claiming the national leadership. For many, this was the worst legacy of the Old Left—infiltration, rigid ideological lines, unprincipled fights for control.

In response to PL's challenge and deeply radicalized by the resistance of the Vietnamese, SDS leaders turned to their own version of revolutionary theory. Led by Bernardine Dohrn and National Secretary Mike Klonsky, they called for a Revolutionary Youth Movement (RYM) that would ally with the Vietnamese Communists abroad and the Black Panthers at home. At SDS's final, tumultuous 1969 convention in Ypsilanti, Michigan, Dohrn and the RYM faction expelled the Progressive Labor faction. In control of the name, prestige, and resources of SDS, they proceeded to wreck it. Believing themselves part of a worldwide guerrilla war against U.S. imperialism, they decided to convert a loosely organized public organization with hundreds of thousands of sympathizers into an underground network of disciplined armed cells. They called themselves Weatherman, after a line in a Bob Dylan song, "You don't need a weatherman to know which way the wind blows" (later the name was changed to the Weather Underground Organization). While they may have admired charismatic leaders like Dohrn, very few in SDS's base were ready for armed struggle "in the belly of the beast." When a few hundred of them went underground at the end of 1969, most SDS'ers just walked away. The rest of this story is sad, if not pathetic. While receiving enormous media attention, Weatherman accomplished almost nothing, other than some disastrous streetfighting with police in so-called "Days of Rage" in Chicago in late 1969, and bombing a bathroom in the Pentagon. Their best-known exploit was when a cell hiding in a Greenwich Village townhouse in New York city blew themselves up in late 1970. After that, the organization declined rapidly. Eventually most of its members turned themselves in to the FBI, their revolutionary dream no more than wishful thinking.

The collapse of SDS had no effect on the antiwar movement: 1969 was a banner year, culminating in the nationwide Moratorium (see below). The real effect of this organizational disaster was to free up thousands of experienced young organizers just as they were getting ready to graduate. These ex-SDSers were a major component of the New Communist Movement of the early 1970s, joining with thousands of young people of color coming from revolutionary nationalist organizations like the La Raza Unida Party, the Congress of African Peoples, the League of Revolutionary Black Workers, the Young Lords Party, and the African Liberation Support Committee (see chapter 13).

VIETNAMIZATION AND POLARIZATION, 1969–1975

Richard Nixon's presidency marked a fundamental shift in the war and in the direction of the antiwar movement. His tenure in office (1969–1974) saw both the peak of mass protest in the streets and the movement's gradual incorporation into conventional politics, via Congress and the Democratic Party. In 1969–1970, Nixon and his chief strategist, the former Harvard professor Henry Kissinger, "Vietnamized" the war by replacing American troops with heavily-armed South Vietnamese troops backed up by crushing applications of U.S. air power. Their goal was to hold back the National Liberation Front guerrillas (severely weakened by their losses during Tet) and the increasingly aggressive People's Army of [North] Vietnam, to buy time for a diplomatic solution preserving South Vietnam. Nixon also escalated the war in new ways. Under presidential orders, the U.S. Air Force began secretly bombing neutral Cambodia and Laos, hoping to smash Communist supply lines, the famous "Ho Chi Minh Trail." This campaign violated both international and U.S. law, as senior Air Force officers lied to Congress and altered documents. In time, these criminal actions in violation of the Constitution came back to haunt Nixon, and destroyed any remaining congressional support for continuing the air war after the final withdrawal of U.S. troops from Vietnam in January 1973.

At home, Nixon and his tight circle of personal aides initiated what scholars have called a "domestic counterinsurgency," treating the antiwar movement, and even respectable Democratic liberals, as if they were the Viet Cong—an enemy to be destroyed. He ordered the full power of government into this effort, including the FBI, the CIA, Army Intelligence, and the National Security Agency. Electronic surveillance covering thousands of people was stepped up, and *agents provocateurs* were widely deployed. One such agent, known as "Tommy the Traveler," moved around the country, joining local groups where he would taunt activists into discussions of violent actions, whereupon they were indicted for conspiracy. Planted letters and phone calls encouraged mutual distrust among radicals, which inside the Black Panther Party led to paranoia, violent factionalization, and the killing of real and imagined informers. Eventually this pattern of illegality degenerated into the Watergate affair.

Though Nixon's Justice Department and allied local prosecutors pursued dozens of indictments intended to disrupt the antiwar movement, the most famous was the trial of the Chicago Eight. Using an old statute that made it a felony to cross state lines for the purpose of inciting a riot, the U.S. attorney in Chicago indicted a cross-section of the New Left's leadership for organizing the demonstrations at the 1968 Democratic Convention, including the Mobe's Dave Dellinger, Black Panther Chairman Bobby Seale, SDS veterans Tom Hayden and Rennie Davis, and Yippie agitators Jerry Rubin and Abbie Hoffman. The trial dragged on for two years, with violent courtroom confrontations; Judge Julius Hoffman, who openly despised the defendants, had Seale chained and gagged in his chair. Although eventually their convictions were thrown out, the trial of the Chicago 8 and numerous other prosecutions added to the New Left's belief that a revolutionary crisis was approaching, perhaps even a fascist crackdown.

Yet a closer look at Nixon's actual policies indicates that, however devious and corrupt he may have been, he was not a fascist, nor even a true conservative like Barry Goldwater and his disciple Ronald Reagan. The contrast between Vietnamization—a slow-motion retreat, while pretending to maintain national honor—and calculated repression at home, indicates the sophistication of Nixon's intentions. Elsewhere in the world, Nixon played the role of a moderate, a man of peace. He lessened tensions with the Soviet Union and China through a policy of "détente" and signed major arms control treaties, while ordering the CIA to sabotage Chile's democratically elected socialist government and supporting right-wing dictatorships from Greece to South Africa. In his domestic policies, Nixon operated squarely within the Cold War liberal tradition, expanding the scope of social welfare programs in significant ways, and signing breakthrough environmental legislation like the Clean Water Act. For much of his first term, this blend of polarization and progress seemed to work: Nixon was overwhelmingly reelected in 1972. Ultimately, however, the war in Southeast Asia, and his belief that everyone who opposed it was an "enemy" to be destroyed, caused his fall from power in the nation's worst constitutional crisis since the Civil War.

For the first year or so of Nixon's presidency, the Vietnamization policy seemed remarkably successful. U.S. troop levels dropped sharply, and so did television news coverage. Nixon and Kissinger believed they could end the war on their own terms. Like Lyndon Johnson, they simply could not accept that a "third-rate peasant country," in Kissinger's words, could defeat the United States. But fighting on their own land, retaining the backing of the peasantry and, facing an utterly corrupt Saigon regime, the Vietnamese Communists had the strategic initiative, ruining all of Nixon's carefully laid plans. Despite the heaviest bombing in world history, he could neither control the situation on the ground in Vietnam nor end "the war at home." Denounced as traitors who stabbed our troops in the back, the antiwar movement refused to back down. In fact, while Nixon slowly scaled down the war, the movement kept widening its reach, as it came to represent a large section, even a plurality, of the public. This much wider movement included many of the most eminent people in America, yet it was united around the most radical demand—for the unconditional withdrawal of U.S. forces, and "peace now" rather than later. Then and later, many commentators have argued that the main consequence of the polarization of the late 1960s was a backlash on the right; this misses an equally important result, that much of the center moved to the left.

The revived antiwar movement, now a vast citizens' mobilization incorporating pacifists and leftists and reaching deep into the mainstream, made its public debut in the fall of 1969 in a series of historic events. Two major new national coalitions had formed early in the year. Veterans of the McCarthy campaign—mainly white students like Bill Clinton, an intern in the office of Senator William Fulbright—signed up for the Vietnam Moratorium Committee. Their plan was to organize a nationwide one-day strike, when all normal business would cease and people would gather to reflect on the war. At the same time, the radical forces that had built the movement since 1965 formed a New Mobilization Committee to organize a massive national demonstration in Washington. Ultimately both events, first on October 15 across the country, and then November 13–15 in the nation's capital, were called "the Moratorium." Together, they demonstrated a level of antiwar dissent unparalleled in U.S. history. On October 15, 1969, the huge United Auto Workers and Teamsters unions, twenty-four U.S. Senators, Cardinal Richard Cushing of New York (the country's senior Catholic prelate), and millions of Americans from junior high schools to Wall Street all participated in the Moratorium, staying home from work or school, holding vigils, wearing black armbands, attending church services, or turning on their car lights. A month later, at least half a million people from all walks of life rallied peacefully on the Mall in Washington, virtually taking over the city. Thousands walked past the White House over a 36-hour period, reading the names of 45,000 dead GIs, one by one. Earlier that fall, on September 25, New York Republican senator Charles Goodell introduced a motion to withdraw all U.S. troops by December 1, 1969, the first of many such efforts in Congress.

A political infighter like Nixon would not remain silent when challenged. He counterattacked in a televised address on November 3, 1969, invoking the "silent majority" of patriotic Americans and insisting that dissidents, even antiwar Republicans like Goodell, directly aided the Communist enemy. Nixon's willingness to polarize the nation paid short-term dividends. While he had to call off secret plans for a sudden escalation to terrorize the Communists into submission, he rallied much of the public to his side. Once again, the movement seemed in the doldrums as the war dragged on into 1970. The biggest news as 1969 ended was the revelation of the massacre at My Lai in March 1968. The publication of gory color photographs and anguished eyewitness testimony by GIs in *Life* magazine led to court martials where one officer, Lieutenant William Calley, was convicted of "at least" twenty-two murders. Despite a life sentence, he served only three years in jail. Three more senior officers were acquitted, increasing the feeling among the antiwar section of the public that Vietnam was corrupting basic moral decency. Many other Americans supported pardoning Calley and seemed indifferent to the slaughter of Vietnamese civilians.

The standoff of 1969, and the war's apparent lull in early 1970, led many radicalized liberals to turn to Congress, the one institution with legal authority to end the war. Much organizing focused on the fall 1970 elections, with visible results. A number of antiwar leaders were elected to the House as Democrats, including black activist Ronald V. Dellums from Berkeley; Bella Abzug, a New York leader in Women Strike for Peace with roots in the Communist-led Civil Rights Congress of the 1950s; Patricia Schroeder, a Colorado antiwar advocate; and the Reverend Robert Drinan, a Massachusetts Jesuit connected to the Catholic Left. Together, they represented the New Left's entrance into the Democratic Party.

Any lull in the war was short-lived. In spring 1970, Nixon's Vietnamization strategy broke down with disastrous results. Gambling on one last military escalation, Nixon announced on April 30 that American and South Vietnamese troops were invading Cambodia to get at Communist supply bases. In a flash, all of his assertions of "peace with honor" seemed as hollow as Johnson's promises of "no wider war." Campuses erupted in the largest wave of student protest in U.S. history. A nationwide student strike closed down hundreds of schools as 1.5 million students walked out. For many students, nonviolence was no longer an adequate form of protest against the war. They fought pitched battles with police, burned police cars, and firebombed Reserve Officer Training Corps (ROTC) buildings. In Ohio, Governor John Rhodes sent the National Guard to Kent State University in response to violent protests. On the afternoon of May 5 they fired without warning into a crowd of protesters after stones and bottles were thrown, killing four students, including two walking to class. Days later, Mississippi state police shot up a dormitory at all-black Jackson State, killing two more. On May 8, a group of New York construction workers, encouraged by their prowar union leaders, attacked antiwar protesters on Wall Street with pipes and fists, highlighting the cultural and class differences over the war. They were honored by the president, and in return gave him a honorary hardhat.

But the best indicator of Nixon's blunder could be seen in congressional sentiments and in the polls. The Senate Foreign Relations Committee denounced the invasion as illegal. Congressional leaders began seriously considering how to reassert Congress' constitutional prerogatives and limit the president's ability to initiate major military operations without legislative approval. By September 1970, a Senate bill mandating immediate withdrawal, sponsored by South Dakota Democrat George McGovern and Oregon Republican Mark Hatfield, had 39 supporters. Meanwhile, in one poll, the public wanted to get "out now," by a margin of 58 percent to 24 percent. Congress lagged far behind the public in large part because of the power of southern conservatives, representing the one clearly prowar region, plus the fear in both parties of looking soft on Communism by accepting an outright defeat.

The stalemate of a profoundly unpopular war, and an increasingly powerful antiwar movement unable to force a final withdrawal, continued for two more years. Spring 1971 saw the last major national demonstrations, at a point when the country seemed both sick to death of the war and profoundly split by it. Hardly anyone—not even those members of Congress who backed the president—could see any purpose to the fighting and bombing and dying. Discord had spread into families, churches, union locals, workplaces, and schools, creating a sour bitterness and distrust. The National Peace Action Coalition, led largely by the Socialist Workers Party, brought perhaps 750,000 people to Washington in late April. That same week the Vietnam Veterans Against the War staged a legendary protest, in which 800 veterans led by decorated Navy Lieutenant John Kerry threw their medals away on the Capitol steps, repudiating any notion of honor or glory attached to the war. The day before, Kerry had testified before the Senate Foreign Relations Committee, asking a famous question: "How do you ask a man to be the last man to die for a mistake?" Days later, thousands of radicals arrived in Washington for May Day protests intended to shut down the capital completely by blocking roads and occupying buildings. To forestall this disruption, the Justice Department arrested 12,000 people, illegally jailing thousands of them in Robert F. Kennedy Stadium, an action reminiscent of a South American dictatorship. New revelations about U.S. war crimes and the terror practiced by the South Vietnamese government surfaced constantly: the CIA's Phoenix Program, in which 90,000 civilian supporters of the National Liberation Front were systematically assassinated; and the horrific "Tiger Cages" camps for civilian dissidents, uncovered by congressional aide and later Iowa senator Tom Harkin.

From mid-1971 until the January 1973 signing of the peace agreement ratifying the U.S. withdrawal, the antiwar movement became much less visible. There were no nationwide campus rebellions or large rallies. Instead, ongoing opposition to the war became almost a normal activity for both seasoned radicals and the larger number of liberals frightened by Nixon's willingness to make the Vietnamese pay in blood for their independence. The radicals raised money for hospitals in Hanoi, and linked their solidarity with Vietnam to a larger identification with the revolutionary Third World across Asia, Latin America, and Africa. From 1969 on, small underground groups, many never detected, carried out thousands of acts of sabotage against military facilities, sometimes with tragic results, as when a graduate student was killed in the bombing of the University of Wisconsin's Army Math Center in 1970. With growing success, the liberals lobbied relentlessly to push members of Congress into antiwar positions, or worked to replace those still supporting the war. Though the public by three to one opposed any further involvement in Southeast Asia (in one poll, 65 percent believed the war to be "morally wrong"), Congress remained deadlocked. Nixon's Justice Department continued to indict activists on various conspiracy charges. The Berrigan brothers, held in two different federal prisons, were charged with hatching a plan to kidnap National Security Advisor Henry Kissinger and hold him hostage in the sewers under Washington. The ensuing trial of the "Harrisburg Seven" only made the administration look ridiculous, as even a jury in conservative central Pennsylvania refused to convict. More effectively, Nixon orchestrated a private campaign by businessman Ross Perot to publicize the plight of U.S. prisoners of war, mainly downed pilots like the future senator John McCain. Perot and other conservatives stoked rage at both the POW's North Vietnamese captors and the thousands of draft resisters and deserters in Canada who refused to fight. Meanwhile, the Paris talks between the United States and North Vietnam, initiated in 1968, dragged on with no apparent end in sight.

The final stages of the war in Southeast Asia and the war at home took shape in this context of a deeply polarized America. The last big confrontation was the 1972 presidential election campaign—first the fight over the Democratic nomination, and then the lopsided contest between Nixon and the Democratic candidate, Senator George McGovern. Ultimately, Nixon crushed the South Dakotan 61 percent to 37 percent, carrying every state but Massachusetts. To blunt McGovern as the peace candidate, the president authorized Kissinger to make concessions and move the Paris peace talks forward. In other words, to win at home, he finally accepted defeat abroad. But Nixon proved unable to resist the desire to punish, and he turned his rage on domestic opponents. Unknown to the press and voters, the president ordered his staff to recruit undercover operatives with CIA connections (the so-called "plumbers") for illegal operations against the Democratic Party. These included breaking into the Democratic National Headquarters in the Watergate Hotel, and numerous other "dirty tricks" (such as planting false stories to undermine the presidential candidacy of Maine Democratic senator Edmund Muskie). Political crimes stemming from Nixon's paranoia about opposition to his authority eventually led to his impeachment by Congress and fall from power.

By January 1972 the focus of antiwar activism had moved into the Democratic primaries through McGovern's candidacy. The mild-mannered prairie liberal became a national leader because of his unequivocal insistence on "bringing the boys home." Both radicals and liberals saw him as the vehicle to take the party away from the old guard, personified by Muskie, the 1968 vice-presidential candidate and presumed frontrunner in 1972. Further to the right, George Wallace ran yet another time, this time as a Democrat, and proved again to be a powerful vote-getter with his barely veiled racism and populist attacks on elites. Muskie's campaign flagged early and McGovern steadily advanced, competing with Wallace for white working-class votes and drawing in New Left constituencies—students, peace and civil rights activists, feminists, and gays. Union leaders and moderates, horrified by the prospect of a "radical" candidate, convinced Hubert Humphrey to enter the race late, but McGovern beat the former vice president in California and locked up the nomination. The Democratic Convention in Miami looked unlike any before. Movement leaders like Congresswoman Bella Abzug and the Reverend Jesse Jackson, a former aide to Dr. Martin Luther King, Jr., led pro-McGovern delegations that displaced the traditional party and trade union delegates. Together, they passed a platform to the left of any of the Cold War era or since.

Getting the presidential nomination of the nation's majority party was an elusive victory, and from then on disasters piled up. Much of the Democratic Party apparatus walked away from McGovern. The AFL-CIO, led by its prowar president George Meany, refused to endorse the Democratic candidate for the first time in many decades. McGovern made major mistakes, choosing Senator Thomas Eagleton of Missouri as his vice-presidential candidate and then dumping him when mental health problems surfaced. In the fall campaign, Nixon's savvy professionals tore McGovern apart with ads suggesting he would gut U.S. military power. Local Republican operatives coined a handy slogan to characterize the Democrat: "acid, amnesty, and abortion"—meaning hippies, hard drugs, draft dodgers who spit on the flag, and free-loving women's libbers (abortion was still illegal in most states, and McGovern did not in fact endorse legalization). Days before the election, Kissinger returned from Paris announcing an imminent peace settlement, making McGovern's candidacy look redundant. In mid-November, right after his huge win, Nixon rejected the pending treaty and opted for one last massive air campaign, Operation Linebacker. This so-called "Christmas bombing" was the most intensive in world history, with heavy American losses. It was aimed directly at North Vietnam's two major cities, Hanoi and Haiphong, and killed thousands more civilians. Having secured his vengeance, Nixon agreed to terms identical to those available in October, before the election. In January, the fighting ended, and by March 1973, the last U.S. troops and the POWs had finally come home.

The American ground war was over, but the fight over the war dragged on. Despite overwhelming evidence of the military incompetence, repressiveness, and corruption of the U.S.-backed regime in Saigon, Nixon hoped that he could prop it up, denying the Communists a final victory. But the accumulated power of the antiwar movement in Congress proved too much for him. A Coalition to Stop Funding the War, incorporating dozens of mainstream religious denominations, plus an effective grassroots effort, the Indochina Peace Campaign, created by Tom Hayden and the activist movie star Jane Fonda, blocked all of Nixon's efforts. In August 1973, Congress finally cut off all funds for the continuing air war in Indochina. Meanwhile, the administration's criminality caught up with it in the revelations labeled "Watergate." *Washington Post* investigations and congressional testimony revealed that Nixon's plumbers had burglarized a psychiatrist's office to steal information on Defense

Department analyst Daniel Ellsberg; in 1971 he had leaked a secret government history of the war to the *New York Times* and other media, the so-called Pentagon Papers. Nixon had compiled an "enemies list," including top journalists and politicians, and instructed the Internal Revenue Service to harass these citizens. He had subverted the Democratic Party in numerous ways, and accepted massive illegal donations to his reelection campaign from so-called "fat cats." Finally, the president had usurped Congress' constitutional authority through the secret bombing of Cambodia. In summer 1974 a bipartisan House Judiciary Committee voted his impeachment, and on August 9 he resigned in disgrace. Eight months later, the entire South Vietnamese army, one of the largest and best-equipped in the world thanks to U.S. tax dollars, collapsed in a few weeks. Battle-hardened North Vietnamese regulars rolled into Saigon, renaming it Ho Chi Minh City. The thirty-year war for national independence was over, with total victory won at great cost: Americans mourned 58,000 dead, but at least two million Indochinese had perished.

In the United States, the response to this final humiliation—or triumph, depending on your political perspective—was muted, except among core New Leftists, people who had since 1965 defined themselves through opposition to the war. In New York's Central Park, tens of thousands gathered for a victory celebration and peace rally, listening to musicians and speeches from movement leaders. Most Americans, however, just wanted to move on, and from that date through the present, a strange silence has fallen on the topic of the dirty war in Vietnam. Occasionally, the war resurfaces, in Hollywood movies or as a point of comparison with later U.S. wars, or when the military record or failure to serve of a presidential candidate becomes an issue, as with Bill Clinton, John Kerry, and George W. Bush. Those who lived through the war prefer not to dwell on the topic; those too young to remember continue to wonder what happened. This silence contributes to a deep confusion about the New Left, what it was and what it achieved, since Vietnam was its greatest common cause, its claim to honor.

Chapter 9

BLACK POWER: "A NATION WITHIN A NATION?"

National liberation, national renaissance, the restoration of nationhood to the people, commonwealth: whatever may be the headings used or the formulas introduced, decolonization is always a violent phenomenon.

—Frantz Fanon, *The Wretched of the Earth*, 1961

Population experts predict that by 1970 Afro-Americans will constitute a majority in fifty of the nation's largest cities. In Washington, D.C., and Newark, N.J., Afro-Americans are already a majority. In Detroit, Baltimore, Cleveland, and St. Louis they are one-third or more of the population. . . . There are more Afro-Americans in New York City than in the entire state of Mississippi. . . . In accordance with the general philosophy of majority rule and the specific American tradition of ethnic groupings (Irish, Polish, Italian) migrating en masse to the big cities and then taking over the leadership of municipal government, black Americans are next in line. Each previous ethnic grouping achieved first-class citizenship chiefly because its leaders became the cities' leaders, but racism is so deeply imbedded in the American psyche from top to bottom, and from Right to Left, that it cannot even entertain the idea of black political power in the cities.

—James and Grace Lee Boggs, "The City is the Black Man's Land," 1966

In attempting to analyze where the movement is going, certain questions have arisen as to the future roles played by white personnel. . . . The answers to these questions lead us to believe that the form of white participation, as practiced in the past, is now obsolete. Some of the problems are as follows: The inability of whites to relate to the cultural aspects of Black society; attitudes that whites, consciously or unconsciously, bring to Black communities (western superiority) and

about Black people (paternalism); inability to shatter white-sponsored community myths of Black inferiority and self-negation; inability to combat the views of
the Black community that white organizers, being "white," control Black organizers as puppets; insensitivity of both Black and white workers towards the hostility of the Black community on the issue of interracial "relationships" (sex); the
unwillingness of whites to deal with the *roots* of racism which lie within the white
community; whites though individually "liberal" are symbols of oppression to the
Black community—due to the *collective* power that whites have over Black lives.
                    —Atlanta Project, Student Nonviolent Coordinating Committee,
                                        "A Position Paper on Race," 1966

It is often asserted that Black Power resulted from spontaneous combustion in
1965–1966, when the fierce nationalist rhetoric of Malcolm X and anger over
the disrespectful treatment of the Mississippi Freedom Democrats led to separatism and a repudiation of interracial solidarity by frustrated civil rights
activists. There's certainly truth in this popular account. SNCC leader Stokely
Carmichael did make the slogan "Black Power" instantaneously famous by
showcasing it during a June 1966 march in Mississippi because he and others
believed "the Movement" had run out of steam. But focusing on the rage of
young black people, the desire to separate from whites, and a few charismatic
orators like Malcolm X and Carmichael ignores Black Power's deep roots, how
it surged through African American communities, and the complexities of its
competing strategies. Instead of a sudden eruption, Black Power grew slowly
from ideas, organizations, personal networks, experiences, and tactics that
were always under the radar of the national media, in cities and on campuses
from New York to Los Angeles (with stops in Philadelphia, Cleveland, Detroit,
Chicago, and the Bay Area). It flared up like a brushfire after the southern
Civil Rights movement reached its climax in 1963–1965, but the ideologies
and institutions of Black Power had slowly accumulated over the preceding
twenty years since World War II (see chapter 4).

DEFIANCE: BLACK POWER ARRIVES, 1965–1966

The events of 1965 provided a dramatic closure for the Civil Rights
movement, as well as for those black activists who were increasingly
estranged by the leadership's insistence on nonviolence and cooperation with
Cold War liberals—the array of white-led trade unions, churches, and foundations tied to the Democratic Party. Once the Voting Rights Act passed
Congress overwhelmingly in August 1965, the legal and political basis of Jim
Crow was visibly crumbling, and it would only be a few years, or even
months, before white segregationist politicians would begin appealing for

black votes. Equally decisive for Black Power advocates was Malcolm X's assassination in February 1965. Many African Americans had rested their hopes and renewed pride upon this honest, resolute man whom the actor Ossie Davis eulogized as "our shining black prince." His killing by fellow Muslims, and the suspicion that government agencies abetted the murder, propelled many civil rights activists to take a new look at white America. Thousands came to ponder Malcolm's words and example, and to accept his stern injunction that the only viable path to liberation lay in breaking with white liberalism, and consciously identifying with blackness and the revolutionary Third World. In death, Malcolm X brought to life many new black revolutionaries.

Many other factors contributed to the sudden convergence around the Black Power strategy in 1965–1966. The escalation in Vietnam cast a harsh light on American pretensions to lead the Free World. "No Viet Cong Ever Called Me Nigger" was a popular antiwar slogan among young black men, epitomizing the conviction that justice at home required fighting imperialism abroad, instead of the dutiful anticommunism of traditional black leaders. When the heavyweight boxing champion Muhammad Ali refused to accept induction into the armed services in 1967 because of his devout Muslim faith, he made the link between Black Power and opposing the war uncomfortably concrete for whites. Black Power was also spurred by the August 1965 civic insurrection (or "riot") in Watts, Los Angeles' sprawling, blighted ghetto. Thousands of black people sent an unmistakable message that they no longer accepted White Power's legitimacy, filling the streets, jeering at and stoning police, and looting and burning white businesses, until "law and order" were finally imposed by military occupation. Dozens of residents were killed by police and National Guardsmen and thousands were arrested, as the news media and politicians speculated frantically about the anger of the urban black poor. For many white Americans, this was a disturbing, irrational outburst that legitimized their deepest racial fears—hadn't Congress passed bill after bill to "help the Negroes?" Wasn't President Johnson leading a War on Poverty? Of course, very few whites other than policemen had ever seen Watts or any of the decaying, overcrowded, jobless neighborhoods like it across urban America. They ignored the widespread feeling among African Americans that a riot was an effective means of protesting rampant police brutality and forcing white power structures to finally pay attention to poverty and deprivation. For Black Power organizers, Watts sent another message—that the black masses might constitute a radicalized strike force prepared to defend their own streets.

The importance of defiance, even violence, in making a decisive break with the authority of the colonizer was underscored by the book that young black activists everywhere were reading in 1964–1965, Frantz Fanon's *The*

Wretched of the Earth. Over time, it became one of the central theoretical documents for the Black Power movement. Fanon was a black psychiatrist from Martinique, a French colony in the Caribbean. Assigned to a clinic in Algeria in the 1950s, he joined its underground independence movement, the FLN (National Liberation Front), then confronting the French Army and white settlers in a bloody guerrilla war. Fanon defined the struggle by oppressed people of color against colonial domination as the axis of modern world history. With eloquent logic, he insisted that an anticolonial war of liberation required unremitting violence, because only violence would liberate the colonized subject psychologically and make him or her an autonomous human. Fanon's doctrine was pored over by African American activists. Through it they understood themselves not as an ex-slave minority stripped of cultural identity and striving for integration into white society, but as part of a vast global war for self-determination. Black people across America began calling themselves an "internal colony," a "nation within a nation."

Inspired by Malcolm X, Fanon, the Watts uprising, African liberation struggles, and homegrown theorists like the Detroit autoworker James Boggs, ex-Communist social critic Harold Cruse, and the poet and playwright LeRoi Jones, black radicals moved towards seeking not just rights, but economic justice, political power, and cultural autonomy for black people, "by any means necessary," as Malcolm had once put it. LeRoi Jones offered an abrupt example of this transformation. By 1964, he had become famous, as the author of *Blues People*, a foundational study of black culture and American music, and an award-winning Off Broadway play, *Dutchman*. After Malcolm X's death in February 1965, however, Jones left his downtown Manhattan bohemian world of white friends and a white wife, moving uptown to Harlem to create the Black Arts Repertory Theater/School (BARTS). The BARTS lasted less than a year, teaching black history and staging avant-garde plays and jazz street parades, before it fell apart in violent infighting—a hint of Black Power's crippling divisions in the future. Jones then returned to his hometown of Newark, New Jersey, where he set up Spirithouse, a consciously Black Nationalist cultural center, theater, and school. Spirithouse and a network of related organizations like the Committee for a Unified Newark became a local political force and a much-imitated model of total independence from the white establishment. In 1968, Jones changed his name to Amiri Baraka, a forerunner of widespread moves to adopt African names in preference to names inherited from white slaveowners. Baraka's multifaceted effort, embracing black culture as a weapon for radical nationalist politics, was one of many grassroots urban projects that became Black Power's base. His embrace of a homophobic, authoritarian form of male leadership, and his periodic bursts of anti-Semitism, were also influential, if much less positive.

Another local experiment with national impact was Los Angeles' tightly disciplined US group, founded by Ron Everett, who renamed himself Maulana Karenga. Karenga mastered Swahili at a time when hardly any Americans spoke African languages, and he focused exclusively on what he called "cultural nationalism." This meant divesting white traditions in favor of a synthetic African identity, based on a militaristic, patriarchal "traditionalism." The centerpiece of Karenga's politics was a comprehensive doctrine called Kawaida, which offered seven broad principles for leading a culturally liberated African life. For activists schooled in ideologies derived from Europe, whether pacifism or Marxism, Karenga's audacious vision and supercharged machismo were appealing, and he recruited disciples like Baraka across the country.

Meanwhile, during 1965 both CORE and SNCC resolved to move away from interracial liberalism, and in 1966 both became explicitly all-black, jettisoning their white staff people, and thus the white financial support upon which they had relied. At the time, white journalists assumed these well-known organizations were leading the Black Power movement, but in fact they were following the lead of community activists tired of conventional civil rights strategies. Like Women's Liberation, Black Power percolated from the bottom up, as hundreds of unsung local leaders and groups fashioned their own theories and rhetorical calls, competing to lead a cultural revolution. This remarkable diversity explains why Black Power was never led by any major national organizations (with the partial exception of the Black Panther Party), and why it flourished despite the rapid decline of CORE and SNCC from 1967 on.

By spring 1966, the black freedom movement was evidently in transition, and various individuals and groups competed to lead it in a new direction. Dr. King's SCLC brought its style of moral suasion through nonviolent protest to the North, hoping to challenge the de facto segregation and poverty of Chicago, where African Americans elected ten city councilmen, yet lacked meaningful access to power and opportunity. Mayor Richard Daley adroitly finessed King with face-saving gestures, and the badly planned campaign made the vaunted leader look ineffectual. Harlem's outspoken congressman, Adam Clayton Powell, Jr., demanded "black power" in a speech at Howard University's commencement in May 1966, and convened a working group that over led to the first National Black Power Conference in 1967. Powell was positioning himself to take over the leadership of the emerging trend, but Stokely Carmichael preempted this move.

James Meredith, who had integrated "Ole Miss" in 1962, had begun a quixotic one-man walk through Mississippi in June 1966 to confront racist violence. He was promptly felled by a shotgun blast, so Martin Luther King, Carmichael, and CORE's new head, the nationalist Floyd McKissick, agreed to continue his march. Along the route, Carmichael and a fellow SNCC activist,

Willie Ricks, used the moment to provoke a crisis by leading black crowds in a call-and-response chant: "What do we want? Black Power!" The white press, Vice President Hubert Humphrey, the NAACP's Roy Wilkins, and many influential whites and blacks reacted with outrage—as if the words "Black Power" were evidence of what was labeled "racism," "fascism," "a reverse Ku Klux Klan," and violent black supremacy. Carmichael's strategy worked perfectly. He used the mass media, and predictable denunciations by elites, to throw down a challenge, asserting himself and SNCC as leaders of the new direction. Many people picked up that gauntlet, and the Black Power movement was officially launched.

This famous incident revealed the promise and pitfalls of a particular mode of Black Power leadership, sometimes called "Mau-Mauing" or, in derision, acting "more militant than thou." Like Baraka, Karenga, and many others, Carmichael learned from Malcolm X the art of unleashing sharply honed rhetoric like machine-gun fire, in a spectacular display of public anger and masculine charisma, although there was a simplicity and clarity to Malcolm's message that no one else could match. Millions of African Americans (and others too) were inspired by the stinging oratory of tribunes like Carmichael. But oratory often substituted for what SNCC and CORE had pioneered: building self-reliant local movements that could sustain themselves without famous leaders or media attention. In hindsight, this community organizing tradition offered a more durable mode of getting power for black people. Carmichael himself had earned enormous respect as a dogged, wily community organizer in Alabama's poorest, blackest rural counties. In 1965–1966 he helped organize the single most concrete manifestation of local Black Power yet seen in the Deep South—the Lowndes County Freedom Organization (LCFO).

The LCFO was an all-black political party in Alabama's Black Belt that used the emblem of a coiled black panther. It challenged the all-white Democrats who controlled all political offices in Lowndes County, and the entrenched oligarchy of eighty-six white families that owned 90 percent of the land in a county where four out of five residents were black, but not a single one was registered to vote. Over many months, SNCC helped local activists take advantage of the Voting Rights Act to register almost 4,000 black voters. In November 1966, the LCFO ran a complete slate for local offices, but they were narrowly defeated when plantation owners trucked in hundreds of black tenants to vote Democratic. Undeterred, the LCFO eventually took over the county, and in the 1970s brought it into the developed world: running water, electricity, and paved streets in the poor black neighborhoods, and a measure of respect and civility instead of the passive deference whites had demanded from African Americans. In the long run, Black Power's most enduring legacy was the insistence on black people being represented in elected office by their own, controlling their own neighborhoods, counties, and black-majority cities, with the normal benefits of jobs and services that accrue with political control.

The final step in launching Black Power was the appearance, seemingly out of nowhere, of the Black Panther Party for Self-Defense (BPP) in Oakland, California. Like many Black Power activists, Huey P. Newton and Bobby Seale were migrants, born in the Jim Crow South but raised in the urban North, the first in their families to get a college education, growing up in affluent America but stuck in a dead-end world. They met at Oakland's Merritt Junior College in 1962. Subsequently both Newton and Seale sampled various groups (like the Revolutionary Action Movement inspired by Robert F. Williams), but rejected them because none was committed to action in defense of the local community. Newton, who combined intense intellectualism with a reputation for shocking physical audacity, discovered a section of the California Penal Code that permitted carrying weapons in public, even shotguns. Fed up with pervasive police harassment, he and Seale decided to "police the police," arms in hand. In October 1966 they gathered a few young friends, outfitted them in black pants, black leather jackets, black berets, powder-blue shirts, and sunglasses, and set about making themselves known. Newton named himself Minister of Defense of the grandly titled Black Panther Party (BPP), and Seale became Chairman, with other ministerial ranks parceled out. The BPP issued a "Ten Point Platform," which became hugely influential, with its terse, unequivocal demands and final invocation of the U.S. Declaration of Independence:

1. We want freedom. We want power to determine the destiny of our Black Community.
2. We want full employment for our people.
3. We want an end to the robbery by the white man of our Black Community.
4. We want decent housing, fit for shelter for human beings.
5. We want education for our people that exposes the true nature of this decadent American society. We want education that teaches us our true history and our role in the present-day society.
6. We want all black men exempt from military service.
7. We want an immediate end to POLICE BRUTALITY and MURDER of black people.
8. We want freedom for all black men held in federal, state, county and city prisons and jails.
9. We want all black people when brought to trial to be tried in court by a jury of their peer group or people from their black communities, as defined by the Constitution of the United States.

10. We want land, bread, housing, education, clothing, justice and peace. And as our major political objective, a United Nations-supervised plebiscite to be held throughout the black colony in which only black colonial subjects will be allowed to participate, for the purpose of determining the will of black people as to their national destiny We hold these truths to be self-evident, that all men are created equal; that they are endowed by their Creator with certain inalienable rights. . . .

Almost immediately, the handful of Panthers engaged in Old West–style confrontations with scared white policemen in Oakland: Newton liked to carry the Penal Code in one hand and a shotgun in the other. Until May 1967, however, the BPP was mostly a northern California phenomenon. All that changed when they cemented their reputation for daring, gaining national and international notice through an act of extreme bravura. On May 2, the California State Assembly had been debating a ban on any public display of weapons, clearly aimed at the Panthers. Filling several cars with armed party members, Seale drove to Sacramento and marched them straight into the State Capitol, where he read a statement before a phalanx of television cameras, and marched out. Black men with guns in the halls of power? Nothing like that had been seen since the heyday of Radical Reconstruction; it was white America's worst fantasy made real.

REVOLUTIONARY NATIONALISM, CULTURAL REVOLUTION, AND HOME RULE, 1967–1968

Through 1967 and into 1968, Black Power seemed unstoppable, growing with uncoordinated energy as organizations, initiatives, and leaders sprouted in every part of the country. The events of those two years are dizzying and spectacular, hard to assimilate. Weekly denunciations by *Time, Newsweek*, the major television networks, newspapers, white politicians, and traditional black leaders only brought more people into the movement. National Black Power Conferences were held repeatedly—though no coalition structure evolved. Notorious figures like Stokely Carmichael and SNCC's new chairman, H. Rap Brown, traveled the country and the world, calling for revolution before huge audiences. Brown was indicted for inciting a riot in Cambridge, Maryland, and coined the pithy aphorism, "Violence is as American as apple pie," to defend the necessity for armed struggle. Black students rebelled at both white and black colleges, demanding curricula that included the study of black history and culture, with black teachers picked by the new black student unions that proliferated nationwide. In the summer of 1967, the largest riots in the nation's history took place in such cities as Detroit and Newark, leading to full-scale contingency planning by the U.S. Army to suppress an armed black revolution—and also giving many black people the exhilarating sense they were no longer afraid. The Black Panther Party established chapters in thirty cities, powered by a massive "Free Huey" campaign after Newton was arrested because of a shootout in Oakland in October 1967, during which one policeman was killed and another wounded. Newton himself was shot in the stomach (convicted of manslaughter in 1968, he won a new trial, and was released on bail in August 1970 to a tumultuous hero's welcome). Black athletes Tommy Smith and John Carlos, medalists at the 1968 Olympic Games in Mexico City, sent more tremors through white America by lowering their heads and raising black-gloved fists during the playing of the "Star-Spangled Banner."

The events listed above are what most people remember about Black Power, either nostalgically or with a shudder—fists in the air, cities burning, voices shouting. Yet there were other, less spectacular developments that were just as important, such as efforts to organize workers, challenge white political dominance, and generate a cultural renaissance. In Detroit, the Motor City then at the core of America's economy, the all-black Dodge Revolutionary Union Movement (DRUM) took on both the auto companies and the white-dominated United Auto Workers union (UAW). The UAW had long supported civil rights nationally, but it was very cautious about challenging racism in the plants themselves. With more RUM's springing up at Ford and General Motors plants throughout the city, a League of Revolutionary Black Workers (LRBW) soon formed, suggesting a more systematic, canny approach to urban revolution than the Panthers' embrace of "revolutionary suicide" by "picking up the gun."

Equally important, but offering a very different route to local power, was Carl Stokes' 1967 election as mayor of Cleveland. For the first time in U.S. history, an African American would directly govern large numbers of white people, controlling the police and schools that whites had taken for granted as their own. Across the country, city hall became a new target for Black Power organizers, as they slowly learned the ropes of electoral politics. Often defeated on their first try, as Stokes had been, they persevered and by the early 1970s reaped many electoral gains. The tiny black foothold in Congress became a major source of contention, since most black voters were still represented by white politicians. A breakthrough of a new kind came in 1968, when Shirley Chisholm became the first black woman elected to Congress, from a newly created seat in Brooklyn. Chisholm, a West Indian by birth, had fought her way up through machine politics. She faced a formidable challenger when New York's liberal Republicans ran James Farmer, former head of CORE, and second only to King in his leadership of protests in the South, but Chisholm ended up winning easily. (In 1972, Representative Chisholm was the first woman and the first black person to mount a serious campaign for the presidency, in that year's Democratic primaries, but she received little support from either black politicians or feminist leaders.)

Paralleling the political maelstrom was a cultural renaissance in black intellectual and artistic life. Until mid-century, only a tiny handful of black students attended white universities, and hardly any black scholars had ever taught in one. Since the Harlem Renaissance of the 1920s, white America had bestowed recognition on only a select handful of black writers, artists, and performers—the novelist Richard Wright, the actor-singer Paul Robeson, the great classical singer Marian Anderson, and a few others. In the 1950s, that cultural invisibility began slowly changing, due in part to the increasing prestige of jazz, especially the avant-garde bebop associated with Charlie Parker and Dizzy Gillespie, and the advent of writers like Gwendolyn Brooks, who won the Pulitzer Prize for poetry in 1950, and the novelists Ralph Ellison and James Baldwin. However, despite the attention paid to these extraordinary talents, well into the 1960s black people were excluded from the nation's cultural apparatus: the universities, academic journals, museums, art galleries, Broadway theaters, literary magazines, and the lists of major publishers.

Black Power, and the Black Arts Movement that paralleled and fed into it, changed all that. Many of Black Power's forerunners in the decade before 1966 were literary or dance groups, small magazines and publishing houses, and museums and societies devoted to rediscovering African heritage. When the shift of 1965–1966 fostered a new interest in "black consciousness," they were ready to meet the demand, and an artistic flowering took place in urban black America and on campus. Uncountable numbers of young men and women began writing poetry (best known were Don L. Lee, later Haki Madhubuti, and Nikki Giovanni, the most widely read serious American poets of the later twentieth century), and rediscovered the vibrant literary tradition of their elders, epitomized by Brooks, Wright, and Baldwin. Major dance and theater groups formed, like New York's Negro Ensemble Company and the Alvin Ailey Dance Theater, embracing African American vernacular forms. Playwrights, novelists, painters, sculptors, muralists, composers, filmmakers, and musicians all flooded into newly opened college programs, and used university resources to create performance venues and publications by the hundreds. Independent publishers and magazines proliferated, like Third World Press, the *Journal of Black Poetry*, and Detroit's Broadside Press, run by the poet Dudley Randall. Groups like Chicago's Organization for Black American Culture (OBAC) took a holistic approach to culture, embracing historical and political debates, poetry readings, and jazz performances. Its famous south Side mural, the "Wall of Respect," was an early and influential effort to reclaim a community's history.

At the same time, a wave of polemical, highly personal studies of history, theory, and commentary created an indigenous intellectual base for Black Power. Harold Cruse's *The Crisis of the Negro Intellectual* (1967) influenced many through its indictment of the Communist left's manipulations of black activism, coupled with an argument for political and economic autonomy as the only strategy for black people in a country dominated by ethnic group competition. *Soul On Ice*, by the paroled prison writer Eldridge Cleaver, was a huge bestseller in 1968, and Cleaver was named the Panthers' minister of information. Within popular culture, James Brown, the acknowledged "Soul Brother #1" and one of the most innovative American musicians of the twentieth century, produced a 1968 anthem of startling simplicity: "Say It Loud, I'm Black and I'm Proud." Food, clothing, hairstyles, and language itself were all revolutionized. Many whites sneered at Afro haircuts and African-style clothing, but it was a thoroughly political act for African Americans to repudiate the generations spent trying to "whiten up" by straightening their hair, powdering their skin, and mimicking white middle-class mannerisms and dress.

Amid this creative chaos, by 1968 there were two publicly opposed strategies for Black Power, plus a host of lesser alternatives. The first option was that offered by the Black Panthers, the League of Revolutionary Black Workers, SNCC, and similar groups—a "revolutionary nationalism" derived from Malcolm X, Frantz Fanon, and China's Mao Zedong. Revolutionary nationalism called for a conscious linkage of African Americans to the worldwide struggle against U.S. imperialism, strategic alliances with other revolutionary groups (including white leftists, whether in SDS or the Communist Party), and eventually the formation of a disciplined party along Marxist-Leninist lines. The Black Panthers insisted that the white power structure must be confronted and defeated, which required a multiracial alliance. In contrast, "cultural nationalists" looked to Maulana Karenga with his injunctions that they should embrace "Blackness" in all things, and "Think Black, Talk Black, Act Black, Create Black, Buy Black, Vote Black, and Live Black." Cultural nationalists disparaged any alliances with whites and connections to revolutionary struggles globally, other than those in Africa. While supporting armed self-defense, they saw no particular need to confront white power, and emphasized the building of separate black institutions and a liberated black consciousness based in African identity. For cultural nationalists, capitalism and socialism were both European concepts irrelevant to the black world they would build. They were the heirs of Marcus Garvey, though they too claimed Malcolm X's legacy, emphasizing, however, his espousal of total autonomy and black self-worth rather than his support for revolutionary internationalism late in life.

It would be a mistake, however, to stress a rigid dividing line between these two philosophies. Outside of core groups like Karenga's US and the

Panthers, which denounced each other vociferously, many independent local groups assimilated both the revolutionary and the cultural approaches to nationalism into a rich stew of ideas and organizational experimentation. And there were many other ways to define Black Power, not all of them explicitly nationalist. The "territorial" nationalism of the Republic of New Africa (RNA) took Garvey and the Nation of Islam's call for a separate black homeland literally, and urged a military takeover of the Black Belt in the South to create a new nation for all African Americans. Though a group of RNA activists moved to Mississippi, declared the new nation, and defended their turf against local police, they ultimately had little success. At the other end of the spectrum, various would-be entrepreneurs and political operators, including CORE National Director Floyd McKissick, argued that the only real form of power in America was economic, and that required the development of a black capitalism. They received support from Republican presidential candidate Richard Nixon, who endorsed Black Power on those terms in 1968. The Nixon administration, and various white corporations and foundations, were eager to dangle jobs and money in front of black militants, encouraging them to set up businesses so as to tame the movement's radicalism, but so-called black capitalism was never a major current of Black Power. In the long run, it was simply one more source of confusion, one more option, for a movement spreading in all directions.

The distinctions between the strategies outlined above are important, but they soon merged at the local level into a common practice best described as community control, or "home rule," as Baraka would later call it. The term "home rule" evokes the partial independence sought by early anticolonialists in places like Ireland and India. It was based on the recognition that for the immediate future, there was not likely to be either a socialist revolution or a separate black nation in the United States. Nonetheless, black people *could* unite to elect their own political leadership, make deals with white institutions, allocate resources, control hiring and school curricula, and otherwise emulate the successful ethnic machine politics of urban America. The self-evident difference was that the Irish, Italians, Jews, Poles, and others were all part of the white majority, and had never faced the weight of racism and sheer hostility confronting even the best-run, most conciliatory black city government.

REFORM, NOT REVOLUTION: TO (AND FROM) THE GARY CONVENTION, 1969–1976

By 1969, it was clear the Civil Rights movement had come to an end. Dr. King was dead; other movement leaders like Bob Moses or James Forman were exhausted or in self-imposed exile; after losing his congressional race, James

Farmer became Assistant Secretary of Health, Education, and Welfare in the Nixon administration. Black Power had taken the mantle of leadership in the black freedom struggle, but the questions remained. How to achieve it? What kind of power was real, and what was merely symbolic? Should black people gain self-determination in America through revolution, or was Black Power realized by "black faces in high places," and community control of school boards and police departments? Answers to these questions proliferated, and it would take several years of internal struggle and building new institutions—amid sweeping government repression of the Black Power movement's radical elements—before a momentary unity was achieved at the huge Gary Convention of 1972. Gary forecast the nationwide turn to electoral politics in the 1970s, which consolidated the gains of the movement and tamed its radicalism.

The repression, deadly and deliberate, was of greater significance for Black Power than any other New Left movement, though all suffered from continuous surveillance and disruption by the FBI and other government agencies. Since 1956, J. Edgar Hoover's secret COINTELPRO (the acronym stood for Counter-Intelligence Program) had worked to foment distrust and confusion within the Communist and Socialist Workers parties; its official mission was "to expose, disrupt, misdirect, discredit, or otherwise neutralize" the left. In the 1960s, COINTELPRO's purview was extended to New Left groups. In September 1968, Hoover made a major decision: instead of the Communist Party, the Black Panthers now constituted "the greatest threat to the internal security of the country," and he proceeded to use the power of the federal government to destroy the organization. FBI infiltrators were inserted into every Panther chapter, and in 1968 the bureau fanned hostility between Karenga's US organization in Los Angeles and the local BPP, resulting in a shootout on the UCLA campus in which two Panthers died. From 1969 to 1971, phony letters and phone calls were used to exacerbate tensions between followers of Huey Newton and Eldridge Cleaver (in exile in Cuba and later Algeria, following a late 1968 gun battle with police), spurring vendettas in several cities between their two factions of the BPP. The FBI also worked closely with local and state law enforcement agencies to crush the Panthers. Outraged at the BPP's insistent calls to "Off the Pig!" many white policemen decided that preemptive, overwhelming violence was justified. Most infamous was the assassination of Chicago Panther leaders Fred Hampton and Mark Clark, shot in their sleep after their own security chief, an FBI infiltrator, drew maps of their apartment for the police marksmen, pointing out where they slept. Perversely, these years were also the high-water marks of the BPP's influence, as its "survival programs," including free breakfasts for schoolchildren and free medical testing, earned great respect in inner-city communities.

Constant repression and the media's overwhelming focus on the Panthers made simple self-defense seem revolutionary, giving the entire Black Power movement an aura of urgency, desperation, and martyrdom that was illusory in many ways. Teenage Panther organizers lived under siege in their beleaguered storefront offices, while the discipline enforced by their increasingly paranoid leaders included beatings and the torture and execution of informers. Newton declared that his option was "To Die for the People," as one book title proclaimed. Famous young poets like Giovanni asked "Can you kill, nigger, can you kill?" Indictments, trials, and convictions mounted up. The "Panther 21" were jailed in New York City, accused of a massive plot to assassinate policemen. Bobby Seale was charged with the murder of a presumed informant in the BPP's New Haven chapter, spending several years in jail until he was finally acquitted. George Jackson, imprisoned for eleven years in California's Soledad prison for a minor robbery, became famous through his 1970 book *Soledad Brother*, and joined the Panthers from his cell. He developed a relationship with the University of California philosophy professor and Communist Party member Angela Davis, whom Governor Ronald Reagan had purged from the UC system. In August 1970, Jackson's seventeen-year-old brother Jonathan took a judge and three court officers hostage in Marin County, in a failed attempt to force his older brother's release, but police killed them all in the courthouse's parking lot. Angela Davis had bought the weapons used in the failed jailbreak, and was charged with murder and kidnapping. She escaped capture during a two-month nationwide dragnet. Finally imprisoned, she was found innocent in a celebrated trial, but in August 1971 George Jackson was killed by guards in the San Quentin prison yard, supposedly while trying to escape. Such was Jackson's mystique among radicals of all races that Bob Dylan immediately released a single commemorating his martyrdom.

In the early 1970s, the increasing number of what many activists regarded as government murders legitimized a move beyond armed self-defense to actual armed struggle and revolutionary terrorism. A small number of Panthers from Eldridge Cleaver's faction formed a miniscule Black Liberation Army. Their most famous leader was Assata Shakur (originally Joanne Chesimard), who was badly wounded in a highway shootout with New Jersey State Police in 1973 in which one officer died. She escaped from prison in 1979 and found asylum in Cuba, as had a significant number of other black radicals over the course of the 1960s and 1970s.

After 1970, as the frequency of urban rebellions waned and the Panthers slowly imploded under tremendous internal and external pressure, several directions emerged for the Black Power movement. First, the "cultural" part of the revolution was clearly a success, as black studies programs spread nationwide, and self-educated working-class intellectuals like Harold Cruse, James Boggs, and John Henrik Clarke were invited to lecture at Ivy League schools and in Europe. Some were offered professorships at prestigious universities. Out of a mixture of guilt, genuine liberalism, and clumsy paternalism, American higher education integrated itself almost overnight. Hundreds of thousands of African Americans were recruited onto campuses formerly attended by tiny handfuls of black students. The hope was that bringing young, gifted black people into the middle-class professional world would channel their militancy into more constructive avenues. The result was that black studies programs, often poorly funded and intensely politicized, and the black student unions backing them up, became little fortresses of Black Power in the white academic world. In California and other western states, Chicano, Asian American, and Native American students were similarly recruited, and ethnic studies programs blossomed as political spaces on campus.

Second, as municipal home rule and political empowerment became the common thread of most Black Power organizing, a power base was consolidated at the national level for the first time in American history: the Congressional Black Caucus (CBC), formed in 1969–1971. As late as 1964, there were only a few hundred black elected officials in the entire country, a statistically insignificant number. With the exception of Harlem's powerful Representative Adam Clayton Powell, Jr., and the handful of other black congressmen, African Americans were not represented at all in national politics. Democrats and moderate Republicans wanted their votes, but felt no obligation to provide seats at the table of power. This stark reminder of black powerlessness begged for redress. Black representation began to grow, and the congressional delegation increased exponentially, from six in 1964 to thirteen by 1970. Breaking a tradition of "color blindness" where black members of Congress submerged their identity, this newly enlarged group took the radical step of caucusing separately, telling Democratic party leaders (all were Democrats, since Massachusetts senator Ed Brooke, an old-style liberal Republican, did not join the caucus) that they alone represented the concerns of black people. As with Carmichael's call for "Black Power!" in 1966, the liberal Establishment was shocked. Senate Majority Leader Mike Mansfield, a leading liberal, called the idea of a separate black legislative caucus "racist." But the CBC did not back down—their time had come, and they rapidly made their influence felt. In 1971, Congressman Ronald V. Dellums of Berkeley, an antiwar leader close to the Panthers, decided there should be an African American on the all-important Armed Services Committee, which controlled vast budgetary resources and was a traditional preserve of white southerners. Over the vociferous objections of its chair, the

Congressional Black Caucus forced the Democratic leadership to appoint Dellums, the first avowed radical in Congress since the 1940s, to the committee. Eventually, in the 1990s, he would chair it, to wide acclaim—one indicator of how the world had changed since Black Power's heyday.

The creation of the CBC was closely linked to a general turn towards electoralism by even the most radical wings of the Black Power movement. In Newark, Amiri Baraka led a process of community-wide consultation on how to take power from the corrupt, mob-connected Democratic Party machine of Mayor Hugh Addonizio, which ruled by using black lieutenants to get out the black vote. After careful planning, African Americans and Puerto Ricans coalesced around a mayoral candidate. In 1970, the moderate Kenneth Gibson triumphed with support from black celebrities nationwide, plus a huge ground campaign run by Baraka's forces. This effort was widely emulated. In Detroit, the entire black community and progressive whites rallied behind state senator Coleman Young, electing him mayor of America's fifth-largest city in 1973 (the same year that Maynard Jackson became mayor of Atlanta and Tom Bradley was elected mayor of Los Angeles). Young had been a leader of the black left in the 1940s and 1950s, close to the Communist Party, but this baggage had little effect on his rise within Democratic Party politics. In 1968, he became a member of the Democratic National Committee, and in 1976, he played a central role in Jimmy Carter's primary campaign.

Even the Panthers followed the electoral turn. Reeling from defections, killings, FBI infiltrations, and violent splits, in 1972 Newton shut down his party's national network of chapters and retreated to Oakland, where BPP Chairman Bobby Seale ran a strong race for mayor in 1973. During the 1970s, the BPP transformed itself into a local urban machine with a criminal side; Newton told his followers that Mario Puzo's bestseller *The Godfather*, mythologizing the Mafia, was the best guide to getting power in America.

Less dramatically than in the famous races in Newark, Detroit, and Oakland, in hundreds of cities and counties, especially black-majority areas of the rural South, African Americans ran for office and won. The number of black elected officials grew exponentially, from a few hundred in 1964 to 2,600 by 1973. African Americans suddenly had a toehold in mainstream politics through this new leadership class, gaining access to resources and rewards. But that process of inclusion had sharp consequences for earlier hopes of revolution or at least autonomy. Most of those politicians were elected as Democrats, and found themselves incorporated into a much larger, more powerful, deeply rooted institution.

The process of electoral inclusion and the potential for home rule accelerated the demand for unity in the black community. Since 1967, annual National Black Power Conferences took place, but their results were minimal. Baraka, at the zenith of national influence because of successes in Newark, decided to unify the movement around Karenga's Kawaida doctrine, combined with strategies for practical community control. In August 1970, he and other cultural nationalists convened a Congress of African Peoples (CAP) in Atlanta, attended by 3,500 delegates. An astonishing array of black leaders spoke, from the Urban League's Whitney Young, the embodiment of moderate civil rights activism dependent on white corporate support, to the Nation of Islam's Louis Farrakhan, to the Reverend Jesse Jackson, a former aide to Dr. King and aggressive head of Chicago's Operation Breadbasket. That same weekend, the Black Panthers made a final bid to unify the multiracial "anti-imperialist" left by calling a Revolutionary People's Constitutional Convention in Philadelphia. While widely attended, it produced little other than rhetoric. CAP, on the other hand, set itself up as a permanent national coalition, promising to unite the hundreds of local urban projects and student groups that came to Atlanta. CAP also had a major international dimension, playing a key role in the Sixth Pan-Africanist Congress held in 1974 in Tanzania. It helped organize the African Liberation Support Committee (ALSC), the last significant Black Power organization, which from 1972 to 1977 mobilized tens of thousands of black people to demand the final end of European colonialism in the remaining white-controlled states in Africa—the Portuguese colonies of Angola and Mozambique, the former British colony of Rhodesia (now Zimbabwe), and the Republic of South Africa.

Baraka did not stop with CAP, however. In an audacious move, he reached out to the other major new institution born of Black Power, the Congressional Black Caucus, to propose something far grander than the Congress of African Peoples' attempt to coalesce all black nationalists. In concert with CBC members like Detroit congressman Charles Diggs, Jr. and Richard Hatcher, the mayor of Gary, Indiana, Baraka developed a plan to unify all of Black America—businesspeople and integrationists, radicals and revolutionaries, students and professionals, elected officials and ministers—into a grand assembly, an embryonic nation. In March 1972, 8,000 black people representing every constituency of African Americans convened in Gary as the first National Black Political Assembly (usually called the Gary Convention); the NAACP was the major hold-out, sticking to its repudiation of nationalism. For a moment, Gary presented an extraordinary vision of unity, as the militant poet and conference co-chairman Baraka led the huge crowd, even Coretta Scott King, in chanting "it's nation time!" Ambitious plans were approved for a permanent assembly, with projects and campaigns in every area of politics, culture, the economy, and society. The central goal was to negotiate as a separate political-economic entity with white America, seeking economic development and real community control.

But it was not to be. First, by the time the convention met, the Congressional Black Caucus was already backing away from CAP's sweeping agenda, and it refused to endorse the Gary Convention's program. It proved impossible then or later to pry black elected officials out of their strategic niche in the Democratic Party—a body that could accommodate a degree of Black Power but could hardly incorporate Black Nationalism. Second, after 1972, Baraka and many other nationalists moved in a new ideological direction, towards Marxism-Leninism and the New Communist Movement (see chapter 13) and away from the insistence that all black people were natural allies, regardless of their class. Once they accepted that there were real divisions in the black community, and that a working-class revolution required a strategy to unite working people of all races in struggle, the rationale for the National Black Political Assembly became contradictory. It soon fell apart, as the remaining nationalists and newly converted Leninists denounced each other bitterly.

This paralyzing conflict from 1973 to 1976 was the final stage of the Black Power movement that had shot to prominence in 1965–1966. In some ways, it was an ignominious ending. It destroyed the once-promising African Liberation Support Committee (ALSC), and broke up many long-time political relationships. Some activists withdrew from politics, disillusioned with the loss of solidarity, and many others accommodated themselves to the mainstream. In 1976, former Georgia governor Jimmy Carter, a New South white moderate, made deals with various black leaders and garnered the majority of black votes in the Democratic primaries, despite his minimal program for civil rights or social justice. In this context of accommodation and patronage politics, there was a tendency to view the Black Power movement as an aberration or a failure.

But in light of later events, it seems clear that the mass mobilization at the heart of Black Power was only temporarily halted. The Rainbow Coalition campaigns in support of Jesse Jackson's presidential campaigns in 1984 and 1988 reignited that insurgency, though with the same tendency to submerge independent radicalism into inner-party deal-making for shares in patronage and "access." In that sense, Jesse Jackson represents both the culmination of the Black Power imperative, and its limited and partial success. But the degree of change should be clear. From the most token representation in the political system even where they could vote, black politicians and activists emerged in the late 1960s and 1970s as recognized players whose allegiance required far more than a few minor jobs. Instead of outright exclusion from the pantheon of American culture, African Americans moved to the center, with black history, music, and literature recognized (often grudgingly, sometimes with great sincerity) as a major force in American life. A substantial African American middle class developed, often through access to well-paid public sector jobs opened up by electoral clout—urban home rule was no pie-in-the-sky to thousands of black teachers and civil servants.

All of these gains were far less than what most Black Power advocates demanded. While many highly skilled professionals are now integrated into the corporate, political, and military elites, as symbolized by the rise of General Colin Powell, millions of poor African Americans remain locked out of the opportunities available to most white Americans, marginalized by the new racial stereotype of the "underclass." Endemic police brutality and grossly disproportionate rates of incarceration and sentencing of black men remain, in the twenty-first century, impervious to any Black Power expressed through electoral politics, even in cities where black mayors exert formal authority over white police and prosecutors. Black parents still must warn their male children of the very real dangers of DWB ("driving while black") in America. In that sense, Black Power remains an idea, a challenge, and a hope, rather than a reality.

Chapter 10

RED, BROWN, AND YELLOW POWER IN "OCCUPIED AMERICA"

We are not free. We do not make choices. Our choices are made for us; we are the poor. For those of us who live on reservations these choices and decisions are made by federal administrators, bureaucrats, and their "yes men," euphemistically called tribal governments. Those of us who live in non-reservation areas have our lives controlled by local white power elites. We have many rulers. They are called social workers, "cops," school teachers, churches, etc. . . . They call us into meetings to tell us what is good for us and how they've programmed us, or they come into our homes to instruct us and their manners are not always what one would call polite by Indian standards or perhaps by any standards. We are rarely accorded respect as fellow human beings.

— Clyde Warrior, President, National Indian Youth Council,
"We Are Not Free," February 2, 1967

The Asian American Political Alliance is an organization formed this year for the purposes of redefining the Asian American role, historically and contemporarily, in this country; of exposing and destroying the glaring myths concerning orientals; working to eliminate the insidious racism which permeates all levels of this society.

— Asian American Political Alliance leaflet, San Francisco State
College, Fall 1968

In the spirit of a new people that is conscious not only of its proud historical heritage, but also of the brutal "Gringo" invasion of our territories, we, the

Chicano inhabitants and civilizers of the northern land of Aztlan, from whence came our forefathers, reclaiming the land of their birth and consecrating the determination of our people of the sun, declare that the call of our blood is our power, our responsibility and our inevitable destiny. . . . Brotherhood unites us, and love for our brothers makes us a people whose time has come and who struggle against the foreigner "Gabacho" who exploits our riches and destroys our culture. . . . We are Aztlán.

—National Chicano Youth Liberation Conference, *El Plan Espiritual de Aztlán*, March 1969

1. We want self-determination for Puerto Ricans, liberation on the island and inside the United States.
2. We want self-determination for all Latinos.
3. We want liberation for all Third World people.
4. We are revolutionary nationalists and oppose racism.
5. We want equality for women, down with machismo and male chauvinism.
6. We want community control of our institutions and land.
7. We want a true education of our Afro-Indio culture and Spanish language.
8. We oppose capitalists and alliances with traitors.
9. We oppose the Amerikkkan military.
10. We want freedom for all political prisoners and prisoners of war.
11. We are internationalists.
12. We believe armed self-defense and armed struggle are the only means to liberation.
13. We want a socialist society.

—Young Lords Party, "13 Point Program and Platform," 1969

The black freedom movement has been incorporated into the official history of America. Politicians routinely invoke it, as do advertisers. Students learn about Dr. King and Rosa Parks in grade school, and most people know who Malcolm X was, even if they do not know much about him. Streets in hundreds of cities and towns are named for these famous Americans. Many historians and movement veterans feel that a sanitized version of the black struggle is taught, such as the ubiquitous posters for Black History Month in fast-food restaurants, but even this popular narrative is a vast improvement over how black people were rendered invisible while Jim Crow prevailed until the 1960s.

The tendency of this kind of popular history, however, is to present America as a *bi*-racial society, simplifying the story into an inevitable evolution from slavery to full citizenship for the one group that is "non-white." Even in the twenty-first century, we are just beginning to acknowledge how America's history encompasses *multi*-racial struggles against white supremacy.

This more complex history of racial oppression and resistance is the context for the least-studied aspects of the New Left: how the civil rights movement and Black Power were linked to similar struggles among the other dispossessed, subjugated racial minorities in America: Native Americans, Chicanos (Mexican Americans), Puerto Ricans, and the multiple ethnicities that came together as the Asian American movement. Each of these struggles and movements has its own distinctive history, yet they share some significant common features. First, all four of these movements had a particular regional, spatial, or cultural location within white America. In that, they both resembled and differed from the larger African American movement. The latter had two major locations: first, as a substantial minority, sometimes a majority, throughout the South; second, as a concentrated presence in northeastern, midwestern and West Coast cities. No other people of color could match that one-two geographic punch, but each had its own specific place and location.

Native Americans had been confined to reservations, often barren prisonlands, after the Indian Wars ended in defeat. A post-1945 generation moved to cities, and their experience with discrimination and police brutality fused with cultural resistance by reservation "traditionals." From this combustion came a fierce campaign for survival and renewal.

Similarly, the Chicano movement was spearheaded by first-generation college students, who reasserted their culture's history of resistance to the invading "Anglo" power since the 1830s and 1840s, when the United States conquered what was then northern Mexico. Whereas there were Indian peoples in every part of the United States, the Chicano movement had a specific regional locus—the southwestern states stretching from Texas to California.

The Puerto Rican movement was also distinctly regional, oriented to New York and along the northeastern seaboard, with outposts as far west as Chicago. It too evolved from youthful militancy and anticolonial consciousness, evoking independence for their island seized by the United States during the 1898 Spanish-American-Cuban War. It too reflected a postwar migration, as hundreds of thousands of *puertorriqueños* used their U.S. citizenship to emigrate to the mainland.

Hardest to define in its location is the Asian American movement. A distinctly American phenomenon, it brought together numerous different peoples—Japanese, Chinese, Filipinos, and Koreans, in particular—with their own languages, religions, cultures, and histories. In Asia, these peoples had warred on and sometimes conquered each other. American racism and nativism, specifically 1920s legislation barring all Asian immigration, the World War II internment of Japanese Americans, and the wars in Korea and Vietnam, created a pan-Asian identity and a potential movement. Its location was urban—those neighborhoods (the Chinatowns, Japantowns and Little Manilas) where Asian peoples were ghettoized, mainly on the West Coast.

These movements shared more than the immigrant experience and a particular regional focus. Each suffered from the assumption of white liberals and radicals that white supremacy oppressed only black people. Of course, Euro-Americans knew that Indians had been crushed militarily, that Chicanos were among the poorest of the poor, that Japanese Americans had been shunted into concentration camps during World War II. Simply put, they did not take these experiences seriously. It took a whole new set of forceful movements to make white Americans, including leftists, respect these other struggles for self-determination, liberation, and power. In each case, a key impetus came from the first wave of young people entering college in large numbers in the 1950s and 1960s, through the G.I. Bill and War on Poverty programs. Not surprisingly, all four of these movements had an intense interest in culture and identity—in rediscovering, remaking, and reimagining the peoples they had been, the history in which they had suffered and fought. None had submitted passively to their second-class status in America. All had traditions of civil rights activism in the 1930s, 1940s, and 1950s. The younger people associated with Red Power, Chicano Power, and Yellow Power did not start from scratch, though in the red-hot atmosphere of 1968–1973 the struggles for identity and pride took on the new militancy characteristic of the times.

There is one final connection to be made between the multiple upsurges for power—black, brown, red, and yellow. At a decisive moment, they emerged both practically and symbolically as a new common front of "Third World peoples" inside the United States. In 1968, as the country polarized, Cold War liberalism imploded, and the New Left turned sharply left, a new struggle broke out in the San Francisco Bay Area, the locus for so much of youth activism in the 1960s. African American, Chicano, Native American, and Asian American students had organized as their numbers increased exponentially in area colleges like Berkeley and San Francisco State. In the fall of 1968 and winter of 1969, they came together to demand a radical reform in their schools' curricula and governance: the creation of ethnic studies programs controlled by students. These Third World Liberation Front (TWLF) strikes at San Francisco State University and Berkeley became a central moment in late 1960s radicalism, influencing students nationally and even globally. They highlight how self-consciously all students of color linked their struggles against white supremacy, and the dynamic interaction across these movements, even as we later study them as separate phenomena.

RED POWER AND THE NATIVE AMERICAN MOVEMENT

Often, the Native American movement is reduced to its most famous organization, the American Indian Movement (AIM), which reminded many of the Black Panthers. AIM played a central role, but it neither founded nor led the grassroots movement. Like other struggles of the late Sixties, the cultural revolution of Red Power could not be channeled into a single organization. It spread of its own accord, often through the actions of small groups or individual self-discoveries.

Pinning down a beginning for the new Native American activism is difficult. For the press and most of the larger New Left, it began with the seizure of the abandoned federal prison on Alcatraz Island in San Francisco Bay in November 1969. But organized campaigns to restore Indian treaty rights and sovereignty over tribal lands went back to the early Cold War years; they remain the central issues in "Indian Country" in the twenty-first century. The National Congress of American Indians (NCAI), founded in 1944, a moderate civil rights group, focused on influencing the notoriously inefficient Bureau of Indian Affairs (BIA), which controlled the reservations. Well before the heyday of the late 1960s, however, direct-action protests had begun. During the 1950s, groups of militant "traditionals" around the country used nonviolent civil disobedience to block takeovers of tribal lands, notably in New York State. The term "traditionals" described Indians who resisted assimilation into white society, instead continuing to speak their languages, practice their religions, and follow elders and spiritual leaders rather than BIA-funded tribal governments. Their alliance with young urban radicals in the later 1960s led to a wave of protests, occupations, and armed resistance, culminating in the 1973 standoff at Wounded Knee.

In 1961, 460 Native Americans from 90 tribes attended the historic Chicago American Indian Conference, a clear sign of mounting concern. Ten of the student delegates were disturbed by the conference's moderate tone, and agitated for an activist program. Afterwards, they met and declared themselves the National Indian Youth Council (NIYC), a key bridge between older reformers and younger firebrands. NIYC initially raised used the term "Red Power" in the mid-1960s, meaning a direct confrontation to maintain the Indian way of life. It published *ABC* (Americans Before Columbus), a groundbreaking magazine, and attracted thousands of members. Its best-known leader was Clyde Warrior, a young Ponca from Oklahoma, who became a hero to younger Indians because of his passionate, articulate exposition of the need to take pride in being Indian (he died prematurely in 1968). NIYC helped instigate another major impetus towards radicalism with its 1963 Washington State Project, modeled in some ways on SNCC's southern community organizing drives. This campaign focused on maintaining historic treaty rights to unrestricted fishing in certain Pacific Northwest rivers, in the face of state legislation abrogating those rights. "Fish-ins" met violent police responses, but Hank Adams, later a major movement leader and theorist, brought in celebrities like Marlon Brando to generate national press attention. Over time, this campaign succeeded in restoring treaty rights, leading to many similar efforts in subsequent decades—a tangible mark of how Native Americans have radically improved their legal position in the United States since the 1960s.

After 1965, it was increasingly clear that a "New Indian" had arrived, unwilling to accept BIA or even War on Poverty–style paternalism. In the Oklahoma hills (the state had been a congressionally designated Indian Territory for tribes displaced from the East until it was overrun by whites early in the century), poor Creek farmers armed themselves. The staid National Congress of American Indians appointed a new executive director, Vine Deloria, Jr., who became the recognized voice of pragmatic radicalism, reaching white Americans with his 1969 bestseller, *Custer Died for Your Sins: An Indian Manifesto*. In 1967, tribal leaders, after generations of coming to Washington and dutifully submitting to whatever the U.S. government wanted, walked out of a White House conference on poverty.

If one side of the emerging Native American movement was growing conflict on the reservations, even more important was a major demographic shift towards urban America, paralleling the migration of African Americans out of the South into northern and western cities. Native Americans moved to cities in large numbers in the 1950s and 1960s because of federal "relocation" programs that offered a bus ticket and the promise of job training, with the goal of depopulating and eventually "terminating" the poverty-stricken reservations. In response, the Quakers and other liberal white church groups founded local legal and health clinics and community centers to aid these immigrants. In the Bay Area and Minneapolis-St. Paul, especially, this growing web of social service centers became seedbeds for radicalism. Spurred by movements like Black Power, mixing together in new urban neighborhoods among whites who neither knew nor cared to know the distinctions between a Lakota Sioux from South Dakota and a Catawba from the Carolinas, a new pan-tribal Indian identity germinated. For most of American history, Indians had seen themselves as members of separate nations, speaking different languages and inhabiting widely scattered regions of what became the United States. Now they began to define themselves as Indians first and tribal members second. This was the context for the emergence of the Indians of All Tribes coalition that staged the Alcatraz occupation.

In a sense, Alcatraz was just waiting to happen. 1969 was the highest point of the Sixties' mass radicalization—with Nixon elected, no end to the war in sight, regular gun battles between Panthers and police, and new movements springing up on all sides (Women's Liberation, Gay Liberation and more). The Bay Area was universally understood as the cutting edge, where the wildest countercultural movements all flowed together. Following the Third World Liberation Front strikes that united all the students of color, the first Native American studies programs had just opened at Berkeley and San Francisco State. Across California, young Indians were entering college for the first time, creating the same recruiting pool of unmarried, marginally employed, intellectually adventurous, mobile young people that SNCC, SDS, the Panthers, the Resistance, and the rest of the New Left drew upon for shock troops. For this new generation of Native American radicals, Alcatraz was the rallying cry.

In the years since the federal government closed the island prison in 1963, the Bay Area's newspapers and population had held a wide-ranging debate about what to do with the notorious island, with its ideal location in San Francisco Bay. In 1964, a small group of Native Americans had unsuccessfully attempted an occupation. In November 1969, with modest planning and few supplies, an *ad hoc* group drawn from community leaders in the Bay Area Native Americans Coalition and college students led by Richard Oakes, a Mohawk from New York, borrowed a boat and sailed near the island one night. Desperate to avoid an embarrassing failure, Oakes and a few others dived into the bay and reached the island, where they surprised the one caretaker. The occupation was on.

The next day, dozens of Indians from many tribes came to the island, along with a flood of reporters, spectators, and celebrity visitors. An eloquent proclamation was issued to the press, money flowed in, the band Creedence Clearwater Revival donated a boat, and occupation spokespersons appeared on television and traveled widely. Across the country, Native Americans were inspired by a vision of rebirth. The occupation itself became increasingly chaotic as months went by; it lacked effective leadership, and people of all sorts drifted on and off the island while the Nixon administration played for time. In June 1971, it finally collapsed, and the lofty hopes for a Native American university, a cultural center, and much else were forgotten. In larger terms, what mattered was that it happened at all. In its wake came dozens of occupations of vacant federal facilities (which Indians had a right to use, according to various treaties), as well as Mount Rushmore, missile bases near reservations, and more. Suddenly, Native Americans were in motion, and the question became where they would strike next.

In the national upsurge following Alcatraz, the American Indian Movement (AIM) proclaimed itself the vanguard of Native American resistance. It began in 1968 as a local Minneapolis organization, organizing an AIM Patrol to monitor the police (much like the Panthers in Oakland) and pressuring governmental and charitable agencies to treat Indians fairly. AIM's example of effective, militant leadership spawned groups elsewhere, and it became a national organization in 1969—the major rival to the National Congress of American Indians, the National Indian Youth Council, and other more moderate groups. Its leaders included Dennis Banks, an Ojibway, and the telegenic, controversial Russell Means, whose mother was an Oglala Sioux from South Dakota's Pine Ridge reservation, the nation's largest and poorest. These were seasoned, smart agitators, who had been through the BIA boarding schools (where Indian youths were beaten for speaking their own languages), gone to jail for petty crimes, and known all the degradation Indians suffered in white-run cities. Reveling in their ability to face down the teachers, policemen, and storeowners who treated all Native Americans as pathetic drunks, the AIM cadre evoked both Third World guerrillas and the traditional "warrior society" that protected the tribe. Lacking a detailed plan for either revolution or reform, they were looking for a fight, to show that Indian peoples were still unbeaten. They found their battleground at the symbolic center of Native America—the Sioux reservations in South Dakota.

AIM's sudden fame and extraordinary appeal was based on an event symbolizing the low value of Indian life. In February 1972, Raymond Yellow Thunder, a fifty-one-year-old Sioux, was found dead in Gordon, Nebraska, a white bordertown that lived off selling liquor to Indians. He had been beaten by whites outside a bar, and then froze to death. No significant legal action was taken, and his grieving relatives, who were Pine Ridge "traditionals," asked AIM to step in and force some kind of justice. Hundreds of angry young AIM members from several states flooded into Gordon, shutting it down completely and imposing a boycott. After a week, the town's power structure capitulated, promising a range of legal changes and reforms. Nothing like this had been seen since the days of Crazy Horse. AIM became magnetic. Like the Panthers, it adopted a simple but identifiable uniform (levis, red bandannas, sunglasses), and drew enormous press scrutiny from white reporters who highlighted any suggestion of violence. Also like the BPP, it paid a very high price for the willingness to engage in armed self-defense.

The next stage of the Native American movement was another occupation, but on a larger scale and with even less planning. In fall 1972, AIM and many independent groups decided to organize a Trail of Broken Treaties Caravan, to converge on Washington, D.C. and confront the federal government. Starting on the West Coast, and then meeting in St. Paul, several hundred tired Indians finally reached the nation's capital on November 1, six days before the presidential election. Their representative had failed to set up housing or provide for food. Almost accidentally, the group occupied the auditorium at the

Bureau of Indian Affairs headquarters. Faced with police threats, they took over the entire building, renaming it the Native American Embassy. Molotov cocktails were assembled, and young Indian men made crude spears and clubs from table legs, standing on the steps ready to take on the U.S. government. At the last minute, on Election Day, an armed assault was barely averted, and Nixon administration officials negotiated a withdrawal. With government money for gas, the caravan straggled out of Washington. They had won no concessions from the government, but from another perspective, it was like Alcatraz—a great gesture of symbolic resistance.

Each of these famous events, and many other local protests, occupations, and confrontations, led to the most symbolic action of all—the declaration of an Independent Oglala Nation in the village of Wounded Knee, on the Pine Ridge reservation. For Native Americans, and for the millions of whites who read Dee Brown's 1972 bestseller, *Bury My Heart at Wounded Knee*, the emotional weight of this act was enormous. In 1890, the last Indian resistance to the white invasion of the plains came to a bloody end at this site. Troopers from Custer's old unit, the Seventh Cavalry, used their new Gatling guns to massacre an entire band of Sioux during a frozen winter confrontation. As many as 300 men, women and children were shot down in the snow as revenge for the Seventh Cavalry's 1876 defeat at the Little Big Horn. That slaughter lived on in Indian memory, and AIM leaders knew that their choice of Wounded Knee as a site for armed defiance would give their demands great power.

The occupation did not begin with AIM. Pine Ridge—bigger than Delaware and probably the poorest place in America—had a long history of bruising intratribal factional strife. The latest instance involved tribal chairman Dick Wilson, a conservative supported by the Bureau of Indian Affairs, against the "traditionals" and young activists in OSCRO, the Oglala Sioux Civil Rights Organization. They charged that Wilson was a corrupt dictator, using a paramilitary Special Operations Group of U.S. Marshals and his own private vigilantes to intimidate opponents. OSCRO asked AIM to help them stand up to Wilson and his "goons," as AIM called them (Wilson said the acronym GOON stood for Guardians Of the Oglala Nation). AIM had already cut a swath through South Dakota, promising to completely shut down Rapid City and waging pitched battles with police in the town of Custer after another Indian was killed in a bar fight. In late February 1973, Means and other AIM leaders met with five respected chiefs and OSCRO. In response to their pleas, AIM led a caravan of several hundred men, women, old people, and children into Wounded Knee. Building crude fortifications, they created the appearance of an armed camp, issuing fierce statements demanding Wilson's ouster and Senate hearings on the plight of the Sioux. The government treated this action as a full-scale rebellion, with the potential for turning into a guerrilla war between Native Americans and whites—though AIM and its supporters had only hunting rifles. Illegally, U.S. military personnel deployed on American soil, along with FBI agents and marshals in armored personnel carriers, BIA police, Wilson's "goons," and white vigilantes, all periodically shooting into the small village. Remarkably, only two Native Americans died, despite numerous firefights as the standoff dragged out over seventy-one days. National and international attention has focused on the twentieth century's first major armed resistance by Native Americans. Finally, after negotiations leading to face-saving gestures, it was over, as AIM surrendered themselves and their meager armory.

In the aftermath of Wounded Knee, federal and state authorities mounted a massive, well-planned legal assault to tie up and bankrupt AIM by indicting 562 activists. Native American radicalism went into severe decline. A low-level war continued on Pine Ridge, as Wilson's GOONS killed several dozen militants. In a 1975 gun battle, two FBI agents died, for which AIM member Leonard Peltier is serving a life-sentence today. Yet these same years also saw what one historian calls a "Native American renaissance," with a series of landmark congressional bills restoring various tribes to full status and granting basic rights of self-determination. New Indian-led legal, cultural, educational, economic development, and civil rights organizations multiplied during the 1970s, and major court cases began the process of restoring those lands and privileges granted in old treaties but long-ignored. The number of people identifying themselves as Native Americans in the census grew three or four times in a single generation—a remarkable renewal of Indian life, given that for much of the twentieth century, even sympathetic observers believed Indians would soon be entirely extinct. The relationship of this demographic surge and mainstream civil rights reforms to Red Power, the spectacular, sometimes violent protests begun at Alcatraz and then symbolized by the warriors of AIM, is complex. Did the occupations and confrontations, the threat of resistance, prod the government and Congress to pay attention and make concessions? Or was the main function of the radicals simply to stir the cauldron, to goad a new generation and a new consciousness into being, burning out in the process? In later years, veterans of the Native American movement would criticize the emphasis on action, and the anti-intellectualism and disregard for long-term planning that accompanied that impulse to confront. But no one could deny that the years from Alcatraz to Wounded Knee had transformed Native America.

CHICANO POWER IN *AZTLÁN*

Activism by Mexican Americans certainly did not begin in the late 1960s, when the Chicano Power movement suddenly appeared. In the World War I years, an undeclared guerrilla war raged in the Rio Grande valley between Mexican ranchers and the Texas Rangers, who murdered hundreds of people. In 1929, the League of United Latin American Citizens (LULAC) formed in Texas to defend the dignity and rights of Mexican Americans. Over the next twenty years, a range of moderate, assimilationist organizations appeared, as well as a radical wing led by Communists in the Congress of Spanish-Speaking Peoples and various CIO unions. As with other movements, the return of veterans from World War II spurred a new political consciousness and a focus on building ethnic electoral power though the G.I. Forum, the Mexican American Political Association (MAPA) in California, and later the Progressive Association of Spanish-Speaking Organizations (PASSO) in Texas. In the latter state, Henry B. González was elected to the state senate in 1956 and then to Congress in 1961, while Raymond Telles became mayor of El Paso in 1957; in Los Angeles, Edward Roybal was the first Mexican American elected to the city council. These efforts culminated in a wave of grassroots Viva Kennedy Clubs in 1960. They dramatically increased turnout among normally Democratic Mexican American voters, but Mexican American politicians were ignored once JFK took office.

During these years, many Mexican Americans insisted on their precarious legal status as whites, denying any indigenous identity as a mixed-race people of color, despite the fact that throughout the Southwest they were segregated into separate-and-unequal schools and "Jim Crowed" in public establishments. A further complicating factor were the regional and cultural differences, even within one state. South Texas had heavy Mexican majorities in its white-run plantation counties. In California, Mexican Americans were one more minority in a pluralist urban society, while the poorest Chicanos and many undocumented migrants from Mexico worked in rural areas like the Central Valley. Finally, in New Mexico and southern Colorado, a culturally distinct community called Hispanos lived in ancient mountain villages settled by Spanish settlers centuries before the United States took over the Southwest after the war with Mexico in 1846–1848. After 1965, when a new radicalism flourished, the focus of protest and national attention would shift from one state or city to another, each with its own distinctive political style, and it proved difficult to unite the many local and regional currents into a coherent national organization or campaign.

The move towards a different politics—defiantly Chicano rather than Mexican American—came in 1965. The word "Chicano" was a pejorative term for un-Americanized, working-class Mexican Americans; it was adopted by student activists as a badge of pride, as was the term *la raza* (the race) to mean all of the peoples of Latin America. The new movement had several inspirations, including the surging radicalism of African Americans, and the sense that the dam was breaking in conventional politics. Key to the nation's discovery of Chicanos and the new Chicano consciousness was the United Farm Workers union (UFW), led by the veteran community organizer and devoutly Catholic pacifist César Chávez. For generations, poor Mexicans had crossed the border to labor alongside other immigrants for the vast agrobusinesses of the West Coast. Unionizing this huge but dispersed, desperately poor constituency of noncitizens seemed impossible. Starting in 1962, Chávez and a group of colleagues built a small membership for their would-be union. In 1965, they joined a strike of Filipino lettuce pickers in Delano in California's Central Valley. Chávez made this strike (or *huelga*) into a national cause, proclaiming the "Plan of Delano," a call for nonviolent struggle and social justice for all agricultural workers. A pattern was established in Delano that lasted into the 1970s: first the strike, which provoked unyielding employer resistance leading to constant violence on the picket lines; then the UFW's rallying support from the union movement and among liberal Catholics, like the Kennedy family; finally, a nationwide consumer boycott. At key moments Chávez, who was often compared to Dr. King, went on lengthy fasts to focus the nation's attention. Bit by bit, contracts were won from some major growers, though the UFW never unionized more than a fraction of California's agricultural labor force and had difficulty organizing elsewhere. Chávez became by far the best-known Chicano leader, featured on *Time*'s cover in 1967, and was a close friend of Senator Robert Kennedy, who was then moving to the left. Chávez and the UFW acquired an extraordinary mystique among radicals and many liberals, all of whom tended to assume the farmworkers embodied the entire Chicano movement.

In fact, Chavez never claimed to speak for all Mexican Americans. His focus was on building a viable union in the fields rather than a national Chicano movement encompassing the cities. The UFW acted as a spur to the larger movement but remained distinct from it. It was connected to the larger movement through activists like Luis Valdéz, a radical student who moved to Delano to create the union's *Teatro Campesino* (Peasant's Theater), which symbolized the new Chicano consciousness, proudly *mestizo* (mixed race) and working-class. Much more directly involved in steering the efforts to create an organized national movement was Rodolfo "Corky" Gonzáles, a one-time boxing star and later a businessman and rising Democratic Party activist in Denver. By 1965, he was disgusted by the habitual manipulation of Mexican voters by white Democrats. Declaring his independence, Gonzáles founded the Crusade for Justice, the first radical civil rights organization of Mexican Americans since World War II. Militantly nationalist, the Crusade quickly became a major player in Denver and the emerging Chicano politics. Gonzales himself wrote "I Am Joaquín," a long poem evoking the history of

Mexican and Chicano resistance, which deeply influenced many young Chicanos who had grown up learning only Anglo history.

Equally inspiring was the revival of the oldest cause of Mexicans within U.S. borders—the struggle to hang onto their land. In northern New Mexico, traditional farms and villages dated from land grants given by the King of Spain long before there was any United States. Since the United States conquered the territory in 1848, those lands had been stolen or expropriated by businessmen, government officials, and eventually the National Park Service, and the Hispano *pueblos* had declined as their impoverished inhabitants fled to Albuquerque. In the late 1950s, an itinerant evangelical Baptist minister, Reies López Tijerina, began agitating to recover the land. In 1963 he formed the *Alianza Federal de Mercedes*, and built a militant movement of small farmers. In 1966, the *Alianza* occupied sections of a National Forest and declared an autonomous government, arresting two Rangers who tried to stop them. Events came to a head when Tijerina led twenty armed men into a courthouse in the village of Tierra Amarilla on June 5, 1967, to perform a citizen's arrest of the local district attorney. A jailer and a state policeman were shot and wounded, and Tijerina's small army retreated into the mountains, chased by 2,000 National Guardsmen and police. After surrendering, Tijerina was acquitted by a jury. The *Alianza* continued for a few years, roiling New Mexico with its assertion of independence from the state and even the United States. Nationally, Tijerina made connections with Black Power and Native American activists who shared his belief that they were a conquered race in what the historian Rodolfo Acuña, one of the founders of Chicano Studies, defined as "Occupied America."

Like César Chávez and Corky Gonzáles, Tijerina offered a new model of leadership. Contemptuous of assimilation and conventional politics, he was willing to fight and die to defend his people. These examples sparked the next wave of Chicano politics—the youth revolt that flared from 1967 to 1971. First came the creation of dozens of Mexican American student organizations at Texas and California colleges, an unprecedented development. Since the 1960s, groups of every possible ethnic, religious, and cultural stripe have flourished on American campuses with the backing of administrators, but this embrace of diversity and multiculturalism is quite new. Formerly, any assertion of a separate ethnic or cultural identity, especially by a racial minority, was highly suspect. So the simultaneous appearance in fall 1967 of the Mexican-American Youth Organization (MAYO) at St. Mary's College in San Antonio, the United Mexican American Students (UMAS) at colleges around Los Angeles, and the Mexican American Student Confederation (MASC) at colleges in northern California, among others, was a major departure. At first, these groups focused on helping Mexican American students get into and stay in college, and organized support for the UFW. But all that changed in March 1968, with the "blow outs" of Los Angeles high schools, where 15,000 Mexican American students walked out to protest pervasive racism in the curriculum, abusive teachers, and lack of community input. UMAS played a leadership role in this historic action, the first large-scale public protest organized by Mexican Americans in U.S. history, reversing decades of assimilationism. The student movement grew by leaps and bounds, even though thirteen leaders of the strike were indicted on felony charges. At the same time, another Los Angeles group, the Brown Berets, consciously modeled on the Black Panthers, attracted considerable media attention with their paramilitary style and goal of organizing street youth, though they never became a national organization like the BPP. The Berets and the various student organizations played key roles in the largest single protest by Mexican Americans in U.S. history, and an important extension of the anti–Vietnam War movement: the Chicano Moratorium on August 29, 1970, in which 25,000 Chicanos rallied peacefully in Los Angeles against the war. They were assaulted by the notoriously repressive, nearly all-white LAPD, which killed three demonstrators, including a much-admired *Los Angeles Times* journalist, Ruben Salazar, who was hit in the head by a tear-gas canister when policemen fired without warning into a restaurant.

The Chicano Moratorium was part of the brief moment, 1969–1971, when it seemed as if a radical, student-led Chicano Power movement was unstoppable, part of a revolutionary upsurge. In March 1969, Corky Gonzáles convened a National Chicano Youth Liberation Conference in Denver, which was attended by more than a thousand. The conference adopted *El Plan Espiritual de Aztlán* (the Spiritual Plan of Aztlán). *Aztlán* was an Indian name for the area that became the southwestern United States, and its widespread use in these years signaled an intense cultural nationalism, rooted in the assertion of an indigenous identity much older than the "America" imposed by the *gringo* colonizers. One month later, one hundred student leaders from key campus groups met in Santa Barbara and formed *El Movimiento Estudiantil Chicano de Aztlán* (MEChA, the Chicano Student Movement of Aztlán), asserting an ideology of *Chicanismo* based in the "ancient communalism" of the Mexican people, and before them, the Nahuatl Indians who had fought the Spanish. MEChA saw itself as the vanguard of Chicano liberation, and proposed to use the universities and student-controlled Chicano studies programs as a base for organizing in local communities, bringing the poor and the disenfranchised (the *vatos locos* or "crazy kids," who otherwise joined gangs) into a mass movement. They succeeded in California, as every college campus in the state created a Chicano studies program. However, within a few years, as undergraduates moved on and became graduate students and professors, the burdens of institutionalization and professionalism greatly reduced the radical thrust of *Chicanismo*. By 1973, MEChA had become simply a loose nationwide network of Chicano campus groups, as it remains to this day. Many mainstream Mexican American politicians, like California's former Lieutenant Governor Cruz Bustamante, trace their political awakening to this student organization.

In these same years, the vanguard role passed to the last major expression of Chicano Power—*La Raza Unida Partido* (LRUP, or United Race Party), a spectacular but short-lived attempt to assert an independent electoral option outside of the Democrats or Republicans. Whereas MEChA was based in California, with its emphasis on militant protest and campus politics, *La Raza Unida* began in south Texas, where for years Mexicans had dreamed of gaining local power through their numerical majorities in many towns. In May 1969, MAYO student leader José Angel Gutiérrez picked the town of Crystal City (where in 1963, Mexican Americans had briefly won office) as the site for a takeover. Beginning with a student strike to polarize the town, he diligently assembled a voter registration and mobilization organization, found candidates to run, and won all local races in a clean sweep in January 1970— the first time Mexican Americans controlled a town government in the twentieth century. The LRUP spread rapidly in Texas, and branches were formed by the Crusade for Justice in Denver and by MEChA activists and others in California. Like MEChA, LRUP espoused a mixture of cultural nationalism and practical, piecemeal reforms. As with Black Power, revolutionary rhetoric accompanied a pragmatic attempt at community control and home rule.

LRUP did not last long. Its different state and local branches each adopted their own program, with radically different emphases. Outside of parts of Texas, its main effect was to draw votes from liberal Democratic candidates, themselves often Mexican American. Some activists saw its role as mainly educational, whereas others hoped to gain office. As with other movements in the early 1970s, the rediscovery of Marxist-Leninist theories led to sharp debates and polarization, as the premises of cultural nationalism were challenged. In September 1972, *La Raza Unida* held its first and only national convention, where José Angel Gutiérrez, favoring a practical emphasis on elections, contended with Corky Gonzáles, who had moved toward a more ideological socialist politics. The factional battles soon split LRUP and by the mid-1970s it ceased to exist. However, many former organizers moved into Democratic Party politics. New institutions proliferated, like the Southwest Voter Registration Education Project, the Mexican American Legal Defense and Educational Fund, and the National Council of La Raza. In the 1980s and 1990s, Chicanos became an increasingly respected component of the remade Democratic Party coalition.

The Chicano movement forcefully ended the silence and shame of those decades during which socially mobile Mexican Americans denied their heritage, embracing the Anglo definition of America. The history and culture of Mexican people became part of our national story, just as Chicano studies got a berth in the academy. Mainstream politicians and organizers, some calling themselves Chicano and some using the more neutral "Hispanic," moved into the space opened by radicals. In 1976 a Hispanic Caucus was formed in Congress, and by the 1990s, Mexican Americans like former San Antonio Mayor Henry Cisneros, former Denver Mayor Federico Peña, and former U.S. Representative Bill Richardson headed major cabinet departments. Yet Mexican Americans (like the Central Americans who have joined them in the Southwest and elsewhere), remain on average one of the poorest groups in U.S. society, working in sweatshops, as janitors and day labor, and toiling in the fields. As with each of the struggles by peoples of color, the Chicano movement had ambiguous results. It changed the consciousness of the oppressed, and forged a new identity, without ending the oppression itself.

THE ASIAN AMERICAN AND PUERTO RICAN MOVEMENTS

The Asian American and Puerto Rican movements were less visible than the Native American and Chicano movements. Neither movement produced a nationally known figure, like the saintly César Chávez or the notorious Russell Means, or confrontations on the scale of Wounded Knee or the Chicano Moratorium. Yet within their own communities, and within particular cities, they had major impact.

Though asserting a pan-Asian consciousness, the Asian American movement was led by Chinese and Japanese Americans, the largest groups in what was still a very small minority in American society (in 1960, the census showed fewer than a million Asian Americans of all ethnicities; by 1970, that figure reached 1.4 million, and the increase in the next two decades was over 500 percent, to 7.3 million). Its two major goals were similar to those of the Chicano movement: to recover and insist upon the study of Asian American history and culture through the establishment of Asian studies; to empower and reform the poor immigrant neighborhoods where many Asians still lived, the world of tenements and sweatshops that tourists visiting Chinatown restaurants never saw. Another similarity was the pattern of movement-building. Like Chicanos, the radicalization of Asian Americans began with the formation of new, overtly political student organizations that coalesced into a national movement. Vietnam was another major impetus, as Asian Americans grew angry over a deeply racist war where Vietnamese men, women, and children were all reduced to inhuman "gooks" by an increasingly vengeful U.S. military machine. Asian American contingents began appearing at the major antiwar demonstrations with their own slogans and demands focusing on solidarity with their Indochinese brothers and sisters.

The Bay Area proved once again to be the site of confrontation and self-realization. For Asian Americans, the Third World Liberation Front strikes had a special meaning: never before had they come together as "Asians" in America, not just as Japanese, Chinese, or Filipino Americans. A new identity was formed in struggle, across great cultural and historical barriers. An Intercollegiate Chinese Students Association had formed citywide in November 1967, and Asian American Political Alliance (AAPA) formed at both Berkeley and San Francisco State in 1968, but the TWLF mobilizations created a sense of urgency that spread across the country. AAPAs surfaced at Yale and Columbia on the East Coast, and similar groups formed elsewhere. In January 1969, a conference on "Yellow Identity" was held at Berkeley, attended by 900 people. The next month, five undergraduates at the University of California-Los Angeles founded a monthly tabloid called *Gidra*, which became the informal newspaper of the new movement. *Gidra*'s offices were in the newly created Asian American Studies Center at UCLA, the vanguard of a new academic discipline that put down solid roots over the next decades.

Not surprisingly, these student radicals felt an urgent need to return to their ghetto communities to campaign for social justice. In many cases, they were actually visiting for the first time, since middle-class Asian Americans had the same pattern of dispersed assimilation as many other ethnic groups. Chinese American youth opened community centers along the West Coast and in New York City, taking on the ultra-conservative business establishment that dominated Chinese America in alliance with the anticommunist KMT (Nationalist) party government of Taiwan. In San Francisco, young activists even formed Red Guards, emulating Mao Zedong's youthful followers. Simply by showing films from the mainland People's Republic of China they attracted large crowds, anxious for news and sights from home. These community groups organized theater and dance performances, provided substance abuse counseling and legal aid for undocumented immigrants, supported union campaigns, protested racist imagery in advertising, and more. Smaller communities of Filipinos, Koreans, Vietnamese, and others also organized in their respective communities. At the same time, the campaign for reparations and a public apology to thousands of Japanese Americans interned in squalid camps during World War II gathered force.

The radicalism of the Asian American movement waned in the mid-1970s, but the movement itself did not end. Instead, it took on a more institutional, moderate form, as Asian American studies programs struggled for funding and academic legitimacy, and community groups tried to gain permanent grounding in their neighborhoods. Some of the most dedicated radicals joined small New Communist groups, asserting a special affinity for the Great Proletarian Cultural Revolution in China that claimed to mobilize the people against bureaucratic inertia, but these tightly disciplined organizations fought each other bitterly and alienated many in the Asian communities. The positive results of the movement's first phase (1968 to roughly 1975) were clear, however: a new consciousness of a common ethnic experience, a willingness to confront racism, many new organizations, and the beginnings of political activism, including in the electoral arena.

The New York–based Puerto Rican movement had a similar trajectory, with two significant differences. First, Puerto Rico was and is a colony of the United States, in the legal sense of a dependent territory controlled by an external government. Second, because of this fact, Puerto Rico has historically had an independence movement, which included a current of armed struggle—and as one-third of the island's population moved to the United States after World War II, that movement emigrated as well. In the first half of the twentieth century, revolutionary *independentista* sentiment was represented by the Nationalist Party, led by Don Pedro Albizu Campos. At several points in the 1930s and 1940s, the Nationalists staged local uprisings, which were forcibly repressed. In 1950, the Nationalist Oscar Collazo tried to assassinate President Truman near the White House, and in 1954, four Nationalists stood up in the gallery of the U.S. House of Representatives and started shooting, wounding several congressmen. These attacks were responses to the formal establishment of Puerto Rico as a self-governed commonwealth under U.S. control, tying it more permanently to Yankee rule. The "five," as they became known, received life sentences, and their imprisonment remained a *cause célèbre* for a later generation of militant Puerto Rican youth who drew inspiration from Malcolm X at home and Cuba and other revolutionary nationalist struggles in the Third World.

The question of underground guerrilla warfare versus legal protest and election campaigns remained a major debate among Puerto Rican radicals, because of the fundamental differences between conditions on the island and those in the United States. In Puerto Rico, the *Partido Independentista Puertorriqueño* (the PIP, or Puerto Rican Independence Party) was founded in 1946 as a legal party to campaign in elections. Since then, it has attracted a small but solid minority of voters. On the island Puerto Ricans, whatever their political views, are the overwhelming majority, including the political and business elites. Spanish is the primary language. In the United States, Puerto Ricans were and are a Spanish-speaking minority, overwhelmingly poor or working-class, in a sea of English speakers who know little and care less about the island or its possible future as an independent nation. What then was the role of the immigrant community in the United States? Should it serve as a support base for independence struggles on the island, or should it campaign for civil rights and self-determination for mainland Puerto Ricans in New York and other U.S. cities in alliance with other oppressed groups? That question was never satisfactorily resolved for the new Puerto Rican movement of the late 1960s and 1970s, but it provoked multiple approaches to organizing.

The Puerto Rican population in the United States grew 500 percent from 1950 to 1970, reaching almost 1.5 million, nearly half of whom were born in the United States. This younger generation was the base for the new movement. The most famous organization of the Puerto Rican New Left was the Young Lords, later the Young Lords Party (YLP). The Young Lords were little-known outside of New York, except among Puerto Ricans, but became famous in that metropolis. The original Lords were a politicized street gang in Chicago, who in 1969 entered into a Rainbow Alliance organized by the Black Panthers that also included the Young Patriots, a white gang. Various student groups in New York heard of this novel development and traveled to Chicago, asking if they could form their own branch of the Lords. The New York–based Young Lords quickly surpassed the founders. They broke into the public eye in 1969 with dramatic protests and savvy media tactics in *El Barrio*, Spanish Harlem— piling garbage in the streets to force the city's Sanitation Department to do its job; taking over a local church and turning it into a community center with free breakfasts, a health clinic, and classes in Puerto Rican history; publishing a tabloid newspaper and selling it in Central Park and at Rockaway Beach; and marching through the streets in improvised uniforms and purple berets to protest the police killing of one of their members. In September 1970, the Lords and the Puerto Rican Student Union organized a national student conference at Columbia University that drew more than 1,000 activists and led to an October 30, 1970 march on the United Nations by 10,000 people, calling for Puerto Rican independence—the first large-scale protest by Puerto Ricans in U.S. history.

Overwhelmingly youthful, mixing college students with street kids, blending Marxism, anticolonialism and community organizing rhetoric and tactics, the Lords were often compared to the Black Panthers. They were less militaristic than the BPP, however, more open to discussions of machismo and sexism, and lacked a single dominant figure like Huey P. Newton. Their heyday was brief, only a few years, but they were very influential in New York and opened branches throughout the northeast and even on the island. After 1972, the YLP declined rapidly as it became part of the New Communist Movement, changing its name to the Puerto Rican Revolutionary Workers Organization. Most of the key founders had left by that time, including Pablo "Yoruba"

Guzmán, Juan González, and Felipe Luciano, all of whom went on to major careers in New York city journalism (González, for instance, is a columnist for the *Daily News*). In 1972, the Lords' lawyer, César Perales, founded the Puerto Rican Legal Defense and Education Fund, which more than thirty years later remains a central advocacy organization for this community.

The Young Lords' most significant rival in the U.S.-based Puerto Rican movement was almost a mirror image: the *Partido Socialista Puertorriqueño*, or Puerto Rican Socialist Party (PSP). The Lords were teenagers, mostly born in the United States, focused on direct action against racism in *El Barrio*. The PSP and its predecessor organization, the *Movimiento Pro Independencia* (MPI, or Movement for Independence), were led by middle-aged intellectuals in Puerto Rico who had a strong commitment to Marxist-Leninist ideology and building a disciplined, mass party to struggle for national liberation on the island. For the PSP, Puerto Ricans stateside remained a part of the Puerto Rican nation, and their primary task was to work toward independence. That priority guided their strategy even in the United States, with results that were impressive in the short term but destructive of the PSP's long-term ability to put down roots among the immigrants.

The MPI was founded in 1959, and steadily built strength in Puerto Rico, led by its charismatic founder, Juan Mari Brás. It opened a United States office in 1964, and after the decision to formally adopt Marxism-Leninism and become the PSP in 1971, it took off. The first Congress of its U.S. section took place in April 1973, with 3,000 people attending the final plenary. Throughout this period, the PSP's strategy emphasized building a movement among the larger New Left to back its call for independence. It convinced Representative Ron Dellums to introduce a decolonization resolution in Congress, and lobbied extensively at the United Nations. It was the main force behind the Puerto Rican Solidarity Committee, founded after an enormous rally at Madison Square Garden on October 27, 1974, the National Day of Solidarity with the Independence of Puerto Rico, when 20,000 people cheered numerous radical leaders and celebrities, from Jane Fonda to Geraldo Rivera. In 1976, during the Bicentennial celebrations in Philadelphia, most of the remaining New Left converged behind the PSP-inspired call for a Bicentennial Without Colonies. But soon thereafter, the PSP's U.S. branch declined—like the Young Lords, unable to sustain itself and riven by disagreements.

The Puerto Rican movement was never united around a single organization, coalition, or strategy. Like other movements, many local groups operated, outside of the YLP or the PSP, which helped them survive when those groups weakened. A major campaign for the entire movement was the effort to free the five Nationalist prisoners, which culminated in their release by President Jimmy Carter in 1979. A small group founded the underground

Fuerzas Armadas de Liberación Nacional (FALN, or Armed Forces of National Liberation), which began a bombing campaign, including explosions at Fraunces Tavern on Wall Street in 1973 that killed several office workers. More generally, however, the radicalism of the Puerto Rican movement faded after 1975 as it institutionalized itself in a host of community, cultural, and political organizations, and focused on taking control of its own neighborhoods and achieving electoral representation in city halls, state legislatures and Congress.

Looking back from the perspective of the early twenty-first century, when Latinos, Native Americans, and Asian Americans serve in Congress, head Cabinet departments, and anchor television news programs, it may seem as if their ascent to full citizenship is simply one more story of ethnic assimilation and assertion—the comforting story we tell ourselves about American history. This is a fable. Just as much as African Americans, their defeat of white supremacy is a fragile bridge into a more democratic future. In the 1990s, as the United States felt the impact of the largest wave of immigration in its history, primarily from Asia and Latin America, a new nativism surged. Anti-immigrant ballot referenda and "English-Only" campaigns became one more part of the toolkit of the New Right. As the white majority shrinks to less than three-fourths of the population, with European Americans now merely the largest minority in California, it is clear that what the once-famous racist theorist Lothrop Stoddard called "the rising tide of color" will be a central dynamic of twenty-first century politics in the United States.

Chapter 11

WOMEN'S LIBERATION AND SECOND-WAVE FEMINISM: "THE PERSONAL IS POLITICAL"

Objectively, the chances seem nil that we could start a movement based on anything as distant to general American thought as a sex-caste system.
—Casey Hayden and Mary King, "Sex and Caste," November 18, 1965

Women are an oppressed class. Our oppression is total, affecting every facet of our lives. We are exploited as sex objects, breeders, domestic servants, and cheap labor. We are considered inferior beings, whose only purpose is to enhance men's lives. Our humanity is denied. Our prescribed behavior is enforced by the threat of physical violence. . . .

We identify the agents of our oppression as men. Male supremacy is the oldest, most basic form of domination. All other forms of exploitation and oppression (racism, capitalism, imperialism, etc.) are extensions of male supremacy; men dominate women, a few men dominate the rest . . . All *men* receive economic, sexual, and psychological benefits from male supremacy. All *men* have oppressed women. . . .

We identify with all women. We define our best interest as that of the poorest, most brutally exploited woman. . . .

The time for individual skirmishes has passed. This time we are going all the way.
—Redstockings Manifesto, 1969

[T]o the white women's liberation groups we say . . . until you can deal with your own racism and until you can deal with your OWN poor white sisters, you will never be a liberation movement and you cannot expect to unite with Third World peoples in a common struggle. Most white women involved in liberation groups come from a middle-class and student thing. They don't address themselves to the problems of poor and working class women, so there is no way in the world they would be speaking for Third World women. . . . They call for equality. We answer, equal to what? Equal to white men in their power and ability to oppress Third World people??

It is difficult for Third World women to address themselves to the petty problems of who is going to take out the garbage, when there isn't enough food in the house for anything to be thrown away. Fighting for the day-to-day existence of a family and as humans is the struggle of the Third World woman. We are speaking of oppression, we don't need reforms that will put white women into a position to oppress women of color or OUR MEN in much the same way as white men have been doing for centuries.

—"Equal to What?" Statement of the TWWA, 1969

Many different activist and intellectual currents fed into the mass women's movement of the late 1960s and 1970s, which built upon the underground organizing and hard-won legislative successes of the 1950s and early 1960s, but had much greater visibility and influence. The new feminism included everything from lobbying campaigns for the Equal Rights Amendment (ERA) to clinics, battered women's shelters, and publishing companies. Its constituencies ranged from informal groups of suburban married women to lesbian collectives. Many of its most important victories took place in workplaces and families where women spoke up to change the sexual division of labor, and in personal struggles to enter traditional male preserves, from construction sites and coal mines to law and engineering schools. Ultimately, this new or "second wave" feminism became the largest and longest-lasting of all the movements of the New Left, with an unbroken trajectory that stretches into the twenty-first century. Perhaps not surprisingly, it has aroused the deepest opposition, even among women themselves.

It may not have included all women—a nearly impossible task—but the women's movement brought about clear benefits for all, white or black or brown or yellow, young or old, rich and poor, pro- or antifeminist. The best jobs could no longer be advertised as "men's"; women could not be fired because they were married or past a certain age limit, or denied credit simply because they were female; men no longer had the legal right to rape their wives; women stopped dying from illegal abortions; hundreds of shelters and rape-crisis centers were opened for victims of male violence; schools from kindergarten to college were required to provide athletic facilities for girls as well as boys; finally and not least, though demeaning terms like "broad," "babe," and "bitch" hardly disappeared, they became much less acceptable in public. These changes affected the texture of life everywhere, though the movement's influence took longest to reach rural and small-town America.

In the movement's early years, activist women divided themselves into liberal, radical, lesbian, and socialist strands, while African American and Chicano women built their own separate feminist movements, and fierce conflicts raged over sexual orientation and organizing strategy. Indeed, the term "Women's Liberation" was originally used to distinguish "radical feminists" (who wanted to abolish the "sex-gender system") from "liberal feminists" (who worked to end discrimination in schools and employment). But these distinctions blurred very quickly, at least among white women activists. Married, older, and professional women who considered themselves liberal feminists took up radical issues like abortion and rape, while younger radicals found a home in the main liberal group, the National Organization for Women (NOW). There were significant distinctions between the many varieties of feminism, yet they also shared a newly awakened, intense awareness of the personal consequences of male domination, coupled with the excitement and power of sisterhood. As we shall see, however, the tensions between a universal sisterhood and the fundamental differences between women divided by race (and thus class) produced distinctive varieties of feminism.

NOW AND EQUAL RIGHTS FEMINISM, 1965–1968

"Second wave feminism" (the "first wave" was the struggle for suffrage and basic citizenship rights from the mid-nineteenth century through the 1920s) was the product of conscious organizing by thousands of women during the postwar decades when feminism was denigrated (as described in chapter 7), combined with demographic and economic shifts that began in the 1950s and accelerated in the 1960s. The scope of these changes is crucial to understanding why so many women reacted with spontaneous agreement when first exposed to feminist ideas.

The postwar changes in the lives and expectations of American women can be grouped into two major categories: education and career opportunities, and sex and family life. In 1950, only one in four students receiving college degrees was female. By 1968, almost half of graduates were female, while the student population itself grew massively. But these millions of well-educated women faced a very low glass ceiling, and were shunted into the "pink collar" ghetto of low-wage clerical work. Women with bachelor's degrees were systematically shut out of the graduate training that provided access to the professions—law and medical school professors often barred women from their classes because they took places from "more deserving" men. In 1960, only one in ten Ph.D. degrees were awarded to women, a significantly smaller proportion than earlier in the century. Alongside open discrimination, and men's exclusive access to the best jobs in the professions, skilled trades, and public employment, was the constant assertion by academic experts, journalists, politicians, and the producers of movies and television shows that a woman's natural role in life was motherhood and keeping house. Further limiting women's options was the sexual double standard, which encouraged girls to be "sexy" and seductive to get and keep a husband, but punished them severely if they enjoyed the experimentation and sexual freedom that was encouraged in boys.

By the early 1960s, well before the new feminists began questioning traditional marriage, young women were taking a different road from the prescriptions of 1950s neo-Victorianism. They flocked into universities and sought autonomy by congregating in cities and defining women's sexuality as more than procreation. From 1959 on, the percentage of women in their twenties who remained single increased dramatically, and the percentage who stayed childless grew sixfold in ten years. In 1960, "the pill" became available—the first reliable, simple contraceptive that a woman could use without men's knowledge. The sweeping success of Betty Friedan's *The Feminine Mystique* in 1963 demonstrated the potential constituency for a revival of feminism among younger college-educated women, married and single.

In hindsight, the origins of the massive women's movement that developed after 1965 seem modest. Building on several decades of behind-the-scenes agitation for equal pay and equal rights, which had culminated in Title VII of the 1964 Civil Rights Act, older professionals and seasoned government and labor activists decided they needed their own national organization to lobby against the legal and social discriminations against women. Younger women in civil rights, antiwar, and student organizations wanted their voices respected, and their male comrades to share in the "shitwork" of making coffee and getting out mailings. They felt deeply alienated from their mother's traditional roles, and were inspired by women fighters in Third World liberation movements. The coming together of the youthful radicals into a handful of local "women's liberation" groups in 1967–1968 has received much attention, but the liberals actually initiated the new women's movement by forming the National Organization for Women (NOW) in late 1966. NOW is especially important because in the 1970s it became the main grassroots organization for all types of feminists, and the one major organization formed in the 1960s that has remained a political force through the present.

NOW originated almost spontaneously. In 1964 and 1965, the fifty state advisory councils set up by President Kennedy's Commission on the Status of

Women held annual national conferences. By 1966, many of the experienced female academics, professionals, writers, trade unionists, and civil servants who participated in these meetings were angry because the Equal Employment Opportunity Commission (EEOC), set up to enforce the 1964 Civil Rights Act, refused to deal aggressively with open sex discrimination. The officials who controlled the agenda of the August 1966 conference barred discussion of a resolution criticizing the EEOC. Over lunch, urged on behind the scenes by key women within the EEOC itself, Betty Friedan convened a caucus to plan a national equal rights lobby to pressure the government, media, and Congress on behalf of women, just as the NAACP was the recognized voice for African Americans. NOW was born, with a clear goal to enforce a single gender-neutral standard of equal rights, and "bring women into full participation in the mainstream of American society now, exercising all the privileges and responsibilities thereof in truly equal partnership with men," in the words of its original October 1966 Statement of Purpose.

NOW started off with a splash, aided by Friedan's considerable fame. In December 1967 it organized the new movement's first protests, picketing EEOC offices in five cities to demand a ban on sexually discriminatory employment advertising. But questions of strategy and sexual politics kept it off balance, and it took years to develop a national structure. Originally, NOW was modeled on the NAACP's mainstream, legalistic focus. Just as the latter did not exclude whites, so NOW included men; it was "for women," not "of women." But it lacked the NAACP's apparatus of hundreds of local chapters and thousands of activists. Minus members, chapters, and money, NOW's first office was a desk in the women's department of the United Auto Workers (UAW). In those early years, at least one third of the membership was concentrated in New York City, reflecting the organization's narrow base among well-connected professionals. Besides lack of experience, NOW also suffered from internal disagreements. In 1968, it lost the backing of the powerful UAW when it endorsed the Equal Rights Amendment, long opposed by unions because it might end special legal protections for women workers. In 1968, a group left to form the Women's Equity Action League when NOW decided to back legalized abortion. It was not until 1970 that NOW stepped into the forefront of the suddenly mushrooming movement.

RADICAL WOMEN DEFINE THEIR OWN
LIBERATION, 1965–1968

NOW wanted equality with men in jobs, career choices, and ultimately political offices, and paid less attention to how men exercised power over women in families and sexual relationships. The more radical call for a total "women's liberation" came from a younger group of white women schooled in the southern-based Civil Rights movement, especially SNCC, and its northern white allies like SDS. With little awareness of the history of the National Women's Party, the President's Commission on the Status of Women, and the coalescing of liberal feminism into NOW, they developed their own sharp critique of male supremacy from personal experience.

From the antebellum Abolitionists through later anti-lynching campaigns, a small minority of southern white Christian women had spoken up to defend the humanity of black people. After World War II, groups like the Young Women's Christian Association and the Methodist campus federation were leaders in civil rights activism among southern whites. From this faith background, several white women became important SNCC activists, including Casey Hayden, Mary King, and Jane Stembridge. From black women in SNCC like Ruby Doris Smith Robinson, Diane Nash, and Fannie Lou Hamer, they learned lessons in endurance and courage. Yet over time, white and black women in SNCC noticed that SNCC men often relegated them to roles as secretaries and assistants. The sexual double standard was very much in force, as male activists slept around freely while monogamy was expected of women. Even women hailed for their courage in jail did not have the policy-making and intellectual authority accorded to men.

In November 1964, 200 SNCC organizers met in Waveland, Mississippi for a major retreat. Almost thirty papers were circulated in advance, including an essay, "Position Paper: Women in the Movement," submitted anonymously by King and Hayden after talking with others. But rather than discussing the paper's assertion that SNCC women were forced into subservient roles just as black people were deemed inferior in American society, the paper was ignored and ridiculed. In a comment that became notorious (and that he repeated in subsequent years), the much-admired Stokely Carmichael cracked that "the only position for women in SNCC is prone." Late in 1965, after they had left SNCC, King and Hayden circulated another paper to women activists around the country, again raising how even in "the Movement" women were treated as a separate, inferior caste. Their analysis had little immediate effect, but served as an alarm bell, or what would later be called a "consciousness-raiser."

The difficulty of getting both men and women to take women's oppression seriously was mirrored in the subsequent efforts of SDS women. Bolstered by women from SNCC, and reacting against the aggressively macho style of SDS's young male "heavies," from 1965 to 1967 they tried to make "male supremacy" an issue. At national conferences they fought to hold women-only workshops, and were jeered by men for raising women's oppression as a serious political question. These were the years that the Vietnam War rapidly escalated out of control, inspiring thousands of men to burn their draft cards and join The Resistance. Young radical women felt tremendous pressure to be supportive of antiwar men, who often regarded feminism as a selfish distraction.

At the same time, multiple influences encouraged women in SDS and other student-based groups to assert themselves. Community organizing projects highlighted how poor women kept their families and neighborhoods together, and relied on women organizers' personal skills to make connections. Women in national liberation struggles, especially heroic Vietnamese women, received international attention, and Black Power demonstrated forcefully the need for self-assertion, pride, and self-empowerment. The hippie counterculture, with its derision of all forms of middle-class propriety, penetrated quickly into the lives of young whites, undermining respect for traditional marriage and family life.

In mid-1967, SDS grudgingly recognized the need for "Women's Liberation" (or "chicklib" as one male leader called it), but by then hundreds of women were tired of arguing for their right to speak. The time had come to organize as women, outside existing organizations. The catalyst was the National Conference for a New Politics in Chicago in November 1967, a failed attempt to unite the New Left's diverging strands. Two thousand activists attended from every part of the left. A women's caucus led by Shulamith Firestone demanded a slot on the agenda to present proposals for discussion and a vote like other groups, but the man chairing the meeting decided there was no time for them to speak, and cut them off. The next week Firestone and others formed the first local Women's Liberation organization in Chicago, called simply the Westside Group. They sent out a manifesto, "To the Women of the Left," initiating the wave of autonomous local committees that were radical feminism's backbone.

During 1968–1969, the Chicago women were joined by newly formed "small groups" in cities across the country, composed mainly of young white veterans of the student and antiwar movements. Because of media coverage and a convergence of powerful personalities, the best known were in major eastern cities like New York (first New York Radical Women, which spawned Redstockings, the Radical Feminists, and The Feminists) and Boston (Cell 16, Bread and Roses), each of which included major feminist theoreticians and activists. The New York Radical Women alone included the key leaders and thinkers Ellen Willis, Rosalyn Baxandall, Kathie Sarachild, Robin Morgan, Kate Millett, and Shulamith Firestone; though it lasted only a year, this was an extraordinary concentration of insight and energy. These groups proliferated through personal networks, as women moved from city to city and looked up old friends and roommates. A newsletter, the *Voice of the*

Women's Liberation Movement, was started in Chicago by "Joreen" (Jo Freeman, later an important scholar of the movement), and several free-wheeling national conferences were held, but there was no effort to create a nationwide Women's Liberation organization, or hammer out a shared political program. After years of watching men use organizational structures to fight for power, radical feminists distrusted all hierarchies and any high-profile individual leadership. Key to radical feminism in its early years was this extremely decentralized character, which allowed great political and intellectual flexibility and freedom for completely original ideas, new organizations and manifestos proliferated. It also promoted what Freeman characterized as the "tyranny of structurelessness," where private cliques and personal charisma sometimes replaced democratic decision-making.

The early women's liberation groups engaged in highly creative protests, including a hilarious counter-demonstration during the September 1968 Miss America Pageant, where girdles and brassieres were thrown into a trash can, giving rise to the taunt of "bra-burner." They published colorful, militant magazines like *Off Our Backs* and *No More Fun and Games*, and organized emotionally wrenching "speak-outs" where hundreds of women talked about their own abortions, rapes, and other injuries at the hands of men. These activities gave the movement visibility in the media, attracting a grassroots nationwide base. Less dramatic but more crucial was "consciousness-raising" (CR), which spread with tremendous speed in 1968 and 1969. CR was a process carried out by a small group of women meeting regularly for months, sometimes years, to talk about the conditions of their lives, and about men: fathers, employers, professors, boyfriends, husbands. Men often derided these groups as "girltalk," or called the women who organized them "homewreckers," seeking to convince wives to leave their husbands. In truth, the CR groups invoked the female world of kitchen-table talk, but with a fundamental difference. Women joined them because they wanted to discuss openly their anger and frustration about sex and power, all traditionally off-limits subjects. The earliest feminist groups developed CR guidelines to guarantee respect and equal time, and exported this methodology around the country; its principal advocate was Kathie Sarachild of the New York Radical Women and later the Radical Feminists. CR sprouted everywhere—requiring no formal name, structure, or organizational affiliation, just a few women to take the lead and some agreement about the process, which could be gotten easily from a newsletter or pamphlet. Like other strategies and approaches derived from radical feminism, it crossed over into mainstream liberal feminist circles, helping to create a shared understanding of women's oppression.

FEMINISM EXPLODES INTO THE MAINSTREAM, 1969–1974

From 1969 to 1974 the new feminist movement enjoyed an extraordinary, meteoric success, rapidly overturning cultural shibboleths and legalized forms of discrimination that had been unchallenged for centuries. Yet this same period saw a series of wrenching schisms and growing divisions within feminism itself as it grew rapidly and diversified ideologically. Telling these two stories of political triumph and internal conflict, and their relation to each other, is crucial to understanding the politics of feminism and women's liberation.

The tidal wave of success was heralded by a remarkable burst of media attention in late 1969 and 1970. Suddenly, national newspapers, magazines, and television networks were seeking out radical spokeswomen and theorists, taking them far more seriously than a year or two before, when even left-wing publications featured cartoons that demeaned feminists as braless girls in miniskirts. Kate Millett, author of *Sexual Politics*, one of many groundbreaking books appearing in 1970–1971 (including Shulamith Firestone's *The Dialectics of Sex*, Robin Morgan's groundbreaking collection *Sisterhood Is Powerful*, and Germaine Greer's *The Female Eunuch*), was featured on the cover of *Time*. This celebrity (which caused considerable tensions within the movement itself) was accompanied by major political victories. NOW's president, Betty Friedan, called for a nationwide Women's Strike for Equality on August 26, 1970, and tens of thousands of women marched in cities across the country around three core demands: reproductive freedom and legalized abortion; twenty-four-hour childcare for all; abolition of all job discrimination. In that same year, the Women's Equity Action League (WEAL) filed a class-action suit against hundreds of universities, using an Executive Order issued by President Johnson in 1967 that barred sex discrimination in institutions receiving federal funding. This suit revealed massive inequalities in women's hiring and promotion, and forced a sea change in higher education. Feminists in New York staged a spectacular "zap action" by occupying the offices of the staid *Ladies Home Journal* for ten hours and debating with its male editor until they won a commitment to publish a special supplement on Women's Liberation, authored by activists. Several million *Journal* readers received in their homes a movement primer and organizing guide—a real coup. With longer-term impact, a group of radical feminists in Boston, fed up with the misinformation and sexism of the male-dominated medical profession, published a newsprint tabloid book called *Our Bodies, Ourselves*, that gave women invaluable practical information about their reproductive and sexual organs, pregnancy, menstruation, puberty, aging, menopause, abortion, and much more. It sold 250,000 copies in three years, and when republished by a major company in 1973 (with profits going to movement groups), another four million over the next decades, helping to bring about a national and international women's health movement.

All of these milestones took place in just one year, 1970, and the momentum did not slow over the next few years. A new group of activist women were getting elected to office, often on antiwar platforms, including representatives Bella Abzug, Elizabeth Holtzman, and Shirley Chisholm (the first black congresswoman) from New York City and Patricia Schroeder from Colorado. In 1971, they joined Friedan and the prominent feminist writer Gloria Steinem to form the National Women's Political Caucus, with the explicit goal of electing feminist women to office, an unimaginable development only a few years before. 1972 proved to be a banner year: Chisholm made a creditable run in the Democratic presidential primaries, breaking two barriers as a woman and an African American, and Congress finally approved the Equal Rights Amendment and sent it to the states for ratification. Title IX was added to the Civil Rights Act, requiring equal athletic facilities for girls from kindergarten to college. The trial issue of a new magazine called *Ms.*, after the new courtesy title feminists invented so women would no longer be known by their marital status, sold out its 300,000 run in eight days, demonstrating the vast popular market for feminism. And NOW had grown to 15,000 members from a mere 300 at its founding (it would reach 40,000 by 1977, and several hundred thousands in the 1980s). More important than its paper membership was the development of a dense network of self-supporting state and local NOW organizations, with over 700 individual chapters by 1974. Along with thousands of independent local groups focused on single issues, from forced sterilization of poor women to women's bookstores and music festivals, the NOW network brought feminism as an organized political force into middle America, giving women outside of the major cities a vehicle for activism.

1973 brought second-wave feminism's single most important victory, with the Supreme Court's *Roe v. Wade* decision establishing a constitutional right to privacy, including a women's right to control her body, and thus to legal abortion. Back in 1961, a California activist, Pat Cody, had formed a Society for Humane Abortion. She and others, including progressive male doctors and ministers, organized the National Association to Repeal Abortion Laws in 1966, and campaigned state-by-state, winning many victories. They were joined by clandestine referral services like the group known as "Jane," the code name for the abortion counseling service run by the Chicago Women's Liberation Union, which helped 11,000 women get safe, affordable procedures. As feminism advanced, the movement for legal abortion grew steadily. Groups on the right correctly understood that the Supreme Court's bowing to one of Women's Liberation's most radical demands constituted a massive attack on traditional sexual morality based on patriarchal control over women's bodies. "Abortion on demand," as it was called, broke the final link between sexuality and procreation, which meant that women could be as independent as men, a horrifying prospect of societal chaos for many. *Roe v. Wade* provoked a massive antiabortion or "pro-life" movement which became as institutionalized and powerful as feminism in subsequent decades—a permanent counter-force ensuring that women's liberation and women's oppression would stay focused on the personal politics of sexuality and reproduction.

Throughout the rest of the 1970s, important new groups kept forming, like the Coalition of Labor Union Women in 1974. The United Nations–sponsored international women's meeting in Houston in 1977, attended by 2,000 official U.S. delegates from all fifty states and another 18,000 observers, was a triumph for second-wave feminism, demonstrating its move from the margins of political life to the center. Former congresswoman Bella Abzug, a veteran leftist activist and avowed women's liberationist, was appointed by President Carter to chair the U.S. delegation, and a strongly feminist platform was approved.

But as the 1970s progressed and feminism moved from success to success, two things became increasingly evident: its constituency was largely middle-class and white, and its political success was due to the degree that formerly radical ideas were adopted by mainstream middle-class organizations. The passage of the ERA, and the grassroots pressure that brought about a host of pro-woman legislation, came about because groups like the American Association of University Women, the League of Women Voters, the YWCA, the Girl Scouts, churches, unions, and professional and scholarly groups all made feminist demands a priority, and built an effective lobbying network based in Washington, D.C. *Ms.* magazine perfectly represented both the success and the limitations of the new feminism. It quickly acquired a large subscriber base, and was extremely effective in popularizing core feminist ideas and politicizing women outside the reach of organized groups. But 90 percent of its readers had graduated from college (versus 20 percent of women nationally); of the three-quarters who worked for wages, two-thirds were professionals, and nearly all were under fifty. Similarly, NOW members were overwhelmingly college-educated white women, and half of them were under thirty.

By the mid-1970s, the weight of liberal feminism's success, both legislatively and in converting respectable organizations to openly feminist positions, meant that some radical feminists felt their movement had been hijacked. *Ms.* was attacked for diluting Women's Liberation, and editor Gloria Steinem, perhaps the most famous feminist in the country, was labeled a CIA agent. However, divisions and charges of treachery had been part of second-wave feminism since its beginnings. The original split was between women who identified with the larger New Left and wanted to organize within it on the one hand, and others who labeled them "politicos" and believed it was imperative for women to organize as women, outside of male-led organizations. These were the self-identified "radical feminists." There was also a fundamental difference of opinion regarding the central source of women's oppression. The so-called politicos, influenced by Marxism, argued that women had internalized their oppression and participated willingly in preserving patriarchy (the historical structure by which some men dominated other men and all women). Radical feminists adopted a "pro-woman line," insisting that women were aware of and resisted their subjugation. From that point, however, different strategies proliferated: should women focus on direct action against repressive laws regarding abortion, marriage, and rape? Or should they put the priority on changing themselves via consciousness-raising? Were marriage and ongoing sexual relationships with men acceptable or was sex itself the problem, suggesting that women should become celibate and withdraw from contact with men? Ultimately, should women emphasize their common humanity and total equality with men, or their different and superior natures, as the creators and nurturers of life? The first suggested making men into allies, and educating them in feminism; the second pointed to building a separate women's culture and way of life.

The earliest radical feminists experimented with all of these approaches, as new groups formed and then subdivided, new recruits flooded in, and new leaders found their voices. It was not until 1970, however, that the increasing emphasis on an autonomous women's world raised the question of lesbianism as the correct form of feminist politics. Already, in 1969, Betty Friedan and her allies in NOW had purged some women from leadership in New York NOW whom they considered a "Lavender Menace," fearing that their lesbianism would be used by a hostile media to delegitimize feminism. More and more activist women began to define themselves as "woman-identified," influenced by charismatic young leaders like Rita Mae Brown, and the slogan "feminism is the theory, lesbianism is the practice." At the NOW-sponsored Second Congress to Unite Women that May, a group of women stormed the stage wearing tee-shirts identifying themselves as the Lavender Menace and encouraging women to "come out," wherever they were. Among the best known groups was Washington, D.C.'s The Furies, which cut off all contact with men and defined itself as "lesbian-feminist," a challenge to all other groups. Ultimately, however, liberal feminism proved able to incorporate respect for sexual freedom into its agenda. After a struggle, NOW in 1971 voted to support women's right to choose their own sexuality, and the "gay-straight split" lost its edge.

In the early and mid-1970s, liberal feminists more and more accepted the radical feminist analysis that the "personal politics" of sexuality, rape, and abortion were just as important as discrimination against women in employment and education. At the same time, many radical feminists moved towards a purely cultural feminism that emphasized the permanent difference between men and women. In essays like the "Fourth World Manifesto" and "Mother Right," they called for a matriarchal "gynocracy," a world ruled by women—or the retreat of women into a self-sufficient world of their own. One result was that over the course of the 1970s and 1980s, every possible kind of woman-run institution proliferated: bookstores, cafes, publishing houses, record companies, clinics, music festivals, and so on. Often staffed and led by lesbians, they appealed to a larger middle-class constituency of white women who enjoyed the safety and comfort of an all-women's environment. Once again, liberal feminism's all-inclusive acceptance of women's empowerment had incorporated the most radical impulses, strengthening the broad women's movement while softening its revolutionary impulses.

At the same time, one more current surged and then ebbed—a socialist feminism that grappled with the relation of capitalism to patriarchy, and focused on the problems of working-class women. Several dozen Women's Liberation unions spread around the country in the early 1970s, and socialist feminists made some of the strongest contributions to feminist theory, as in the 1981 book *Women and Revolution: A Discussion of the Unhappy Marriage of Marxism and Feminism*. As late as 1975, more than a thousand women attended a socialist-feminist national conference in Yellow Springs, Ohio. By the 1980s, however, socialist feminism became essentially an intellectual trend.

ORGANIZING ON THEIR OWN TERMS: BLACK AND CHICANA FEMINISMS

Liberal feminism may have been absorbed and been transformed by the politics of radical feminism, but both of these wings of white feminism proved largely incapable of dealing with the racial divide that limited their movement's reach. The entire history of second-wave feminism and Women's Liberation, as described in this chapter, is remarkably defined by color. Despite all of the battles between liberal, radical, gay, and straight women, it is painfully accurate to describe the Women's Liberation movement as some black women did at the time as "white Women's Liberation." Meanwhile, less visibly and facing a radically different set of political challenges, both African American and Chicana women developed their own feminisms, with a politics that differed in fundamental ways from white feminism. They challenged key premises of Women's Liberation as articulated by white feminists: that all women shared a common oppression and a common sisterhood; that "men dominate women, a few men dominate the rest"; and "all other forms of exploitation and oppression (racism, capitalism, imperialism, etc.) are extensions of male supremacy," to quote the Redstockings Manifesto. From the perspective of women of color, the idea of a women's movement focused only on women's struggles and ignoring other forms of oppression was difficult to accept, and any affiliation with such a movement opened them up to charges of collaborating with the enemy.

In retrospect, it seems obvious that women of color would refuse the claim of Women's Liberation that all women were oppressed in the same way. To do so would have implied a denial of the racism they had faced all their lives. It was one thing for a young white woman to leave her SDS chapter or campus antiwar group to finally confront her own oppression; it was a very different act for a black woman or a Chicana to leave the struggle of her own people against white supremacy to wage a separate battle against sexism—the sexism of her own male comrades. In this context, any kind of feminist activism often was construed as a betrayal, as "acting white." The tensions over the legitimacy of feminism in communities of color was exacerbated by the intensely patriarchal and homophobic attitudes of some black and Chicano nationalists, and their insistence that men must lead and women must follow.

White feminism was marked by a consistent failure to consider the linkage of race and class to gender—at best, race and class were treated as add-ons to the overriding issue of Women's Liberation. A woman of color could hardly escape the linkages that defined her own life. Not only was she and the women she knew just as much victims of racism as of sexism; most were poor. Access to graduate schools and professional jobs—a core issue for the women who founded NOW—was at best a secondary issue for a black or Chicana woman. And while sexism, patriarchy, and male violence might be just as real and oppressive for women of color, the men they knew were often viciously oppressed as men, humiliated on the job, beaten by police, and scorned in the larger world. Asserting one's manhood was a very real concern in communities of color, not just for men but for the wives, mothers, girlfriends, and daughters who lived with those men.

In all these ways, women of color lived the reality of what sociologists call "intersectionality," the unavoidability of linked oppressions. If they chose to struggle against their oppression as women, they would do so in very different ways, in and around their communities. Certainly, African American women and to a lesser extent Chicanas and other women of color were active in the major feminist organizations: black trade unionists like Addie Wyatt and Aileen Hernández helped form NOW, and the outspoken, dashing New

York black activist Florynce Kennedy was a major presence in radical feminist circles. Generally, however, women of color went their own way and formed their own organizations, stressing the particular character of their feminism and how it differed from white feminism.

The first major initiative by women of color paralleled the growth of the white small groups. In late 1968, women in SNCC formed a Black Women's Liberation Committee. Within months, they had decided to expand their reach to all women of color, and become an independent organization, the Third World Women's Alliance (TWWA). Led by Frances Beal, TWWA published pathbreaking essays like "Equal to What?" and "Double Jeopardy: To Be Black and Female," and put out a magazine, *Triple Jeopardy*. The TWWA made a foundational criticism of white feminism: that it encouraged white women to liberate themselves so they could join white men in oppressing everyone else. The explicitly anticapitalist, anti-imperialist TWWA also confronted the sexism of black men, accusing them of aping both "bourgeois" and "white" values in their desire to force women into subservient roles. It had several chapters around the country, but never became a national organization. The TWWA was not the first independent black feminist group; earlier in the 1960s, a local organization had formed in Mount Vernon and New Rochelle, outside New York City, to campaign for black women's rights and confront efforts by black men to push them into traditional roles as "mothers of the race." In a well-known essay, "Poor Black Women" (published as "Statement on Birth Control" in *Sisterhood Is Powerful*) they denounced attempts to brand birth control a white conspiracy, and mocked the pretensions of would-be male revolutionaries.

In 1970, the poet Toni Cade Bambara published a major collection, *The Black Woman*, with a wide range of perspectives on whether or not African American women were oppressed by black men, and what they should do about it. More and more informal local groups formed, to discuss what a black feminism would look like. As one woman put it, "white women were groomed to be ladies. I came from a history of women groomed to be workers," underlining the deep differences in historical experience defined by race. Because of grinding economic oppression and the necessity for most black women to work for wages simply to keep their families fed, the white feminist prioritization of issues like the ERA and abortion rights seemed less relevant than winning economic security and legal protections for working-class women. Similarly, while many white feminists saw the family as a source of oppression, for women of color the family had more often been a refuge, a source of strength, and something to be defended.

In May 1973, thirty black women in New York city announced the formation of the National Black Feminist Organization (NBFO), though they had no national structure, money, or staff. An August press conference produced a flood of unexpected phone calls and requests from around the country to form chapters. Near the end of 1973, 400 women attended a NBFO conference, and a dozen chapters soon were formed. A powerful manifesto was issued that defined the distinctive combination of gender and racial oppression that confronted black women:

> Black women have suffered cruelly from living the phenomenon of being black and female, in a country that is both racist and sexist. . . . The black woman has had to be strong, yet we are persecuted for having survived. We have been called "matriarchs" by white racists and black nationalists. . . . We will continue to remind the Black Liberation Movement that there can't be liberation for half the race.

But throughout this process, questions of whether black women should employ the term "feminist" surfaced repeatedly, and the NBFO dissolved by early 1976, paralyzed by internal disagreements. Another key black feminist organization formed in 1974 out of dissatisfaction with the NBFO's moderation: the Boston-area Combahee River Collective (CRC). This group was explicitly open to lesbians and supportive of their self-liberation, an extremely contentious issue within the black freedom movement. Its best-known public figure was Barbara Smith, who for many years headed Kitchen Table Press, an important black feminist publishing house. Other groups survived the breakup of the NBFO, such as Black Women Organized for Action, founded by Aileen Hernández (who had been NOW's second president) and others in San Francisco in 1973.

Chicana feminism had much in common with black feminism, in terms of the attacks it faced from men and some women within the larger Chicano movement, and the distance it maintained from white feminism, yet it evolved in a distinctive way. Mexican American women did not have black women's history of slavery and sexual exploitation as domestic workers, nor had they been stigmatized as black women were in the notorious 1965 Moynihan Report, by Harvard sociologist and later U.S. senator Daniel Patrick Moynihan. Produced for the U.S. Labor Department, *The Negro Family: A Case for National Action* claimed that a pathological "matriarchy" had damaged black families since slavery, and was the main cause of poverty in the black community. But they faced the same accusations from male cultural nationalists of selling out (*vendidismo*) to white feminism and betraying their community. In response, Chicana feminists insisted that their feminism was entirely their own, drawing on indigenous Mexican traditions of women revolutionaries and community leaders. Somewhat more successfully than

African American women, they carved out a women's space within the Chicano movement by insisting that female liberation was a necessary part of Chicano liberation.

The first Chicana feminist organization was formed in early 1969 at Long Beach State in California, just as MEChA came together on the same campus and statewide. It was called *Las Hijas de Cuauhtémoc* (the Daughters of Cuauhtémoc, named for the last Aztec emperor to defy the Spanish colonizers) and lasted for several years as a prototype for groups that worked effectively within the larger movement, while propagating a distinctly feminist politics. Their newspaper of the same name became a national magazine in 1973, *Encuentro Femenil* (Women's Encounter). But *Las Hijas* still faced vilification and scorn from men: its founder, Ana Nieto-Gómez, was hanged in effigy after she was elected president of the local MEChA chapter.

More groups formed, gradually cohering into a national movement. In 1970 the *Comisión Femenil Mexicana* (Mexican Women's Commission) was formed during a National Mexican American Issues Conference, and *Concilio Mujeres* (Women's Council) was founded at San Francisco State University. In May 1971, 600 women gathered in Houston at the *Conferencia de Mujeres por la Raza* (usually translated as the National Chicana Women's Conference). This was only the beginning: one scholar estimates there were three dozen national workshops, meetings, caucuses, and conferences of Chicana feminists by 1977, as well as almost a dozen newspapers and journals. The Chicana Rights Project was set up by the Mexican American Legal Defence and Education Project (MALDEF), the mainstream civil rights group, and a National Chicana Political Caucus founded in 1973. This proliferation of institutions established a visible presence for women within the larger Chicano movement.

Chicana feminism had several distinctive features. In an explicit repudiation of "Anglo" or white feminism's claims of universality, Chicana *feministas* located their roots in the legacy of Indian women leaders, nuns, *soldaderas* (women soldiers) during the 1910–1920 Mexican Revolution, and more contemporary figures like Dolores Huerta, a widely respected leader of the United Farm Workers union. They also vigorously asserted the necessity of strong, united families premised on gender equality as the foundation of the whole community's liberation—a claim that would have seemed quite strange to white feminists. Some Chicanas even denied that machismo was an authentic part of Chicano culture, insisting that Mexican American men had taken on the sexist attitudes of white society. What is striking in retrospect, however, is that (like black feminism) Chicana feminism had to define itself outside of, and even on occasion against, the ideology and politics of white feminism. Thus, while we talk of "the women's movement," it is much more accurate to speak of multiple women's movements and many feminisms.

THE PERMANENT REVOLUTION (AND THE COUNTER REVOLUTION)

There is no end or closure to second-wave feminism. It is impossible to chart any significant downturn in subsequent decades. The militant small groups of the late 1960s and early 1970s spawned thousands of committed feminists with jobs in the professions and government; NOW kept growing, as a meeting place for activist women of all persuasions; new organizations kept forming to meet new needs. Feminism as a sophisticated, pluralist way of seeing the world from a woman's viewpoint and exposing women's oppression became a permanent part of American life, culture, and politics, one of the most visible consequences of the New Left.

Yet if the women's movement led to a fundamental revolution in gender relations—a deep crisis in traditional, transhistorical notions of patriarchy—like most revolutions it also stimulated a profound counterrevolution, often led by women themselves. One way of understanding the basis of women's own antifeminism is to compare feminism to the black freedom movement. Both challenged an entrenched system of supremacy. Just as white supremacy was defended as a traditional "way of life," male supremacy was held up as an unchanging natural order, rooted in the basic biological fact that only women can bear children. Early on, this similarity between the struggles of black people and women was an important factor in stimulating the new feminism. Over time, however, the differences between these two movements became apparent.

Most evidently, the black freedom movement could legitimately speak for all African Americans, since very few black people endorsed Jim Crow segregation and disenfranchisement, and none accepted the pseudoscientific arguments that they were biologically inferior to whites. In contrast, many women still embrace their difference from men, and a necessarily dependent status, because their identity as housewives and mothers remains a source of respect and security in a male-dominated world. Thus, while it is hard to imagine a constituency of blacks opposed to civil rights, there are visible organizations and leaders (such as Phyllis Schlafly's Eagle Forum or the multi-million-member Concerned Women of America) who identify themselves as antifeminist women. For decades, pollsters have noted that a large majority of women endorse basic feminist goals, like the right to equal pay for equal work, while much smaller numbers consider themselves "feminist." This paradox of profound change and widespread acceptance of what feminists called for, and deep hostility and resistance to the fact of the movement itself, indicate how revolutionary Women's Liberation was, and that the revolution is hardly over.

Chapter 12

GAY LIBERATION: "OUT OF THE CLOSETS AND INTO THE STREETS!"

We are a revolutionary homosexual group of men and women formed with the realization that complete sexual liberation for all people cannot come about unless existing social institutions are abolished. We reject society's attempt to impose sexual roles and definitions on our nature. We are stepping outside these roles and simplistic myths. We are going to be who we are. At the same time, we are creating new social forms and relations, that is, relations based upon brotherhood, cooperation, human love, and uninhibited sexuality. Babylon has forced us to commit to one thing . . . revolution.

        —Gay Liberation Front, Statement of Purpose, July 31, 1969

What is a lesbian? A lesbian is the rage of all women condensed to the point of explosion . . . . Lesbian is the label invented by the Man to throw at any woman who dares to be his equal, who dares to challenge his prerogatives, who dares to assert the primacy of her own needs. To have the label applied to people active in women's liberation is just the most recent instance of a long history; older women will recall that not so long ago, any woman who was successful, independent, not orienting her whole life around a man, would hear this word. For in this sexist society, for a woman to be independent means she can't be a woman—she must be a dyke. It says as clearly as can be said: woman and person are contradictory terms. And yet, in popular thinking, there is really only one essential difference between a lesbian and other women: that of sexual orientation—which

is to say, when you strip off all the packaging, you must finally realize that the essence of being a "woman" is to get fucked by men.
                    —Radicalesbians, "The Woman-Identified Woman," 1970

By 1965, the homophile movement had traveled a long, painful road. A new breed of reformers, epitomized by the defiant, unashamed Frank Kameny of the Washington, D.C. Mattachine Society, had taken leadership. Public protest had begun, if only in the most careful and restrained fashion—Kameny himself was known for admonishing female couples to stop holding hands on the picket line. In San Francisco, a beachhead was established into electoral politics, via the Society for Individual Rights (SIR), and homosexual activists had created alliances with liberal Protestant churches, though nowhere else did gay people have this small measure of legitimacy.

Still, these were meager gains compared to other movements at mid-decade. A tiny percentage of the gay and lesbian population participated in the homophile movement (one historian estimates 5,000 members in homophile groups in the late 1960s, out of millions) and only the top leaders were "out of the closet," willing to acknowledge publicly their same-sex orientation. There were hardly any gay people to look to with pride—in those days, even Walt Whitman's homoeroticism was ignored. Gay men and lesbians still suffered from the stigma that they were mentally diseased and prone to sexual crime, specifically child molestation. Liberal cities like New York had policies barring the employment of any teacher deemed homosexual, and many businesses fired gays outright if they were discovered. Across the country, police forces asserted that "public safety" required harassment of anyone overtly engaging in what straights believed to be homosexual behavior. Lesbians who adopted the butch style of short hair, jeans, and other putatively nonfeminine attire were routinely arrested for "impersonating a male," and men caught talking and drinking in gay bars were rousted, often beaten, and prosecuted, with their names printed in newspapers. Worst of all, even in the late 1960s and early 1970s, psychiatrists and psychologists continued to produce studies that diagnosed homosexuality as a form of mental illness. Thousands of gay men and women spent years in anguished therapy, sometimes including electroshock treatment, trying to convert themselves to heterosexuality.

HOMOPHOBIA AND THE LEFT

In this context, the homophile movement cautiously spread its wings from 1965 to the summer of 1969, when it finally emerged as a political force via the mythic riot at New York's Stonewall bar. From that point on, a small civil rights movement was transformed into a vastly larger movement for Gay Liberation and then, simply, gay rights. Until then, while Black Power, Women's Liberation and other movements focused on identity, consciousness, and self-determination mushroomed, homophile activists remained in their own separate, tiny political arena. One reason was the rampant homophobia and "compulsory heterosexuality" of the Left—Old, New, and in-between. Homophobia unified the left. It was one thing people could agree on. Communists and Marxists, from the Soviet Union to Cuba to the United States, had long viewed homosexuality as a prime example of the decadence bred by capitalism. Communists in power offered no protection, rights, or recognition to the homosexual minority, and Communists far from power, including those in the United States, did not acknowledge the reality of homosexual oppression. The New Left simply upped the ante: while the Old Left mostly ignored gay people (Harry Hay, founder of the Mattachine Society, was not expelled from the Communist Party, but left voluntarily), the New Left made a point of baiting them. Black nationalists of all persuasions were vocal in their denunciations of "faggots" and the "faggotry" of wimpy, emasculated white men and black men acting white. White men in groups like SDS aped this tough-guy behavior, and, anxious to demonstrate their masculine credentials, enjoyed gay-baiting each other. Finally, many feminists, acutely aware of the old insult that powerful women were really "man-haters," went to great pains to assert their heterosexuality. As discussed in chapter 11, Betty Friedan even attempted to purge what she called the Lavender Menace from NOW. Yet all of these organizations and movements, from the Communist Party to Women's Liberation, contained many gay people deeply in the closet, unable to be honest with their straight friends, and frightened to even attend a homophile meeting. When many of those closeted gays finally "came out" in 1969 and after, it was as if an army of organizers, skilled and savvy, suddenly appeared. ("Coming out," the defining political act for the Gay Liberation movement, meant no longer hiding one's sexuality—letting family, colleagues, comrades, and friends know, at whatever cost to one's relationships.)

Another reason for the isolation of the homophile movement was that its leaders saw no advantage in alliances with other movements. They believed it was hard enough to be homosexual without also being labeled a communist or a radical. Their goal was uniting gay people, so bringing in other issues seemed divisive. In time, this single-issue perspective was challenged vociferously by young leftist gays, but it would surface repeatedly, in the early 1970s when gays entered mainstream politics, and later in the 1990s, when prominent gay leaders urged an assimilationist strategy. In the late 1960s, even militant homophile reformers like Frank Kameny, the leaders of SIR, and Dick Leitsch, the president of New York's Mattachine Society, focused on lobbying liberal politicians and newspapers. Their model was the NAACP, and like the NAACP, the leaders of Mattachine and the Daughters of Bilitis (DOB) were mainly middle-class and middle-aged. Actually confronting the police, taking to the streets, engaging in civil disobedience and disruption, seemed pure folly. It was in this context that Gay Liberation appeared, out of nowhere, when young street runaways and transvestites, the most despised gays of all, charged the police lines outside the Stonewall Inn just after midnight on June 28, 1969, beginning several days of streetfighting. Their model was something else entirely—more like those moments in Watts, Detroit, and Newark when the police, performing one more routine arrest, suddenly found themselves confronted by huge, angry crowds.

BEFORE STONEWALL: A MOVEMENT GATHERS, 1965–1968

The shock of Stonewall, and its cultural significance in the decades since— June 28 became Gay Pride Day, the occasion for annual marches nationwide— relegated the earlier work of the homophile movement to the shadows, obscuring how much it had grown in the four years before Stonewall. In retrospect, we can see that new demands were brewing among homosexual Americans and some kind of radicalization was imminent. By 1968, the plea for basic civil rights, so radical in 1962 or 1964, seemed out-of-date. In part this was because homophile activism was finally becoming a nationwide movement. Until the late 1960s, it had been confined to New York and San Francisco, with outposts in a few cities like Washington, Denver, and Los Angeles. There was no national structure, no annual conferences or regular communication except through the pages of *ONE* and *The Ladder*, and personal letters between individual activists. After 1965, however, because of more respectful attention in the media and because homophile leaders had announced their commitment to fight for equal rights, gay people (especially men) began forming new groups in heartland cities like Houston, Phoenix, and Cincinnati. In 1966, leaders of fifteen local organizations convened a "planning conference" in Kansas City, which led to the formation of NACHO, the North American Conference of Homophile Organizations, the first national coalition for gay rights. By 1969, it would grow to fifty local groups— though still small in relation to the thousands of gay organizations that formed in the 1970s and 1980s. In 1968, the Student Homophile League was formed at Columbia University, the first campus gay group (adult homophile organizations were wary of the charge of pedophilia, and barred anyone under twenty-one). Also in 1968, NACHO endorsed the slogan "Gay Is Good," as innocuous today as "Black Is Beautiful," but just as shocking then.

Here and there after 1965 homophile leaders began winning concrete political victories and recognition from liberal politicians. In 1966, the Daughters of Bilitis convinced officials from various departments in San Francisco's municipal government to hold public meetings with the gay community. SIR's candidate nights drew important Democrats, who declared themselves allies, including Representative Philip Burton, one of the most powerful liberals in Congress in the 1970s, and Assemblyman Willie Brown, California's most influential black politician in the latter half of the twentieth century. In New York in 1966, the Mattachine Society successfully lobbied Mayor John Lindsay, a liberal Republican, to end the widespread policy of police entrapment that ruined many gay men's lives. In 1967 the New York City Civil Service Commission began eliminating restrictions on gay employment by the city.

In the late 1960s, pillars of Establishment liberalism like the American Civil Liberties Union and the Americans for Democratic Action endorsed an end to discrimination against gays, and the right of consenting adults to do what they wanted in private. At a time when all but two states still made sodomy (usually defined as *any* oral or anal sexual contact between two people) a felony, this was an important breakthrough. The National Council of Churches, representing the mainline Protestant denominations, began formal meetings with gay activists to reconsider its stance. Finally, several central institutions of today's mainstream homosexual community were initiated well before Stonewall. In 1968, *The Advocate* began publishing as a mimeographed newsletter in Los Angeles. It has grown into the major gay weekly newspaper, read by hundreds of thousands. Also in 1968, the Reverend Troy Perry founded the Metropolitan Community Church in a Los Angeles living room. It has since become a recognized Protestant denomination with several hundred MCC churches around the nation.

From the perspective of homophile leaders, all of this indicated steady progress towards toleration and the removal of legal discrimination. There were also early warning signs of a more angry radicalism, of gay people who would not accept invisibility and wanted the right to be different, even flamboyantly so. In early 1967, after violent bar raids in Los Angeles, hundreds of gay men rallied on Sunset Strip, an unprecedented action, especially in the home of one of the country's most openly homophobic and repressive police departments. In 1968, the Committee for Homosexual Freedom was formed in San Francisco as a split from SIR. Simply daring to put the word "homosexual" in its name was a radical act, and its founders vehemently denounced the caution of homophile leaders and called for a "homosexual revolution." They were photographed embracing semi-nude in the *Berkeley Barb*, the area's best-known underground newspaper. These mainly younger activists, too young to remember the McCarthyite 1950s, wanted to become part of "the Movement," the larger New Left. They wanted to claim their own liberation, loudly and joyfully, by any means necessary. Stonewall gave them that opportunity, through the elemental act of self-defense.

THE STONEWALL REBELLION AND THE EMERGENCE OF GAY LIBERATION

Stonewall was many things. First, it was a seedy, unlicensed tavern on Sheridan Square in the heart of Greenwich Village, a favorite of street people, underage runaways, and drag queens—exactly those unruly sections of the gay community that homophile organizers avoided like the plague. But it became something more late on June 27, 1969, when a routine police raid drew an angry crowd. Suddenly, either because several drag queens struggled as they were manhandled into paddy wagons, or just because of long-simmering anger, the gay people watching started throwing bottles, rocks, and coins. The beleaguered police retreated and were penned inside the bar for nearly an hour before reinforcements arrived, as the crowd grew to 2,000. Rioting and violent police responses continued on Village streets for several days, mixing broken heads and a carnival atmosphere—reportedly, transvestites taunted the NYPD's notorious Tactical Police Force by forming a kick-line.

Simply in these terms, Stonewall would have considerable historical significance, since never before had gays fought back in public on this scale, challenging the police for control of the streets. But beyond that, "Stonewall" stands for a sea-change in consciousness, as a battle that defined a new war, like Fort Sumter or Pearl Harbor. In its wake followed a wave of new organizing tactics, and a new language. The term "homophile" instantly became redundant, as did the Mattachine Society and the Daughters of Bilitis. The squeamishness about words like "gay," "lesbian," and "homosexual" was over. Polite meetings with officials were replaced by confrontations, loud and fierce; "Listen to the Homosexual!" became a favorite shouted chant in New York. Assimilation and tolerance were scorned in favor of pride and difference. Freedom from harassment was no longer enough—a share of power was claimed, just as with the other movements by people scorned and made invisible.

Yet despite all the similarities with other liberation movements, whether or not gays and lesbians should ally themselves with the larger left remained controversial throughout Gay Liberation's founding years, from 1969 to roughly 1975. In time, an emerging consensus in favor of a single-issue strategy marked the shift from Gay Liberation to gay rights. Meanwhile, a buried grievance from the homophile movement came to center stage, as lesbians empowered by Women's Liberation forcefully challenged the sexism of gay men. Many "women-identified women" split off into separatist all-women's groups, and a distinct lesbian-feminist movement occupied an uneasy space, somewhere between Women's Liberation and Gay Rights.

The founding moment of Gay Liberation came a month after Stonewall, when a group of younger activists, meeting under the New York Mattachine Society's auspices, decided they wanted to strike out on their own, linking up with the New Left. On July 27, the one-month anniversary of the riot, they staged a protest rally in Washington Square Park, a few blocks from the Stonewall bar, where 500 gays heard militant speeches from new leaders like Martha Shelley, former Yippie Jim Fouratt, and Marty Robinson. On July 31, they met and chose the name Gay Liberation Front (GLF), evoking Vietnam's National Liberation Front. A flyer soon appeared with the provocative head-line, "Do You Think Gays Are Revolting? You Bet Your Sweet Ass They Are!," announcing weekly meetings with the claim "We're going to make a place for ourselves in the revolutionary movement." Almost immediately, the GLF became a wild free-for-all, as some activists stormed homophile meetings to denounce moderation while others organized consciousness-raising sessions; intense debates took place about the relation of Gay Liberation to Third World revolution, Black Power, socialism, and the Vietnam War. GLFers deployed contingents with banners to major antiwar marches, shocking more moderate radicals. Their example spread like a prairie fire, with GLFs forming in Los Angeles, Philadelphia, San Francisco, and Chicago. Similar groups popped up elsewhere. The New York Gay Liberation Front subdivided into nineteen "cells" to pursue different interests, and held weekly dances (as an alternative to overpriced, Mafia-run bars) which proved an enormous political and financial success. They picketed New York's famous alternative newspaper, the *Village Voice*—so homophobic that it called the Stonewall riots the "great faggot rebellion" and censored the word "gay" from GLF classified ads—and won immediate concessions.

The dynamism of the Gay Liberation Front was a product of its connection to the New Left at its peak of mass militancy. 1969 was the year when the Vietnam Moratorium shut down much of the country for a day, when the Panthers dominated radical consciousness and the Young Lords formed, Women's Liberation received enormous media attention, and new revolutionary initiatives sprouted every week. In this context, what would have seemed outlandish a few years before—homosexuals proclaiming not just pride in being gay, but the revolutionary character of their deviance—was just one more shocking development. In New York, and even more on the West Coast, the antiwar movement was the arena for gay liberationists to join the New Left while asserting their own identity, much like Asian Americans and

Chicanos. The huge antiwar rallies of 1969, 1970, and 1971 served as public rallying points for gay contingents, a welcome way to "come out" with a group instead of singly, and ideal times for separate caucuses and conferences. The war defined the clear divide between the new movement and the old homophiles. Not surprisingly, SIR and Mattachine advocated for the right of gays to serve in the armed forces and to be drafted. They took no position on Vietnam. Ironically, draft resistance manuals counseled young straight men on how to avoid induction by acting "swishy" after checking the box on the Selective Service form asking if they had homosexual tendencies. In the new Gay Liberation groups, many leaders came straight from antiwar organizing, like Morris Kight, leader of the local Dow Action Committee and a founder of the Los Angeles GLF in December 1969 (Dow Chemical was the company that manufactured napalm, a prime corporate target for protest).

GETTING POLITICAL: FROM "GAY LIBERATION" TO "GAY RIGHTS"

Before long, some activists in New York's GLF found themselves disagreeing with the strategy of avowing a primary allegiance to the larger New Left. After a bitter December 1969 debate over donating money to the Black Panthers, a section led by Terry Robinson, Jim Owles, and Arthur Evans split off to form the Gay Activists Alliance (GAA). Thereafter, as GLF gradually declined, GAA took off, becoming the nation's single most effective and influential gay organization and the vanguard of the emerging movement. GAA defined itself by two central positions. First, it wrote into its constitution that it was a single-issue organization addressing only gay issues. There would no fights over left-wing theory, the nature of capitalism, or solidarity with the Panthers, this freeing it up to focus on action. Second, it would operate via a formal, written constitution, with elected officers and a dues-paying membership, all of which the Gay Liberation Front disparaged as elitist and hierarchical, preferring to work by consensus, without voting or official leaders.

The emphasis on structure and efficiency did not make GAA any less militant, however. Its reputation was built through an unrelenting crusade to confront liberal policymakers, who were vulnerable to charges of bigotry and might need gay votes at some point. GAA had one focus—passing an antidiscrimination ordinance in New York City. To get it on the radar of the city's political establishment, GAA militants evolved the technique of the "zap"— the sudden, unexpected, in-your-face action, which embarrassed the targeted politician and drew media attention. Mayor John Lindsay, by this time a liberal Democrat preparing to run for president in 1972, was a particular target for GAA zaps. They confronted him at museum openings, during tapings at television studios, and at Gracie Mansion. His top aides were also targeted for attention, including police commanders and board of education leaders. The headquarters of the state Republican Committee was occupied in the first gay sit-in, leading to five arrests for civil disobedience.

Quite quickly, the Gay Activists Alliance began to get results. In 1970, the peace activist and feminist lawyer Bella Abzug, running in a primary against a Democratic incumbent for a Manhattan House seat, campaigned under GAA sponsorship at one of the largest gay men's bathhouses. She embraced gays with zest and they responded warmly, turning out in large numbers as volunteers and voters. When Abzug won in an upset, the message was not lost on other liberal Democrats like Congressman Ed Koch, who moved to take positions against job discrimination and sodomy laws. When another Village bar raid led to the jailing of 167 gay men and angry GAA protests, Koch publicly intervened with the police commissioner on behalf of his constituents. Other liberals who refused to answer questions or pandered to homophobia were verbally assaulted and visibly shamed. GAA extended its presence in New York's gay culture further in May 1971, when it bought an old firehouse in lower Manhattan, hung a big banner outside, and began weekly dances. These events were large, professional, and highly lucrative.

Around the country, young gay liberationists looked to New York. They read GLF and GAA newsletters, invited organizers to visit (GAA called them "Johnny Appleseeds"), and emulated their media-savvy tactics and commitment to establishing public spaces for gay people outside of the bar scene. This wave of protest and organizing made 1970–1971 a tumultuous, liberating high point, with many "firsts." In Los Angeles, the new GLF flexed its muscles by picketing a chili parlor in West Hollywood, Barney's Beanery, which posted signs reading "Fagots [sic] Stay Out," despite its large gay clientele. After months of sit-ins and eat-ins in early 1970, the signs came down. Then, in late 1971, Los Angeles saw the opening of the first-ever Gay Community Services Center as a legally recognized charity, with a modest grant from the Department of Health, Education and Welfare. Earlier, in Minneapolis, in May 1970, two middle-class young men, Jack Baker and Mike McConnell, performed their own "zap" by applying for a marriage license. They became the first poster children for gay rights. When Baker won election as student body president at the University of Minnesota in spring 1971, it made the network news, since no open homosexual had been elected to any kind of office in America before. In Boston, new institutions proliferated, including a newspaper (the *Fag Rag*), regular radio programs, a Homophile Community Health Services Center, and a Gay Speakers Bureau. Controversy erupted over the attempt to hold a "gay mixer" at the Massachusetts Institute of Technology. In June 1970, the first Stonewall commemorations were held in San Francisco, Los Angeles,

Chicago, and New York. These eclipsed any previous demonstrations by gay people. In New York, an astonishing crowd of up to 25,000 people filled Central Park's Sheep Meadow, making the front page of the *New York Times* and sending an unmistakable message that here was a new, politicized, self-conscious minority group.

San Francisco paralleled New York—though in the Bay Area, the Society for Individual Rights had mobilized voters years before Stonewall. Following Bella Abzug, the next politician to openly solicit the gay vote was another straight white woman, Dianne Feinstein. In 1971, as a city supervisor, she ran for mayor of San Francisco, losing but running well; she went on to be elected mayor and then U.S. senator in the 1990s. Most memorable was the winning campaign for city sheriff by Richard Hongisto in 1971. He was a rare phenomenon, a law enforcement officer with leftist leanings. Hongisto beat a traditional, antigay incumbent with a campaign focused on ending police abuses of racial minorities, radicals, and gays. His campaign emblem was a sheriff's badge with a superimposed peace sign. When he won, San Francisco gays had a friend in that wing of City Hall that formerly housed their worst enemies. It was in this atmosphere that a charismatic transplanted New Yorker, Harvey Milk, began turning the Castro district into a base for gay political power. Known as the informal "Mayor of Castro Street," he was elected supervisor in 1977. In 1978, another supervisor, a conservative former policeman named Dan White, murdered Milk and liberal Mayor George Moscone in their offices.

Of all these breakthroughs, the most audacious was the early 1971 campaign to elect Frank Kameny to Congress from the District of Columbia. Congress had granted the District a nonvoting House representative, and a special election was scheduled for March. A cadre of gay men realized this was an opportunity to insert gay rights into local and national politics. They picked Kameny because he was the city's leading homosexual activist, with a track record going back a decade. A hyper-articulate Harvard Ph.D., he also presented a useful stereotype-shattering image. Funds were raised within the gay community from bar and bathhouse owners and a publisher of gay erotica. The first challenge was to get Kameny onto the ballot as the candidate of the Personal Freedom Party, which required 8,000 signatures. This was a formidable task because it required "coming out": anyone soliciting the signatures would be assumed to be gay. At this crucial juncture, New York's GAA jumped in as the shock troops of the national movement, shipping dozens of activists to Washington over several weekends to search for signatures in gay bars and parking lots in liberal neighborhoods. They got Kameny on the ballot and he campaigned aggressively, debating and speaking constantly as a legitimate candidate. He came in fourth with 1.6 percent of the vote, but a moral and symbolic victory had been won. His backers moved immediately to form a Washington D.C. Gay Activists Alliance, and their model of almost entirely male-run campaigns funded by gay businessmen seeking recognition and legitimacy influenced a whole generation of electorally oriented activists.

From 1972 on, the emphasis of the gay rights movement was increasingly towards electoral politics, civil rights, and claiming a space within the Democratic Party nationally, not just in enclaves like New York and San Francisco. The increasing professionalism of gay politics reflected the swing away from militant protest among most "out" gays. The radicalism of 1969–1971 led to more conservative ends: community building in openly gay neighborhoods like San Francisco's Castro, where gay men could enjoy their new freedom and the seemingly unlimited possibilities of sexual liberation it promised before the onset of the AIDS epidemic in the early 1980s. Gay businesses proliferated, and a characteristic lifestyle developed—no longer furtive and afraid, but demonstrative. Where exactly lesbians fit in this new male-dominated, pleasure-seeking world remained an open question and a source of discord.

Particularly important was the creation of the Alice B. Toklas Memorial Democratic Club in San Francisco in early 1972, as the presidential primaries heated up (Toklas and her lover, the writer Gertrude Stein, had been a famous lesbian couple in Paris between the World Wars). Founded by Jim Foster, it swung its weight behind George McGovern's presidential bid, helping him win the crucial California primary. Foster's expectation was that McGovern would endorse a gay rights plank, the major goal of activists from eighty-six different groups who gathered in Chicago in the winter of 1972 to plan strategy. They had considerable success, in that four of the Democratic candidates (McGovern, John Lindsay, black congresswoman Shirley Chisholm, and even former vice president Hubert Humphrey) endorsed gay rights in some form. In Lindsay's case, campaign-trail pressure was the catalyst to an executive order in March 1972 banning discrimination by the city of New York, after GAA "declared war" on him. But at the August Democratic Convention in Miami, McGovern's gay backers were left in the lurch. Already worried about charges of radicalism, McGovern's aides convinced the Platform Committee to defeat planks supporting abortion rights and gay rights. The sole concession was that a gay man and a lesbian were given ten minutes to defend the minority position, at four in the morning. It was another "first"—homosexuals addressing a major party convention—but the delegates ignored or jeered them. Back in New York, GAA leaders were so angered by this insult and subsequent equivocations by McGovern that they occupied his campaign offices and forced a strong statement of opposition to discrimination.

Despite this chastening experience, the McGovern campaign marked a major step into mainstream politics. In Boston, a closeted gay man, Barney Frank, won a seat in the state legislature with gay backing, promising to introduce antidiscrimination legislation. Frank went on to Congress in 1981, and eventually came out. (Today, he is part of the Democratic congressional leadership and the most powerful openly gay politician in the country.) Then, in 1974, an historic victory was achieved when Elaine Noble, an "out" lesbian with a strong community activist record, mustered wide support from progressive groups and won election to the Massachusetts House of Representatives.

The most significant victory for gay rights in these years came through the medical profession, where gays had long sought to confront their stigmatization as "sick." On December 15, 1973, the American Psychiatric Association (APA) voted to remove homosexuality from the list of mental illnesses in its *Diagnostic and Statistical Manual*, the guidebook for the entire profession. Since World War II, the formal designation of gay sexuality as a disease had legitimized systematic discrimination by the military, government agencies, and private employers. Thousands of psychiatrists had studied homosexuality as a pathology during their graduate training, and many of them had spent years treating gay men and lesbians so that they would become "normal" heterosexuals. The process of getting the APA to change its mind was the result of systematic pressure from outside, which prompted considerable soul-searching by doctors firmly convinced homosexuality was a curable illness.

The fight against and then within the APA began at its May 1971 convention, where gay men disrupted a session on homosexuality by shouting down speakers and rushing the stage to discuss their anguish at hearing themselves described as diseased. Their demand was simple: that gay people should be included in a discussion of gayness. This furor led to a panel at the 1972 convention which included leaders like Frank Kameny. A special committee was appointed to study the question, and after voluminous testimony and investigation it concluded that classifying homosexuality as a mental illness was an *a priori* assertion, rather than a provable hypothesis. In 1973, the APA voted to remove it from the *Diagnostic and Statistical Manual* and to pass a strong statement in favor of equality and full civil rights for gays. This decision was as much of a milestone for gays as the *Roe v. Wade* decision was for feminists. It fundamentally changed the position of homosexuals in American society, removing a huge barrier to their recognition as citizens.

These two events, Elaine Noble's election in 1974 and the APA decision in 1973, showed how far gay people had come in a few years. In 1968, the prospect of a lesbian state legislator would have seemed impossible to anyone; yet it happened in 1974, and with little disturbance. To everyone's surprise, gays moved into liberal Democratic politics almost as easily as had black radicals, antiwar activists, and feminists, though soon New Right organizers in the Republican Party began targeting what they called "San Francisco Democrats" as the party of decadence and immorality. Similarly, the assumption that gay men and lesbians were "sick," perverted, and neurotic was so widely shared, common-sensical, and constantly reiterated by professional, medical, and legal authorities, that undermining it in one stroke seemed a long-term goal. Indeed, many homophile activists had internalized the perception of their own sickness and deviance—and simply asked to be left alone with their own kind. In the mid-1970s, those days seemed very far away, like much else, a relic of the 1950s.

LESBIANS AND THE GROWTH OF A "WOMYN'S CULTURE"

Yet this seemingly triumphal story of new acceptance, of rights claimed and power asserted, of visible gay communities and neighborhoods sprouting on both coasts, is not the whole story of the years from 1969 to 1975. One major conflict simmered and sometimes boiled over during these years—the anger over gay men's domination of the movement. Most of the leaders of GLF, GAA, and other groups and campaigns of the period were men. While a few women like Martha Shelley and Elaine Noble were prominent, white men dominated the movement, much in the way they dominated the New Left until first Black Power and then Women's Liberation went their own ways. Many lesbians felt a similar anger and eventually pursued a similar strategy. Older activists in the Daughters of Bilitis had long-established grievances over the Mattachine Society treating them as a women's auxiliary. Now they and younger lesbians coming into the movement were assailed on two fronts, since moderate feminists like Betty Friedan and even many radical feminists were embarrassed by their presence.

In response, lesbians fought a two-front war, with mixed results. Within the burgeoning feminist movement, they demanded legitimacy and solidarity, and largely won it. Beginning with the famous "zap" of NOW's Second Congress to Unite Women in May 1970, they confronted straight women. As already discussed, after Friedan's brief success in purging gay women from the flagship New York NOW chapter, she was defeated at the 1971 convention, and the nation's largest feminist group firmly endorsed gay rights. A significant number of radical feminists took seriously the concept that "feminism is the theory, lesbianism is the practice," and renounced their relations with men. Before long, a new type of feminist appeared, the "political lesbian," who identified with women, and might or might not have sexual relationships with them. Some lifelong gay women, for whom their sexuality had never been a matter of choice, were offended by this approach. It was one aspect of the "gay-straight split" which roiled Women's Liberation, but it indicated the degree to which heterosexuality was no longer taken for granted among feminists—a major gain.

Lesbians had less luck in their relations with gay men, as sexism proved to be a problem regardless of a man's sexual orientation. The gay male subculture, historically oriented to bars and cruising for sex, was repugnant to many gay women. As the free public space for gay men rapidly expanded in the early 1970s in neighborhoods like the Castro, filled with discos and bathhouses, lesbians increasingly withdrew into their own "womyn's" world. Even in the early days of New York's GLF and the GAA, male domination of the weekend dances became a source of contention. The women first organized their own dances, and then in many cases, just left. Another divisive issue was "drag," the visible identity of a minority of male transsexuals. Radicalized by feminist analysis, some lesbians found men aggressively claiming the apparatus of femininity (dresses, makeup, high heels, wigs, and padded brassieres) deeply offensive—a parody of their own oppression, akin to whites wearing blackface. The result was that within a few years, a self-identified "lesbian feminist" movement put down roots, outside of the gay rights movement, and uneasily coexisting within organized feminism. As radical feminism increasingly evolved into a less-confrontational cultural feminism that focused on women's fundamental difference from men and sisterhood with each other, many lesbians found the company of other women more congenial than that of any men, gay or straight. In later years, the tensions between gay men and lesbians were patched up to present a common political front, but the differences in their experiences are still profound.

As the 1970s progressed, gay rights took on more and more of a mainstream coloration. In 1973, the National Gay Task Force (later the National Gay and Lesbian Task Force) was formed as a consciously elite lobbying group, eschewing the confrontational tactics that made the Gay Activists Alliance famous. In later years, along with groups like the Human Rights Campaign, it became the respectable face of gay America, in perpetual tension with the drag queens, "leather boys," and other unreconstructed sexual liberationists. For these organizations, and for the thousands of homosexual men and women who have "come out" since the 1970s, enjoying a precarious citizenship, the quiet years of building the homophile movement, and then the four or five years of all-out mobilization after Stonewall, became a mythic memory. The slow gains and the sudden triumphs are easily forgotten. Like basic voting rights or legally color-blind employment policies for African Americans and other people of color, the political space won by gay & lesbian activists is assumed to be natural, a product of evolution, though horrific incidents like the ritual murder of Matthew Shepard remind us how many Americans still hate and fear gay people, simply because they exist. But if we are going to measure how much the Gay Liberation and gay rights movement achieved, it is vital to remember how American society operated when the law, government, and the medical profession together insisted that a particular sexual orientation was self-evidently pathological and even criminal.

Chapter 13

WINNING AND LOSING: THE NEW LEFT DEMOCRATIZES AMERICA

Why didn't the New Left put down lasting roots? This question has been asked many times, but it rests upon a flawed premise—that the only tangible long-term success for the New Left would have been a new political party, and a corresponding set of established institutions. Clearly, that did not happen. Better questions would be: what permanent presence did the New Left achieve in U.S. society? Which parts of it were most successful, and why? To what extent did it change America permanently, and in what ways did it fail? To frame answers to these questions, we need to step back and look at the New Left's overall evolution from the late 1960s through the mid-1970s, at "the Movement" as a whole.

MERGING INTO THE MAINSTREAM, 1968–1975

In the five years after 1968, existing movements grew enormously and moved to the left, while new movements surged forward with dramatic speed. A whole new political language had to be learned: *Afro-American* rather than *colored* or *Negro*, *Ms.* instead of *Mrs.* or *Miss*, *sexism, patriarchy, homophobia, Chicano, people of color, Third World, solidarity*, and much more. New constituencies pushed their way into the political, academic, and media arenas.

The centuries-old presumption that the normative American was a white, heterosexual man of undefined class status, neither rich nor poor, was over-turned, suddenly and decisively. This cultural, legal, and political revolution met with fierce anger and resistance from many white men, as well as the millions of women who embraced the power women traditionally had exerted within the old order's separate spheres.

Inevitably, the radical upsurge of 1968–1972 began to wane as the war ended and Nixon sank into the swamp of Watergate. Americans across the political spectrum felt a growing political exhaustion after years of division. When President Gerald Ford announced in September 1974 that "our long national nightmare" was over, following Nixon's forced resignation and his pardoning by Ford, much of the nation agreed with him, and desperately hoped for a return to normal life. Large-scale structural and economic changes were a major element in the widespread sense that an era was ending. The New Left's steady rise since the late 1950s was facilitated by the booming economy, where jobs were plentiful and the minimum wage had much greater purchasing power (peaking at $8.17 per hour in 1966, in 2000 dollars). Housing, health insurance, and higher education were vastly less expensive than today, and the cost of organizing was relatively low. An activist organi-zation could be run with a few mimeograph machines and electric typewriters, used furniture, and minimal stipends for staff; SNCC field secretaries got the current equivalent of $50 or $60 per week, when they got anything at all. The so-called Affluent (or "post-scarcity") Society, where making money seemed relatively unimportant to many young middle-class people because there was so much of it to go around, had created an opening for the New Left. All that began changing rapidly with the onset of "stagflation," the endemic recession that began in the early 1970s, combining high unemployment with high inflation. Due in part to the cost of the Vietnam War, it was exacerbated by the oil embargo imposed by the Organization of Petroleum Exporting Countries (OPEC, which included all the major Arab nations) in October 1973 because of U.S. support of Israel in that year's "Yom Kippur war" against Egypt and Syria. The resulting energy crisis, marked by long lines at gas stations and skyrocketing fuel prices, was a cold-water shock for most Americans. For the first time in decades, the majority had real economic worries, putting a chill on the revolutionary euphoria of the late 1960s.

In this context, some scholars assert that the New Left simply died, disappearing like a teenage romance. In fact, its fate was much more complex. Some movements did decline. For obvious reasons, the antiwar movement rapidly faded away once its goal was achieved, though important parts of it contributed to new peace and anti-intervention movements in subsequent decades. Other movements, however, kept growing through the 1970s, 1980s, and 1990s—the women's and gay movements, for instance. The most consistent pattern was for movements to put down institutional roots, seeking to acquire a voice in and access to the seats of power, whether in Congress or city halls. To confuse this institutionalization with the "death" of the New Left is to confuse the goal of politics in the largest sense, which is to acquire power and make change. Therefore, it is essential not to mistake the diffusion of the many movements and their successful moves into the mainstream of civil society with the death of radicalism. After all, the logical goal for serious radicals is to stop being "radical," to cease clamoring for attention from the margins and enter into serious negotiations over governance. By that criterion, the New Left won many victories.

The narrative of the New Left in the decade after 1968 traces how distinct movements went their own way, in multiple surges of self-determination, as the preceding chapters demonstrate. Most attempts to unite radicals across political, racial, and gender lines failed, whether the National Conference for a New Politics in November 1967 (which hoped to run Dr. King for president in 1968, with the peace activist Dr. Benjamin Spock as his running mate), or the Black Panthers' Revolutionary Peoples Constitutional Convention in August 1970. Even more than before, the New Left in the late 1960s was a pluralist "movement of movements," whose common threads were the rejection of Cold War liberalism, white supremacy, and America's imperial role in the world. Having helped wreck the old Cold War consensus, those individual movements could pursue "single issue" politics with considerable success, as they did for the rest of the century. The larger movement came together only episodically, in the great antiwar demonstrations of 1969–1971, legal defense efforts for jailed leaders like Huey Newton, and electoral campaigns in left-wing enclaves like San Francisco and New York, where activists with movement credentials united diverse supporters into winning coalitions.

In the early 1970s, however, there were two significant efforts to coalesce the various movements of the New Left into a single, coordinated, multi-issue movement. One was the attempt to create a *new communist party,* with a comprehensive Marxist-Leninist strategy to bring about a revolutionary seizure of power; this so-called "party-building" effort was part of a more general revival of interest in Marxist theory and socialist practice. Though it drew in thousands of experienced activists, the New Communist project was a signal failure. It profoundly misjudged the political conditions and climate of the United States in the 1970s. The New Communists' stridently ideological tone and organizational rigidity proved to be disastrously out-of-sync with the loose, tolerant pluralism that the New Left itself had brought to American culture, in which everyone was presumed to march to the beat of their own drummer.

The major trend of the early 1970s was a *radicalized liberalism*, which led to the move across the entire New Left, from Black Power to Gay Liberation, into the arena of electoral politics and the Democratic Party. This *new politics* came to prominence in the 1972 McGovern campaign, but long outlasted that effort. Its end result was to establish a credible left-wing voice in national politics for the first time since the 1940s. In a sense, the New Left did finally come together, but only as a set of constituencies within a much broader electoral coalition that in the 1970s still included many moderates and conservatives.

The New Left's last phase, after 1970, also included a slow-motion revolution within higher education. Much of the New Left had grown out of the colleges and universities, and many activists now returned as graduate students and assistant professors determined to institutionalize a new radical scholarship, training young people to be critical thinkers rather than quiescent white-collar workers. This project to take over the academy was notably successful. Whole sectors of the humanities and social sciences were radically reformed from inside, as scholars with left-wing backgrounds achieved commanding positions. Finally, as the New Left's many movements merged into the fabric of American society in the mid-1970s (the Democratic Party, universities, churches, unions, and advocacy groups), newer movements arose around issues of U.S. intervention in the Third World, radical environmentalism, violence against women, consumer rights, housing, and more. Sometimes these were branches emerging from the earlier antiwar, nationalist, and feminist formations, and sometimes they were quite new, but all were bridges into the later 1970s, 1980s, and beyond.

Together, these four phenomena—the "new politics" of radicalized liberalism; the New Communist Movement; the movement of radicals into higher education; and the post-1960s new social movements—constitute the last stage of the New Left. We need to examine each of them briefly before assessing what the New Left did and did not achieve, the degree to which it won by vanquishing Cold War liberalism, and the degree to which it lost by proving to have insufficient political power, popular support, and organizational capacity to move towards a revolutionary restructuring of U.S. society. The late 1960s also saw a larger cultural watershed that must also be noted and analyzed. This chapter's penultimate section will look at the flowering of the white youth counterculture in the late 1960s and early 1970s, its historical roots and connections to the New Left, and how alternative countercultures were accommodated within a new kind of mainstream popular culture in the 1970s and after.

A RADICALIZED LIBERALISM

The histories of the antiwar movement, of Black, Red, Brown, and Yellow Power, and of Women's and Gay Liberation, together document the collapse of the conservative Cold War version of liberalism that had dominated national political life, from Harry Ŝ Truman and Dwight Eisenhower through John F. Kennedy and Lyndon Johnson. Most of these movements pushed for a role in electoral politics, seeking a voice in the Democratic Party and pursuing immediate, tangible gains for their constituencies. A few examples will serve as reminders: antiwar organizers mobilizing for Eugene McCarthy in 1968 and George McGovern in 1972; Black Power leaders like Amiri Baraka and Huey P. Newton concentrating their forces on winning municipal elections; feminists forming the National Women's Political Caucus and mounting massive lobbying efforts to pass the ERA; the rise of the Congressional Black Caucus as a new voice in the Democratic Party; the lobbying power of the Indochina Peace Campaign and the Gay Activists Alliance; the short-lived Raza Unida Party; finally, the increasing number of radicals who got elected to local, state, and national office, almost always as Democrats. Some became famous, like Representatives Ron Dellums and Bella Abzug, but there were many more, at every level of government.

What is so radical about this development, which some leftists bitterly denounced as selling out? One central fact was that elected officials drawn from the peace, feminist, black, and other constituencies simply dispensed with the anticommunist orthodoxy that had been a litmus test for participation in mainstream politics for a quarter-century. They mocked it, ignored it, and fought back hard at any suggestion of reviving McCarthyism. Anyone with an activist background had left-wing allies, including on occasion real live Communist Party members. The new activist-politicians said, in effect, "so what?" They were, in a crucial sense, post-Vietnam politicians, beneficiaries of that defeat. By itself, this marked a vast change in American politics—aspiring political leaders could no longer be intimidated into lockstep support for American foreign policy. It had immediate consequences in pulling older liberals to the left, and making formerly sacrosanct institutions like the CIA the butt of open attacks and popular jokes.

From 1973 to 1975, the national security establishment—the old-boy WASP elite that had created and destroyed governments around the world since 1945 and had led the United States into Vietnam—suffered stunning blows to its prestige. These final victories for the New Left began with congressional hearings investigating U.S. police training programs set up to aid anticommunist military dictatorships in Latin American countries like

Brazil. The hearings exposed American complicity with torture and repression on a vast scale. In August 1973, Congress cut off Nixon's ability to prolong U.S. military actions in Indochina, reasserting its authority over foreign and military affairs. Then, in 1975, Senator Frank Church and Representative Otis Pike convened Senate and House hearings to investigate the activities of the CIA and other intelligence agencies abroad, and the FBI at home. Attention focused on the many attempts to overthrow and kill Fidel Castro, U.S. sponsorship of the September 1973 military coup against the democratic government of Chile headed by socialist Salvador Allende, and the FBI's COINTELPRO program to infiltrate and disrupt left-wing groups at home. In each case, public testimony from State Department, CIA and FBI officials, and documents unearthed by the staff of the two committees, proved devastating. Evidence went into the Congressional record of a massive campaign of sabotage and terrorism against Cuba over many years. The CIA admitted trying to assassinate Castro many times, using Mafiosos and Cuban exiles based in Miami. The CIA and Secretary of State Kissinger were also forced to acknowledge that in 1970 the United States conspired to kill the head of the Chilean armed forces before Allende took office to instigate a coup, and that over the next three years the United States funded the destabilization of Allende's government. CIA Director Richard Helms pleaded "no contest" to a felony charge of lying to Congress about this campaign. A further revelation concerned the Phoenix Program in Vietnam, a CIA effort to exterminate the National Liberation Front's civilian infrastructure in which tens of thousands of unarmed Vietnamese were murdered.

Helms was not the only top official humiliated. Nixon was permitted to resign, but a slew of his cabinet officers were convicted of serious crimes. FBI Director L. Patrick Gray had to resign after admitting he destroyed key documents. Watergate and the revelations about the national security establishment discredited the Republicans and empowered the most liberal Members of Congress. Though the 1970s are commonly described as the decade when America "turned right" after the 1960s, the huge "Watergate class" elected in the 1974 Democratic landslide was the most liberal Congress in postwar history. These younger Democrats took for granted that they had to listen to activist constituencies. Congress's frustration with Nixon's "imperial presidency" and CIA abuses led to several key pieces of legislation that altered the balance of power in shaping U.S. foreign policy and made the Vietnam syndrome a practical reality for decades to come. The opening shot came over Angola, a Portuguese colony in southern Africa where a long armed struggle for independence came to a head in 1974–1975. The CIA, in alliance with white-ruled South Africa, intervened to prevent the most radical group, the Popular Movement for the Liberation of Angola (backed by Cuba), from coming to power. Dismayed by yet another "covert operation" that could get out of control, Senator Dick Clark of Iowa sponsored successful legislation to block any CIA involvement in Angola's civil war—an unprecedented action in the history of the Cold War. In 1976 and after, Congressman (later senator) Tom Harkin of Iowa, along with others, introduced a series of amendments to foreign aid legislation requiring that no U.S. military or economic aid be extended to any government that violated human rights. Though routinely evaded by later presidents, this legislation was the basis for many anti-intervention campaigns in the later 1970s and 1980s.

The restraints placed on U.S. interventionism in the Third World were reinforced during the 1976 presidential campaign. The Democratic candidate was the moderate former governor of Georgia, Jimmy Carter. He used human rights as a wedge in attacking President Ford during a key October 1976 debate, saying "I notice that Mr. Ford did not comment on the prisons in Chile. This is a typical example, maybe of others, that this administration overthrew an elected government and helped establish a military dictatorship." Once elected, Carter positioned himself as a human rights advocate, and appointed former civil rights and antiwar activists to high-level posts in his administration, including as heads of the Action Corps (then including the Peace Corps) and the new Bureau of Human Rights in the State Department. He also reached out to the gay and feminist communities, giving them access to the White House. In a larger sense, though, Carter's nomination showed the limitations of the new radical liberalism as a significant but far from dominant force in the Democratic Party. The Democrats were broken into many pieces in 1976, including large constituencies backing George Wallace's conservative populism and Senator Henry Jackson's neoconservative revamping of Cold War liberalism. On the left, the various liberals appealed to the McGovern constituencies. In a crowded field, Carter slipped through as the centrist candidate.

The 1976 election established a pattern for the Democrats that would last into the next century. They became a party for brokering different interests, from out-and-out radicals to sectors of corporate America. The cooptation of radicals had begun earlier, during the Kennedy and Johnson administrations' efforts to control and benefit from the activist energy of the Civil Rights movement. The Democrats needed black voters to offset Republican gains, and steered money to the movement. From 1964 on, LBJ's War on Poverty pulled in hundreds of activists, from former campus radicals to working-class mothers, to run rural Head Start centers, urban Community Action Programs, and campus offices recruiting black, Latino, and Native American students. If the Vietnam War had never happened, or ended sooner and more successfully, this pattern of accommodation might have continued. But the war put radicals and then a larger number of liberals on a collision course with the Johnson and Nixon administrations. The balance of power shifted, and radicals were no longer recruited as individuals, but now contested for power and office, displacing the old guard. The most notorious evidence of this was the 1972 Democratic Convention, where the national press corps reported with amazement how feminists and blacks filled up pro-McGovern slates from Illinois and New York. In the 1980s and 1990s, the multihued, coalitional character of the Democratic Party as a vehicle for progressive constituencies—feminists, gays and lesbians, environmentalists, labor, African Americans, and Latinos—became familiar. In the 1970s, it was still a shock.

THE REVIVAL OF AMERICAN MARXISM

Further to the left in the 1970s, and generally disgusted by the movement of radicals into the Democratic Party, were a host of socialist, Marxist, and New Communist organizations. For most of the New Left's history, socialism was a minor concern. Many activists expressed a commitment to it, from Dr. King's low-key avowal of "democratic socialism" in 1965 to SDS leader Bernardine Dohrn's 1968 assertion that she was a "revolutionary communist," but actual organizing campaigns revolved around specific issues, not challenging capitalism itself. New Leftists paid considerable attention to the progress of Communists in China and Cuba, and read independent socialist magazines & newspapers like *Monthly Review* or the weekly *Guardian*. Yet this interest was mostly vicarious, as even Marxist parties like the Communists and the Socialist Workers focused on influencing the various movements, not on organizing a revolution, peaceful or otherwise. SDS talked of revolutionizing America, but its loose organization and lack of strategy made that mostly talk, and it fell apart in 1969. The Black Panthers and other revolutionary nationalists were the most ambitious, as their version of Black Power went considerably beyond "home rule," but even they spoke only for a minority within the black minority. In the late 1960s, many radicals of all colors pinned their hopes on the Panthers as the vanguard of a multiracial socialist revolution. This hope proved illusory as the combination of government repression, violent tendencies, and the cult of personality around Huey P. Newton transformed the BPP into a local political gang in Oakland.

Then, in the early 1970s, there was a significant revival of Marxism across parts of the New Left. In some ways this paralleled the emergence of radical liberalism and the McGovern wing of the Democratic Party. In both cases, activists were digging in for the longer haul, looking past the immediacy of the Vietnam War and imagining a different America. The new interest in socialism took various forms. Some of the established Marxist parties were revived by their connections with the New Left. The Socialist Workers Party grew to 2,000 members through its leadership in the antiwar movement. The defense campaign for Angela Davis brought renewed interest in the Communist Party, especially among young African Americans. On the other hand, the Socialist Party, founded in 1900, collapsed when its fiercely anticommunist right wing decided to back Nixon over McGovern in 1972.

The most significant development was that thousands of experienced young radicals adopted a Third World Marxism influenced by China and Cuba, and set out to create a New Communist party to the left of the CPUSA. They came from the wreckage of SDS, from independent antiwar groups, and from organizations of people of color like La Raza Unida, the Congress of African Peoples, the League of Revolutionary Black Workers, the Young Lords, and the African Liberation Support Committee. For all of these organizers, revolution seemed to be in the air as old orders and structures of authority visibly tottered. In 1968, much of the world was in revolt. From Paris to Mexico City to Czechoslovakia, students had defied authority and were brutally repressed. Guerrilla organizations formed in dozens of countries, especially in Latin American states under military rule like Argentina and Uruguay; the Weathermen were not an isolated phenomenon. China was in the grip of what seemed like a continuous grassroots uprising against bureaucracy, the Great Proletarian Cultural Revolution (though in reality the "revolution" was really mob violence stimulated by different Communist Party leadership factions). In the United States too, revolution seemed to be an option, as a significant fraction of the several million college students declared themselves ready for radical change in various national polls. SDS collapsed in 1969, but a cadre of ex-SDSers organized the Venceremos Brigades, which in 1969–1970 sent thousands of young radicals to violate the U.S. embargo on travel to revolutionary Cuba, where they joined work brigades to cut sugarcane.

The Venceremos Brigades were just one part of an apparent revolutionary upsurge, including the "wildcat" strikes led by the League of Revolutionary Black Workers in Detroit's auto plants and similar insurgent efforts among younger white factory workers, many of them returning Vietnam vets. In this context, one more intensely radical movement came to the fore among prisoners, especially African Americans. By 1970, many prisons around the country were becoming schools of revolution, as jailed Panthers and others met up with convicts who had read Frantz Fanon, Eldridge Cleaver, Malcolm X, Ho Chi Minh, the African revolutionary Amilcar Cabral, and Che Guevara. The prison movement seemed the ultimate proof that American society was rotting from the inside and ready to break wide open. One month after George Jackson was shot down in San Quentin's prison yard in August 1971 (see chapter 9), 1,200 convicts in New York's Attica prison rose up, taking guards hostage and demanding negotiations to change atrocious conditions. Governor Nelson Rockefeller responded by ordering state police and guards to stage a massive assault, killing twenty-nine prisoners and all ten hostages. At the time, "Attica" became a synonym for state violence and the resistance of the most oppressed, though within a few years it was forgotten.

This arena of constant, intensifying violence, both of the oppressed and of the oppressor, is what convinced perhaps ten thousand young activists of all races in 1968–1973 that a new Marxist-Leninist party was urgently needed. They disliked the caution of the Communist Party USA, and accused it of "reformism," because its main focus was on influencing mainstream liberal politics rather than actually developing a revolutionary strategy. They were even more hostile to the Soviet Union, charging that it had betrayed Marxism (it was "revisionist," to use the ideological label). Starting in 1968, these militants began getting factory jobs, forming collectives and study groups (or "pre-party formations") in key urban centers, and reading Chairman Mao to learn how to be correct communist revolutionaries. Though often described as Maoist (e.g. pro–Chinese Communist), much of the New Communist Movement was also motivated by the combative spirit of the Cuban and Vietnamese revolutions—small countries that had managed to stand up to the mighty United States. Their Third World Marxism focused more on antiracism and anti-imperialism than the traditional working-class and trade union emphasis of the CPUSA and its Socialist and Trotskyist rivals.

In theory, thousands of highly-motivated, disciplined young activists, fresh from leadership in antiwar, campus, and Black Power organizing, and the Chicano, Puerto Rican, and Asian American movements, were the ideal material to build a new revolutionary force. But after several years of intensive party-building, the results were unimpressive. By 1975, the New Communist Movement was rapidly waning, though it persisted through the 1980s. The most obvious problem was that the New Communists proved incapable of agreeing on a common strategy around which they could unite in a single party. From the beginning, doctrinal splits severely limited this movement's growth. Numerous "leagues" and "parties" formed, including the Revolutionary Union, which became the Revolutionary Communist Party, the October League, which birthed the Communist Party (Marxist-Leninist), the League of Revolutionary Struggle, the Communist Workers Party, the Communist Labor Party, the Line of March organization, and various others. Each of these organizations typically had its own newspaper, a central committee, and a detailed "workplan" for building the revolution, all supported by the labor of a few hundred members. Not surprisingly, their intense sectarianism drove away far more people than they recruited.

In revolutionary times, however, even dogmatic, authoritarian organizations can grow because of their commitment to up the ante and fight for power. The real reason for the failure of the New Communists was that contrary to all their theorizing, the 1970s were not a revolutionary time. Like other radicals in American history, they had a tendency to vastly underestimate the strength of capitalism and "bourgeois democracy" in the United States. Even at its weakest, with the armed forces in severe disarray because of Vietnam, and massive social unrest in urban ghettoes and on campuses, the United States never approached a revolutionary crisis, in which the majority of the population ceases to accept the authority and legitimacy of the state. Indeed, the greatest threat to the established order in the 1970s came not from the New Left but from within the state itself, through the Machiavellian machinations of the Nixon White House, with its use of government power to "get" its enemies. The determination of the bipartisan political elite to investigate the Watergate crimes and force Nixon from power in 1973–1974 should have shown the New Communists how resilient the system really was. By that time, they had suffered the common fate of many would-be revolutionaries. Cocooned in their collectives, schooling themselves in varieties of Marxism with little relevance to the world's most sophisticated capitalist democracy, working feverishly at small-scale local campaigns to try and build a working-class base, they lost touch with America and the pulse of history.

Despite their inability to build a new Marxist-Leninist party, the legacy of the New Communists was not entirely one of failure. Most of them took working-class jobs, on loading docks, in hospitals, in steel and auto factories, even coal mines. There they usually became the most ardent union supporters; many achieved local and later higher office in existing unions. Over the next decades, this hidden harvest of radicals contributed to moving the moribund American labor movement towards a new social consciousness and a revived commitment to organize poor people, women, immigrants, and service workers. Veterans of the New Communist Movement also played major roles in Jesse Jackson's campaigns for the presidency in 1984 and 1988, which tried to build a Rainbow Coalition as a new progressive coalition in U.S. politics.

The New Communist organizers were not the only beneficiaries of a renewed interest in socialism in the 1970s. For the first time in a generation, an ordinary person could walk down the street in a major city or a large college town and find the whole gamut of socialist and radical ideas in the hundreds of underground newspapers, coops, cafes, film series, and bookstores maintained by New Left veterans. College students could take classes across the spectrum and find Marxism and every other variety of leftist thought included in the curriculum. Millions of Americans emerged from the New Left with a susceptibility to socialism or some other form of radical change in society based on the belief that capitalism did not provide the "best of all possible worlds." Most of them stuck with the Democratic Party over the coming decades, and backed various single-issue movements that extended the New Left's legacy. In retrospect, it is hardly surprising that the New Left's multiple movements did not produce a unified political coalition, given the extreme difficulties facing anyone—right, left, or center—trying to break into the government-supported two-party system. In the absence of a new party, the New Left broke through on other fronts, in particular through its ascendancy in much of higher education.

THE LEFT ACADEMY

In the decades since the 1960s, conservatives have denounced the rise of the academic left, or the Left Academy, as some call it. Since the end of the Cold War, right-wing pundits have claimed that the only Marxists left in the world were professors in English Departments at elite American universities. Behind these sneers, however, there *is* the reality that in the New Left's wake, political and intellectual radicalism found a congenial home in many academic disciplines. Interestingly, many left-wing activists outside the academy have also been wary of the academic left.

Conservatives naturally dislike any critique of established order, and are therefore suspicious of critical intellectuals. Their attack on the Left Academy makes sense—they do not want their political opponents teaching the next generation. But the frustration of many practical leftists with professors is more complicated. Activists worry, sometimes for good reason, that the academy becomes a comfortable excuse for inactivity. Years spent in the unsupervised academic life, listening to oneself talk, can lead to self-indulgence and a lack of familiarity with the concerns of working people and the nuts-and-bolts of politics. But this suspicion of intellectuals misses the larger point. First, the fact that conservatives are deeply concerned about the large numbers of "tenured radicals" sends a clear message that teaching itself is a form of activism. There are few more powerful influences on the future of a society than committed teachers, whether their politics are right or left. The many radical scholars who have written textbooks, designed curricula, educated graduate students, and filled classrooms constitute a long-term victory for the New Left. But to understand why this is the case, we need to step back and remember what American higher education looked like, and what professors did (and did not) teach in the 1950s and 1960s.

First, outside of the historically black and women's colleges, classrooms were almost unanimously staffed by white male professors. It was front-page news in the *New York Times* in February 1956 when Brooklyn College hired the distinguished black historian, John Hope Franklin, to head its history department, since very few black scholars had ever taught at white universities. The situation was only slightly better for women academics—they were few and far between, and were usually paid less than men. They had no power in the profession, and most hiring was done informally by older men who hired younger men who were the students of other men, the proverbial "old boys' network." It was entirely possible to go through four years and receive a B.A. without ever encountering a female professor; as late as 1969, only two out of several hundred tenured professors at Harvard were female, a typical ratio. The definitions of scholarship were just as restrictive. Though the postwar years saw remarkable achievement in many academic fields in the United States, notably in the physical sciences, whole areas of intellectual inquiry were forbidden or ridiculed. In 1965, it would have been very difficult to study the long history of socialism and the wealth of Marxist theory at most colleges in the United States. It was not part of academic training in any of the relevant disciplines (economics, history, the various social sciences) and only a few dedicated scholars at places like Madison and Berkeley had the ability to teach these schools of thought. The situation was much worse for women and people of color. The terms "women's studies" or "black studies" would have been considered absurd oxymorons. In terms of the study of literature, history, art, or society itself, the majority of the world's population barely existed, except as a set of social problems. Instead, universities in the United States taught a rigorous but narrow version of the "Western tradition," which excused or ignored the existence of white supremacy, colonialism, and patriarchy.

The New Left changed all that. In the late 1960s and 1970s, radical caucuses were formed in most of the academic and professional associations, and dozens of new scholarly journals and groups sprouted, all dedicated to undermining the old orthodoxies. Thousands of former undergraduate activists returned to campus as graduate students, bringing with them radical ideas and practical experience. With remarkable speed, the academy accepted, accommodated, and in some ways surrendered to this onslaught, in part because New Left scholars pioneered innovative methodologies and were often more cosmopolitan than older professors. Activism aided scholarship, rather than detracting from it. In the aftermath of the Vietnam War, familiarity with Third World Marxism and revolutionary nationalism became an asset in the academy. As universities under pressure from WEAL's class-action suits moved to abandon the all-male premises that had kept women out, scholarly expertise in women's history and struggles acquired a certain value.

In later decades, veterans of the Left Academy took commanding positions in many disciplines. In history, for instance, many presidents of the two major professional associations since the 1970s have been eminent scholars with roots in "radical history," and the same is true for other disciplines. This has led latter-day skeptics to suggest that academic radicalism is no more than a form of careerism, but this charge is unjustified. The untenured assistant professors, graduate students, and independent scholars who created the Union for Radical Political Economics, the *Insurgent Sociologist*, the *Black Scholar*, the Marxist Literary Group, *Social Text*, *Signs*, *Feminist Studies*, the *Radical History Review*, *Radical America*, *Radical Teacher*, the North American Congress on Latin America, the Berkshire Conference on Women's History, the Center for Lesbian and Gay Studies, the Committee of Concerned Asian Scholars, the Middle East Research and Information Project, and the annual Socialist Scholars Conference in New York City believed they were waging a political struggle with real consequences for American society. The decades-long fight to erode their influence, culminating in the assault on so-called "political correctness" in the 1990s, proved them right.

THE NEWER SOCIAL MOVEMENTS

By this point, it should come as no surprise that new radical movements continued to emerge in the 1970s and 1980s, even as the New Left merged into a set of progressive institutions grouped around the Democratic Party's left wing. There had been no revolution, after all. The United States remained the greatest imperial power in world history, even if it had been severely chastened by Vietnam. European colonialism and white settler domination were still being resisted in the Third World, notably in southern Africa. At home, the gains of the New Left were under continuous attack from an increasingly assertive New Right, which since the 1960s had mounted a powerful countermobilization against the left, which brought politicians like Ronald Reagan to national prominence. And finally, new areas of concern arose, notably environmental and consumer politics.

Many of the post-1960s radical movements grew organically out of the New Left. In the 1970s, feminists in several cities decided to focus on the pervasive problem of male violence against women, and created practical responses—including houses of refuge, shelters, and help lines—to protect women when the police would not. The shelter movement rapidly institutionalized itself, spreading into hundreds of cities and towns and changing the face of "domestic relations" in America. Other feminists mobilized to change rape laws and mounted Take Back the Night marches to reclaim urban streets. On another front, veterans of the antiwar movement turned their attention to Latin America after the U.S.-backed coup in Chile, and built a solidarity movement to oppose the dictatorship of General Augusto Pinochet. This campaign evolved into a sprawling Central America movement in the 1980s, when the Reagan administration sought to refight the Vietnam War closer to home by proving it could defeat peasant-based Marxist guerrillas. Solidarity with anticolonial and liberation struggles in Africa also kept expanding, especially opposition to the white supremacist regime in South Africa, leading to a mass anti-apartheid movement in the 1980s.

Other movements that surfaced in the wake of the New Left had fewer precedents, in particular the emergence of environmentalism as one of the largest citizen movements in the nation's history, and a deep opposition to nuclear power. In the later 1970s, local direct action movements surged around nuclear power plants in New England and California, while the international organization Greenpeace pioneered a whole new mode of politics based on spectacular protest like blockading whaling ships and climbing government buildings to hang huge banners. Concerns about nuclear war also came to the fore in the late 1970s, leading to the vast Nuclear Freeze campaign of the 1980s. Consumer rights became a new cause linked to environmentalism, led in large part by the group of organizations created by Ralph Nader, such as Public Citizen and the Public Interest Research Groups. Following a nationwide Earth Day in 1970, and the passage of watershed environmental legislation in the early 1970s, traditional conservation groups like the Sierra Club grew enormously, and were joined by thousands of new environmental organizations at the local, state, and national levels focused on everything from enforcing clean air standards to blocking oil drilling in the Arctic National Wildlife Refuge. Former Activists from SDS's community-organizing wing built huge professional apparatuses based on door-to-door canvassing, like Citizen Action. Veterans of civil rights and Black Power campaigns converged in the 1980s in the Rainbow Coalition led by the Reverend Jesse Jackson, the most significant demonstration of left-wing strength within national electoral politics in the latter half of the twentieth century.

The proliferation of new movements in the 1970s and 1980s is the best evidence of the New Left's lasting success. To reignite passions, recruit new supporters, and raise money, activists instinctively built upon its legacy, evoking Vietnam and the antiwar struggle, the moral dignity of civil rights, the pre–*Roe v. Wade* era of women's subordination, Stonewall, and other watersheds. During the so-called Reagan Revolution of the 1980s, they helped animate a vigorous opposition, even if the power of these tropes later faded, so that by the 1990s they seemed distant and attenuated.

GREENING AMERICA: THE SIGNIFICANCE OF
THE COUNTERCULTURE

Just about everyone knows there was once something called "the counterculture." The 1960s are indelibly associated with images of carefree white youth,
"hippies" and "freaks" dressed in old clothes, with long wild hair and happy
stoned smiles, dancing spasmodically to loud music or gazing off into space.
Often this emphasis on the hippies distorts our understanding of the New
Left, especially when music videos mix up Beatles album covers with antiwar
marches, or combine Jimi Hendrix setting fire to his guitar with footage of the
Black Panthers. Politics becomes a series of visual clichés; jumbling together
the counterculture and the radical movements reinforces the myth that the
New Left was mostly a temporary upsurge by bored, self-indulgent white
kids. The counterculture was never synonymous with the broader New Left—
how could it be, if the New Left was in large part led by people of color?—yet
there were clearly links between them. For millions of people, by no means all
young or all white, the first step towards political involvement was a token of
stylistic dissent like unkempt hair or strange clothes, which visibly separated
the wearer from the dominant pattern in his or her neighborhood or school.
This was especially true for people who lived outside of the cities and college
towns where radicalism flourished.

The popular image of the counterculture actually covers only the period
from roughly 1965 to 1973, during which a significant fraction of the white
youth population publicly rejected their parents' whole way of life. These
were the years when hundreds and then thousands gathered in San
Francisco's Haight-Ashbury neighborhood, New York's Lower East Side, and
other cheap, funky urban settings. They spawned a dropout, casual community, based upon the use of psychedelic drugs, that was imitated across the
country. By 1969, the hippie (now called "freak") way of life had spread so
widely that it resulted in a great tribal gathering, the Woodstock Music
Festival of Peace and Love in upstate New York. The Haight, San Francisco's
Summer of Love in 1967, and Woodstock were key markers of the counterculture, but the movement (if we can call it that) was much larger and more
diffuse, and lasted considerably longer than recognized in the conventional
story, well into the later 1970s in some places. It also had connections to the
rural communalism, and a fascination with spiritual and narcotic exploration
that have surfaced repeatedly in America since the eighteenth century.

While they seemed at the time a spontaneous phenomenon, the hippies
and freaks actually had deep roots extending back into the 1940s and 1950s,
and in some cases much further. Each of the major practices associated with
the late 1960s—anarchist communes, experimentation with mind-altering

substances, the exploration of non-European spirituality, the development of alternative technologies and design principles to simplify life—had precedents in the diverse bohemian subcultures that percolated beneath the surface of American culture after 1945. Beyond these direct antecedents, the counterculture of the late 1960s benefited from a slew of changes in American culture and social arrangements between 1945 and 1965. While the middlebrow culture of television shows, magazines, movies, and newspapers remained staid and cautious, there was remarkable dynamism in the various artistic avant-gardes, from abstract painting to modernist jazz and experimental theater and dance companies. Long-existing legal restrictions on sexuality, from the sale of contraceptives to the distribution of books by authors like Henry Miller and William Burroughs, were successfully challenged in court. Above all, the nexus of expansive consumerism and great social mobility proved remarkably conducive to the incubation of the various scenes and subcultures that fed into the mass "counterculture" after 1965—not just the Beats, folkies, and hipsters, but also the rock'n'rollers, so-called juvenile delinquents or "punks," and surfers.

None of these points of origin was political, however, in any obvious sense. What brought them together as a politicized counterculture was a remarkable convergence of larger social, demographic, economic, and political factors between 1964 and 1966. At the peak of the postwar economic boom, a rising tide of young people assumed enormous weight as consumers, taking over mass popular culture in highly visible ways. By 1965 this demographic fact had such revolutionary implications that one major magazine called it the "Youthquake." Young people assumed a dominant position, in terms of buying power and style. Everyone wanted to be young, acting young and aping youthfulness—what a recent historian has labeled a "culture of rejuvenation" that was underlined by the dynamic, casual charm of the youngest president in U.S. history, John F. Kennedy (a trim, handsome forty-three at the time of his election), and his beautiful, cultured thirty-one-year-old wife Jackie.

By itself, an exaltation of youthfulness was hardly enough to produce a counterculture that rejected wholesale the benefits and privileges of adult power and authority. The startling development was that in vast numbers this wave of youth articulated a passionate desire for something different than what they were offered by the Affluent Society. The word they used to describe their desire was "authentic," meaning a passion for the real and natural rather than the processed and synthetic. Authenticity was what they found absent in the grand new suburbs and the great new "multiversities," and their anguish made figures like Mario Savio a hero. The search for it drove them to experiment with extremely powerful, consciousness-shattering psychedelics, to find a truer self. It motivated their move back into old rundown city neighborhoods like Haight-Ashbury, and then back to the land in thousands of remote rural communes. It explained their cult of simplicity, the contempt for "plastic people, plastic shoes" as a famous Mothers of Invention song put it. It led to their dispensing with suits, ties, haircuts, wingtips, bouffant hairdos, makeup, girdles, and bras in favor of "natural" hair and "natural" (as in unshaven, often unclean, and certainly undeodorized) bodies; squares' obsession with the hippies' dirtiness was mirrored by the ways in which many really did revel in being shaggy and naturally smelly.

Even more than authenticity, however, what the hippies (and their successors, the freaks) wanted above all was to play. In a society that glorified work and responsibility, getting ahead and getting things, they wanted laughter and make-believe and showing off. They played at everything—at being farmers, at being Indians or cowboys or frontiersmen, at being guerrillas and criminals and clowns. The entire counterculture, even at its most serious moments, resembled a great circus or playpen where grown-up children milled around in cast-off costumes. This extraordinary pastiche of images and styles was empowering—you could be Geronimo in the morning, and Davy Crockett in the afternoon—but had severe limitations. As with Peter Pan, the counterculturalists were left proclaiming they would never grow up, even as the world around them changed.

The flowering of hippie culture from 1965 on was driven by larger political and cultural dynamics. It is hardly accidental that it came at the culmination of ten years of mass protest against the institutions of white supremacy and racial segregation. Black activists offered an alternative vision of America, and also a powerful example of authenticity, of acting on one's beliefs. At precisely the same time, the Vietnam War began polarizing American society along generational lines. New drugs (in particular LSD) and new cultural forms (the serious rock band that was capable of powerful popular art, exemplified by the Beatles) appeared in this same moment, further catalyzing the sense of a wholly new way for young people to live their lives. Within only a few years, it seemed as if a significant segment of young white people had become profoundly alienated from the American Dream of stable, homeowning consumer abundance.

To the extent that the counterculture was premised on drugs, orgiastic play, mind-expansion, and free-floating anarchy, everyone doing their own thing, it really was *anti*-political. When Timothy Leary encouraged people to "tune in, turn on and drop out," he was pointing the hippies away from revolution and protest, in the direction of New Age spiritualism and the obsession with "personal growth" that has characterized parts of the white middle-class since the 1960s. The counterculture became, briefly, a political as well as a cultural movement because of the almost hysterical hostility of government

apparatuses and most of the adult, square society, so memorably characterized by Richard Nixon as "the silent majority." Loudly and angrily, cops,
teachers, politicians, and parents all agreed that simple differences in personal
style constituted a deliberate challenge to morality and good order—that
growing one's hair long or uttering a word like "fuck" or smoking marijuana
was political dissent. At the height of the Vietnam War, drawn-out legal
battles were fought out in high schools across the United States over a boy's
right to grow his hair over his ears. When those battles ended in the early
1970s with a general relaxation of the standards of personal appearance,
speech, and consumption, the counterculture lost its political edge—and
indeed, in large part ceased to exist, merging into American society in much
the way the New Left's movements did. Before that, however, for a few years
in the late 1960s, many adults saw the hippies as a threat akin to the Black
Panthers or SDS.

The spectacularly successful 1969 movie *Easy Rider* underlines how the
counterculture played off potent images of youth rebellion, escape, and
martyrdom, with politics that were at best ambiguous. Produced for about
$400,000, it earned over $40 million, defining a whole new kind of Hollywood
system of independent moviemakers. Its plot was simple: a couple of hippie
drug dealers had made a big score, and set off from Los Angeles on their
customized motorcycles, planning to end up in New Orleans and party at
Mardi Gras. On the way, they rested at a desert commune and ran into
dangerous rednecks. On a road in the Deep South, just after the lead character,
Captain America (played by the glamorous Peter Fonda) tells his partner Billy
(played by the dissolute, mustachioed Dennis Hopper) that "we blew it,"
some guys in a pickup blow them away with a shotgun, for no reason other
than what they look like.

Easy Rider expressed (and fomented) the perception that by their very
existence, the freaks were challenging society, or creating something new. The
overall feeling was memorably surreal and grim, as if everything one knew
had been thrown open to question, captured in the advertising slogan was
"A man went looking for America and couldn't find it anywhere." Its politics
were mostly about style, about being, rather than doing. For some, that was
not enough.

Within the amorphous counterculture, which touched the lives of
millions, there were two distinct efforts to develop a new kind of activism.
The first involved a series of once-famous groups: San Francisco's Diggers,
who treated the Haight itself as a stage for utopian political action, giving
away food and taking over the streets for communal rituals; New York's
Yippies, a Digger spinoff, discussed in chapter 8; Detroit's White Panther
Party, who sponsored a famously fierce rock band, the MC5, but also planned

for guerrilla warfare. Each of these groups hoped to make the outlaw status of the counterculture the base for a genuine revolution, peaceful or otherwise. Though they provided some of the most evocative moments of the late 1960s, remarkable pieces of guerrilla theater, all of them failed. A politics based on "sex, drugs, and rock'n'roll" and "fucking in the streets," as White Panther leader John Sinclair put it, only had meaning as long as those activities were repressed and stigmatized. By the mid-1970s straight America had absorbed much of the hippies' style and habits, and being a freak or a longhair no longer meant much; millions "partied" and used drugs, as we know from the later admissions of presidential candidates, congressional leaders, and Supreme Court nominees. Even before then, however, the Diggers and the Yippies had been forced to acknowledge that many of the hippies really did just want to turn on and drop out, and regarded revolutionary politics as a drag.

The spectacular and sometimes goofy escapades of Abbie Hoffman, Jerry Rubin, or John Sinclair were only one version of countercultural politics, however. Less dramatically, an ideology and practice emerged in the late 1960s with greater long-term salience. Epitomized by the remarkably success- ful *Whole Earth Catalogue*, a group of original thinkers that included Stewart Brand and Steve Jobs pioneered a new way of life based around environmen- tal stewardship, the ideas of visionary thinkers like Buckminster Fuller, and "alternative technology." Eschewing revolution, they hoped to render corpo- rate capitalism obsolete via new, low-cost energy sources and personalized information technology. Owning a desktop-size personal computer was then an idea straight out of science fiction: now it's part of ordinary existence. This pragmatic brand of "lifestyle politics" put down deep roots in later decades, moving into the mainstream via organized environmentalism and a wide range of new cultural practices, from organic food production to recycling to, eventually, the epochal changes in social organization and economic life that we associate with the Internet.

Any discussion of the counterculture is complicated by its porous borders. In 1968 was every boy with shaggy, bushy hair, or every girl with patched jeans and granny glasses, or every student who secretly smoked dope or dropped a tab of LSD, a member of the counterculture? Did you have to move to the Haight or a commune to be a real "freak," or did all the little groups of longhairs in small towns across America who bought beads and clay pipes at their local "headshop" and read R. Crumb "comix" also qualify? Ultimately, what mattered most was how you were seen, rather than how you saw your- self: a longhaired boy or girl in jeans might be unremarkable in New York or San Francisco, but would immediately be labeled a "hippie" in rural Indiana or Alabama, and suffer the consequences.

There are many reasons why it is hard to pin down what was "political" about the counterculture, other than the shared sense of acting outside established norms (and outside the law, given how central illegal drugs were to countercultural practice). The most distinctive feature of each of the New Left's political movements was how they related to and managed to force change upon institutions of political power. The most distinctive feature of the white youth counterculture was that despite its very real sense of rejecting mainstream society, it was simultaneously embedded within a commercialized, intensely capitalist popular culture. This connection was most obvious in the ways that extraordinarily successful performers like the Beatles, the Rolling Stones, Bob Dylan, the Doors, the Grateful Dead, Jefferson Airplane, Cream, and Jimi Hendrix were all seen as generational heroes, even while they generated enormous profits for a handful of large corporations like CBS, Warner Brothers, and Capitol Records. The music was the wedge that opened up a whole world of merchandizing and fashion plus other media (movies like *Easy Rider*, magazines like *Rolling Stone*, plays like *Hair*, "album-oriented" FM stations), led by a dynamic stratum of "hip capitalists" who were just as important to the Haight and other hippie enclaves as any political activist. Looking back, some argue that the counterculture's largest political effect may have been to serve as the vehicle linking radical style to the world of commerce—making the New Left hip, or "the conquest of cool," as Thomas Frank put it in a book with that title, arguing that "from its very beginnings down to the present, business dogged the counterculture with a fake counterculture, a commercial replica that seemed to ape its every move for the titillation of the TV-watching millions and the nation's corporate sponsors."

It is much too easy, however, to suggest that the counterculture was merely a stage in the development of niche marketing, and its politics were mainly self-delusion. Powerful figures like Nixon and J. Edgar Hoover, and the tens of millions of people they spoke to and for, took it very seriously. One incident, documented over the decades by the historian Jon Wiener, who forced the FBI to release its massive files on John Lennon (made possible by the Freedom of Information Act, another legislative milestone of the early 1970s), demonstrates the potential power of a "counter" popular culture allied with radicalism. Lennon was always thoroughly conscious of his working-class roots, and moved towards a committed leftist politics in the late 1960s. As the 1972 election approached, he decided to organize a series of concerts to mobilize the new crop of eighteen-year-old voters to vote Nixon out. Lennon managed one concert in December 1971 at the University of Michigan, with Stevie Wonder, Allen Ginsberg, and leading folk and jazz performers. The Justice Department immediately began deportation proceedings against him, which dragged on for eighteen months.

Lennon was a serious artist, not just a rock star. His words and actions had unique weight because he was both. Few embraced the left as deeply as he and his partner Yoko Ono—their 1972 album, *Sometime in New York City*, included songs about John Sinclair (jailed on a drug charge, a common plight of radicals), Angela Davis, the Attica rebellion, and a British massacre of peaceful protesters in Northern Ireland, as well as his still-shocking "Woman is the Nigger of the World." But in different ways, the major musicians, writers, and artists associated with the transatlantic counterculture were authentically *critical* intellectuals. By their stance and their work, they suggested the necessity of dissent, and the imperative of personal honesty. When Bob Dylan put out singles about George Jackson, and the Rolling Stones sang about war, rape, and murder in "Gimme Shelter," and Jim Morrison shouted about breaking on through, and Janis Joplin keened about freedom and loss in "Me and Bobby McGee," and Neil Young mourned the Kent State murders in "Ohio," and Jimi Hendrix turned the "Star-Spangled Banner" into a symphony of dissonant noise, these were hardly the conventional romantic narratives of traditional popular music. For a few years at least, the counterculture in all its dressed-up, trippy excess suggested that the old world was thoroughly corrupt, and that a revolution and a new world were just around the corner. That was and is a dangerous idea.

SUMMING UP: A NEW DEMOCRATIC ORDER EMERGES

Historians describe the political consensus that was born in the 1930s and matured during World War II and the early Cold War years, led by a Democratic Party organized around tax-and-spend liberalism, as the *New Deal Order*. This is a useful way to understand the premises and institutions of Cold War liberalism. The victory of the New Left was to undermine that consensus by forcefully asserting the presence and rights of whole classes of excluded people, who together comprised the majority of American society: women; people of color; gays and lesbians; leftists and bohemians of every stripe. The battles and concessions gained by the various movements in the 1960s and early 1970s constituted a new set of premises and institutions, a *New Democratic Order*, in which racial domination, male supremacy, normative heterosexuality, and mandatory patriotism could be challenged not only in the streets, but in the courts, legislatures, classrooms, and businesses.

In this sense, in terms of its accomplishments, the New Left never ended. Rather, it became part of everyday political life, and that was its greatest success. Protest rallies and civil disobedience actions became normal, even commonplace events; avowing a radical viewpoint was no longer cause for losing one's job and social ostracization; sanctions against racial and gender discrimination were not only legislated but could be enforced. The complacent, self-enclosed world of Cold War America, with its refusal to acknowledge the sweeping oppression faced by many Americans, was broken into pieces. In its place, a decentered, fractured society emerged, with no consensus—just a simmering, bitter "cultural war," as angry conservatives like Patrick Buchanan liked to call it in the 1980s and 1990s.

But the New Left's many movements could hardly claim total victory for the radical reforms they had won, and the cultural revolutions they had launched. Too many men and women among the white, heterosexual majority were hostile to the left's critiques of American power and its demands for equality based on legally enforceable rights. From their commitment to an older racial and sexual order, a deep-seated anticommunism, and hostility to "big government," a New Right movement surged forward in the 1970s. This new breed of radical conservatives built their own "movement of movements" around intense opposition to abortion, school integration, affirmative action, gay rights, the "giveaway" of the Panama Canal, gun control, pornography, bilingual education, sex education, and much more. Demonstrating an unswerving dedication to electoral politics, over several decades the New Right has taken over the Republican Party and steadily encroached on every level of government, from local school boards to the federal judiciary. The result was the so-called Reagan Revolution of the 1980s, extended by Newt Gingrich and others in the 1990s, and brought to its fullest expression under George W. Bush—an unrelenting assault upon the twentieth century's entire legacy of reform, whether under radical or liberal auspices, from its origins in the Progressive Era through the New Deal to the New Left and the 1960s.

The lasting paradox of the New Left is that it made the United States a much more democratic and egalitarian country, while at the same time inequality greatly increased in America. During the 1980s and 1990s, a massive restructuring of postindustrial capitalism shifted wealth towards the top third of the populace, especially the top 2 or 3 percent, while the lower third became much poorer, and those in the middle worked much harder just to stay in place. A whole new class of the super-rich came into existence in Reagan's America, while millions of high-wage unionized factory jobs were exported overseas, and the ranks of poorly paid service workers, often immigrants and women, swelled. Many working-class white men who had lost those good jobs became susceptible to right-wing appeals to blame someone—blacks, immigrants, feminists, gays—for their predicament. These "Reagan Democrats" combined with the defection of the formerly Democratic white South and the rise of a new conservative suburban middle class to provide the votes behind the Republican takeover of much of the government apparatus. Only a steadily increasing number of voters among people of color, and the so-called "gender gap" (that roughly half of white women kept voting Democratic, versus overwhelmingly Republican white men), kept the Democrats competitive. Overshadowing this grinding electoral stalemate was a deep alienation from politics among whole sectors of the electorate, as the percentage of eligible voters who actually voted dropped consistently below 50 percent in the 1990s.

More equal *and* increasing inequality? More democracy *and* greater alienation from politics? This was the topsy-turvy world of post-1960s, postmodern America, and the movements and ideologies focused on the old Cold War America had few answers. The New Left and its political descendants had made cogent critiques of racism, imperialism, and sexism, but they had no coherent alternative to the extraordinarily sophisticated, rationalized world of global corporate capitalism, and its ability to provide genuine abundance to large numbers of people while impoverishing many more. The end result in the 1990s was Bill Clinton, whose political roots were in the antiwar movement. He embraced moderate versions of feminism and gay rights, spoke passionately about racial justice, and defended affirmative action—all the while using Republican votes in Congress to advance a rigorous "free trade" agenda on behalf of multinational interests and his backers on Wall Street.

Early in the twenty-first century, two Americas remain locked in a political and cultural stalemate over the victories of the New Left, while a new generation born in the 1980s find it hard to believe that within living memory people could be denied the vote because of their skin color, or a job because of their gender, or locked up simply because they loved others of their own sex. In that sense, the movements of the New Left are part of a much longer tradition of fighting for democracy, to make a reality of the principle on which the United States was founded, that all people are created equal, equally endowed by their creator with the same inalienable rights to life, liberty, and the pursuit of happiness. As long as the promise of American democracy remains unfulfilled, that struggle is fated to continue.

A Selected Bibliography

This essay is a guide to some important sources I consulted in framing each chapter's narrative. It is in no way definitive; for a more complete examination of the historiography and a comprehensive bibliography (as of 2000), see Van Gosse, "A Movement of Movements: The Definition and Periodization of the New Left," in Roy Rosenzweig and Jean-Christophe Agnew, eds., *A Companion to Post-1945 America-* (London: Blackwell, 2002), pp. 277–302. I also note that the larger international context for the U.S. New Left is only occasionally evoked in this narrative, both for reasons of space and because it is still a very incomplete body of scholarship. Two very different books that an interested reader should consult are Arthur Marwick, *The Sixties: Cultural Revolution in Britain, France, Italy, and the United States, c.1958–c.1974* (New York: Oxford University Press, 1998) and Jeremi Suri, *Power and Protest: Global Revolution and the Rise of Detente* (Cambridge: Harvard University Press, 2003).

Chapter 1

The scholarship that identifies the New Left with white student radicalism, and in particular SDS, is ably represented by three influential books that came out in the same year: Todd Gitlin, *The Sixties: Years of Hope, Days of Rage* (New York: Bantam Books, 1987); Maurice Isserman, *If I Had a Hammer: The Death of the Old Left and the Birth of the New Left* (New York: Basic Books, 1987); and James Miller, *"Democracy is in the Streets": From Port Huron to the Siege of Chicago* (New York: Simon and Schuster, 1987). In "A Movement of Movements: The Definition and Periodization of the New Left," I trace how earlier definitions of the New Left were more ecumenical and inclusive, citing books such as Paul Jacobs and Saul Landau, *The New Radicals: A Report with Documents* (New York: Random House, 1966) and Jack Newfield, *A Prophetic Minority* (New York: New American Library, 1966). It should be noted, however, that my insistence on the multi-generational character of the New Left, and refusal to equate it with what C. Wright Mills called a "young left," is in some ways *sui generis*. It derives from narratives like those of Dorothy Day and the Catholic Worker movement, as chronicled by James T. Fisher, *The Catholic Counterculture in America, 1933–1962* (Chapel Hill: University of North Carolina Press, 1989), and the stories of local struggle led by black mothers and their children, as traced in Charles Payne, *I've Got the Light of Freedom: The Organizing Tradition and the Mississippi Freedom Struggle* (Berkeley: University of California Press, 1995).

My overall understanding of the New Left remains strongly shaped by Sara Evans, *Personal Politics: The Origins of Women's Liberation in the Civil Rights Movement and the New Left* (New York: Alfred A. Knopf, 1979) because of its focus on the connections between different movements over time, including the continuity between earlier traditions, such as Christian social action, and newer movements beginning in the later 1950s. Years ago, I read Lawrence Wittner, *Cold War America: From Hiroshima to Watergate* (New York: Holt, Rinehart and Winston, 1978), and its utility as a framing device stayed with me—a long periodization of the post-1945 period that moves the reader beyond simplistic dividing lines between "the Fifties" and "the Sixties." Around the same time, I was deeply influenced by Manning Marable's *Race, Reform, and Rebellion: The Second Reconstruction in Black America, 1945–1990* (Jackson: University of Mississippi, 1991), both because of its periodization that connects a "Second Reconstruction," beginning in the 1940s, with the revolution and counter-revolution of the 1870s, and his biting characterization of a bipartisan Cold War liberalism that encompassed Truman, Eisenhower, Kennedy, Johnson and Nixon. Marable's *Black American Politics: From the Washington Marches to Jesse Jackson* (London: Verso, 1985) complements this general history with deeper analytical essays that again stress the breadth of a struggle extending from the 1940s to the 1980s. The historiography of the post-1945 period is vast and ever-growing, and these references are intended to show how I arrived at a New Left that extends across the post-1945 period rather than being an episode of the mythic and mystified 1960s.

Chapter 2

William Chafe, *The Unfinished Journey: America Since World War II*, 4th ed. (New York: Oxford University Press, 1999) is the best general history of the postwar decades, and is effectively complemented by the essays in Steve Fraser and Gary Gerstle, eds., *The Rise and Fall of the New Deal Order, 1930–1980* (Princeton: Princeton University Press, 1989), which demonstrate the particular class character and limitations of the New Deal Coalition as it evolved from the 1930s to the 1960s. Thomas Sugrue, *The Origins of the Urban Crisis: Race and Inequality in Postwar Detroit* (Princeton: Princeton University Press, 1996) is indispensable to getting at the fragility of Cold War liberalism, and its inability to acknowledge the consequences of both deindustrialization and racial polarization well before the "white backlash" of the 1960s, which has long been used by some journalists and scholars to put the onus for New Right's electoral success on the supposed excesses of the black freedom movement.

Of course, there is a vast corpus of work examining the Cold War itself. I find Thomas McCormick, *America's Half-Century: United States Foreign Policy in the Cold War and After* (Baltimore: Johns Hopkins University Press, 1995) most convincing, in his refusal to accept that the anti-Communist (or anti-Soviet) imperative was the central dynamic undergirding the United States' rise to global domination. On the domestic front, Elaine Tyler May, *Homeward Bound: American Families in the Cold War Era* (New York: Basic Books, 1988) is the classic study of how a new sexual ideology, intensely familist and pro-natalist, was closely connected to the larger imperatives of the Cold War. A terrific contrast is provided by Lisa McGirr, *Suburban Warriors: The Origins of the New American Right* (Princeton: Princeton University Press, 2001), which examines the political economy, social spaces and ideology of the new world of southern California, and how it birthed a movement opposed to every manifestation of the New Left.

The Red Scare has many chroniclers, but the definitive history is Ellen Schrecker, *Many Are the Crimes: McCarthyisms in America* (Boston: Little Brown, 1998). David Oshinsky, *A Conspiracy So Immense: The World of Joe McCarthy* (New York: Free Press, 1983) helps one understand McCarthyism itself, and why it was so effective. Harvey Levenstein, *Communism, Anti-Communism, and the CIO* (Westport, CT: Greenwood Press, 1981) is particularly acute regarding the intense battles within organized labor, and Philip Jenkins, *The Cold War at Home: The Red Scare in Pennsylvania* (Chapel Hill: University of North Carolina Press, 1999) is a model local study. Norman Markowitz, *The Rise and Fall of the People's Century: Henry A. Wallace and American Liberalism, 1941–1948* (New York: Free Press, 1973) remains invaluable in understanding the disastrous Progressive Party campaign of 1948 and the lost ethos of New Deal leftism. For anyone who wants to explore the depth and complexity of the Popular Front, Michael Denning, *The Cultural Front: Laboring of American Culture in the Twentieth-Century* (London: Verso, 1996) is key.

World War II is more and more understood as a pivot point in American politics, enacting social and demographic (and ideological) shifts that pointed towards the rise of new social movements. Important books which highlight this point of origin include John D'Emilio, *Sexual Politics, Sexual Communities: The Making of a Homosexual Minority in the United States, 1940–1970* (Chicago: University of Chicago Press, 1983), Mario T. Garcia, *Mexican Americans: Leadership, Ideology and Identity, 1930–1960* (New Haven, Conn.: Yale University Press, 1989) and Patricia Sullivan, *Days of Hope: Race and Democracy in the New Deal Era* (Chapel Hill: University of North Carolina Press, 1996), as well as Sugrue's *The Origins of the Urban Crisis*, and others listed later.

Chapter 3

Anyone trying to excavate the myriad strands of what we lump together as the Old Left is well-advised to consult Mari Jo Buhle, Paul Buhle, and Dan Georgakas, eds., *The Encyclopedia of the American Left* (New York: Oxford University Press, 1998), an extraordinary resource on the immigrant anarchists, Socialists and Communists who filled up America's cities from the late nineteenth century on. Paul Buhle, *Marxism in the United States: Remapping the History of the American Left* (London: Verso, 1991) is an important intellectual history. For a broad narrative centered on the American radical tradition from the Revolution on by the historian who has done the most to define it, see Eric Foner, *The Story of American Freedom* (New York: W.W. Norton, 1998).

I would argue that the "black protest tradition," as Manning Marable dubbed it, is the central current in American politics, even before the Civil War, so this essay can only point at some of the monuments of an extraordinary edifice of scholarship developed largely since the 1960s, one result of the liberatory movements of that time. Louis Harlan, *Booker T. Washington: The Making of a Black Leader, 1856–1901* (New York: Oxford University Press, 1973) and *Booker T. Washington: The Wizard of Tuskegee, 1901–1915* (New York: Oxford University Press, 1983) and David Levering Lewis, *W. E. B. Du Bois: Biography of a Race, 1868–1919* (New York: Henry Holt, 1993) and *W. E. B. Du Bois: The Fight For Equality and the American Century, 1919–1963* (New York: Henry Holt, 2000) frame two of the three major strategies developed after Reconstruction. It is difficult to name a single book that adequately captures the distinctiveness of Garveyism, but the reader should consult Edmund David Cronon, *Black Moses: The Story of Marcus Garvey and the Universal Negro Improvement Association* (Madison: University of Wisconsin Press, 1969), Theodore Vincent, *Black Power and the Garvey Movement* (Berkeley: Ramparts Press, 1971), Judith Stein, *The World of Marcus Garvey: Race and Class in Modern Society* (Baton Rouge: Louisiana State University Press, 1986), Wilson Jeremiah Moses, *Classical Black Nationalism: From the American Revolution to Marcus Garvey* (New York: New York University Press, 1996) and Winston James, *Holding Aloft the Banner of Ethiopia: Caribbean Radicalism in America, 1900–1932* (London: Verso, 1997). To understand how black politics moved forward within the larger context of the New Deal, Nancy Weiss, *Farewell to the Party of Lincoln: Black Politics in the Age of FDR* (Princeton: Princeton University Press, 1983) is foundational.

American Communism cannot be understood without the exceptional if deeply anti-communist scholarship of Theodore Draper in *The Roots of American Communism* (New York: Viking Press, 1957) and *American Communism and Soviet Russia* (New York: Viking Press, 1960). Draper's neoconservative epigones like John Earl Haynes and Harvey Klehr have merely added to his argument with their work in the American Party archives discovered in the former Soviet Union. Two books stand out as offering a different view, concerned not with the Party's relationship with the Soviet Union but with its role in American life: Mark Naison, *The Communist Party in Harlem During the Depression* (Urbana: University of Illinois, 1983), and Robin D. G. Kelley, *Hammer and Hoe: Alabama Communists During the Great Depression* (Chapel Hill: University of North California Press, 1990). It is not incidental that both of these books, as well as more recent books like Penny Von Eschen, *Race Against Empire: Black Americans and Anti-Colonialism, 1937–1957* (Cornell: Cornell University Press, 1997), and Martha Biondi, *To Stand and Fight: The Struggle for Civil Rights in Postwar New York City* (Cambridge: Harvard University Press, 2003), focus on the base that the CPUSA established in Black America. To these should be added the prolific scholarship of Gerald Horne—too many books to list here, but also vital for understanding the Black Left and the Communist Party from the 1930s to the 1950s.

There is a voluminous literature tracing the rise and fall of the left-led unions. In particular, one should examine Roger Keeran, *The Communist Party and the Auto Workers Unions* (Bloomington: Indiana University Press, 1980), Ronald Filippelli, *Cold War in the Working Class: The Rise and Decline of the United Electrical Workers* (Albany: State University of New York Press, 1995), Bruce Nelson, *Workers on the Waterfront: Seamen, Longshoremen, and Unionism in the 1930s* (Urbana: University of Illinois Press, 1988), Roger Horowitz, *"Negro and White, Unite and Fight!": A Social History of Industrial Unionism in Meatpacking, 1930–90* (Urbana: University of Illinois, 1997). Very useful for tying up this history is Steven Rosswurm, ed., *The CIO's Left-Led Unions* (New Brunswick: Rutgers University Press, 1992). An especially notable recent work, however, is one that connects the left, labor, and the struggle against Jim Crow in a quintessential New South city, Michael Honey, *Southern Labor and Black Civil Rights: Organizing Memphis Workers* (Urbana: University of Illinois Press, 1993). Very little has been written about the gender politics of the Communist Left, but the interested reader should consult Kate Weigand, *Red Feminism: American Communists and the Making of Women's Liberation* (Baltimore: Johns Hopkins University Press, 2001), Rosalyn Baxandall, ed., *Words On Fire: The Life and Writings of Elizabeth Gurley Flynn* (New Brunswick: Rutgers University Press, 1987), and Dorothy Healey with Maurice Isserman, *California Red: A Life in the American Communist Party* (Urbana: University of Illinois Press, 1993). Finally, a unique vantage point on the Communist Party is afforded by two biographies of its single most important leader, Edward Johanningsmeier, *Forging American Communism: The Life of William Z. Foster* (Princeton: Princeton University Press, 1994) and James R. Barrett, *William Z. Foster and the Tragedy of American Radicalism* (Urbana: University of Illinois, 1999).

Regarding the Socialist, Trotskyist (in particular, Shachtmanite) and, to a lesser extent, pacifist constituencies in the 1940s and 1950s, Isserman's *If I Had a Hammer* is quite useful. Amid the vast literature on the older socialist movement, Mari Jo Buhle, *Women and American Socialism, 1870–1920* (Urbana: University of Illinois, 1982) stands out, as does James Weinstein, *The Decline of Socialism in America, 1912–1925* (New York: Monthly Review Press, 1967). Nelson Lichtenstein, *Labor's War at Home: The CIO in World War II* (Cambridge: Cambridge University Press, 1982), examines the wartime strikes led by Trotskyists during World War II, among other developments. For reasons that remain unclear, most of the historiography of American Trotskyism focuses on intellectuals. Christopher Phelps, *Young Sidney Hook: Marxist and Pragmatist* (Ithaca: Cornell University Press, 1997) and Alan Wald, *The New York Intellectuals: The Rise and Decline of the Anti-Stalinist Left from the 1930s to the 1980s* (Chapel Hill: University of North Carolina, 1987) are central to this historiography. An important overview is George Breitman, Paul Le Blanc, and Alan Wald, *Trotskyism in the United States: Historical Essays and Reconsiderations* (Atlantic Highlands, N.J.: Humanities Press, 1996). To understand the larger ethos of the anti-communist left, and its most impressive leader, see Nelson Lichtenstein, *The Most Dangerous Man in Detroit: Walter Reuther and the Fate of American Labor* (New York: Basic Books, 1995).

On the pacifist tradition, Lawrence Wittner, *Rebels Against War: The American Peace Movement, 1933–1983* (Philadelphia: Temple University Press, 1984), is a good one-volume history. For greater depth, one should consult the scholarship of Charles Chatfield, beginning with *For Peace and Justice: Pacifism in America, 1914–1941* (Knoxville: University of Tennessee, 1971). To understand the connections between peace activism in the 1930s, 1940s and 1950s, it is crucial to read Jo Ann Ooiman Robinson, *Abraham Went Out: A Biography of A. J. Muste* (Philadelphia: Temple University Press, 1981), since Muste was the great bridging figure. Otherwise, the various writings by and biographies of Bayard Rustin are helpful, in particular John D'Emilio, *Lost Prophet: The Life and Times of Bayard Rustin* (New York: Free Press, 2003). Another key individual who awaits a major biography is Dave Dellinger; see his own *From Yale to Jail: The Life Story of a Moral Dissenter* (New York: Pantheon Books, 1993).

Chapter 4

The historiography on the Civil Rights movement is monumental, so I will simply indicate some books that directly contributed to this chapter, beyond those already listed that trace its roots in the 1930s and 1940s. Of all the general histories, I prefer Steven Lawson, *Running for Freedom: Civil Rights and Black Politics in America Since 1941* (New York: McGraw Hill, 1997) because of its chronological breadth, and attention to partisan dynamics. On Dr. King and SCLC, David Garrow, *Bearing the Cross: Martin Luther King, Jr., and the Southern Christian Leadership Conference* (New York: Random House, 1986), pays particular attention to organizational matters. Clayborne Carson, *In Struggle: SNCC and the Black Awakening of the 1960s* (Cambridge, Mass.: Harvard University Press, 1981) remains essential, both in its focus on ideology and the connections it makes between civil rights and the emerging Black Power movement. August Meier and Elliott

Rudwick, *CORE: A Study of the Civil Rights Movement, 1942–1968* (Urbana: University of Illinois Press, 1975) is the most complete organizational history, if undeservedly forgotten, like its subject.

Newer scholarship has broadened our understanding of the international reach of the civil rights (or black freedom) movement, and its profound internal tensions. In this regard, Timothy B. Tyson, *Radio Free Dixie: Robert F. Williams and the Roots of Black Power* (Chapel Hill: University of North Carolina Press, 1999) has been very influential, since Williams was the self-conscious alternative to both Dr. King's nonviolent strategy and the NAACP's institutional leadership. Mary Dudziak, *Cold War Civil Rights: Race and the Image of American Democracy* (Princeton: Princeton University Press, 2000) emphasizes the degree to which the imperatives of anti-communist containment shaped the discourse of the movement, and in turn created opportunities for it. Another important new book is Barbara Ransby, *Ella Baker and the Black Freedom Movement: A Radical Democratic Vision* (Chapel Hill: University of North Carolina Press, 2003), since Baker's articulation of a grassroots approach deeply influenced the entire movement.

A handful of first-rate local studies greatly deepen our understanding of how the Civil Rights movement was really many movements, with profound differences depending on the political economy, existing pattern of racial domination, and location. William H. Chafe, *Civilities and Civil Rights: Greensboro, North Carolina, and the Black Struggle for Freedom* (New York: Oxford University Press, 1980), John Dittmer, *Local People: The Struggle for Civil Rights in Mississippi* (Urbana: University of Illinois Press, 1994), and Robert J. Norrell, *Reaping the Whirlwind: The Civil Rights Movement in Tuskegee* (New York: Knopf, 1985) are exemplary works in this regard. Robert Self, *American Babylon: Race and the Struggle for Postwar Oakland* (Princeton: Princeton University Press, 2003), Suzanne Smith, *Dancing in the Street: Motown and the Cultural Politics of Detroit* (Cambridge, Mass.: Harvard University Press, 1999) and the essays in Jeanne Theoharis and Komozi Woodard, eds., *Freedom North: Black Freedom Struggles Outside the South, 1940–1980* (New York: Palgrave Macmillan, 2003) have begun the crucial work of shifting our focus from the South to the nation as a whole.

These scholarly accounts are inflected in profound ways by James Forman, *The Making of Black Revolutionaries* (New York: Macmillan, 1972), since Forman was the organizer par excellence of the assault on Jim Crow. From a very different personal perspective, a remarkable angle on the urban, usually Northern milieus that bred Black Power is found in Amiri Baraka: *The Autobiography of LeRoi Jones* (Chicago: Lawrence Hill Books, 1997). Equally important is Grace Lee Boggs, *Living for Change: An Autobiography* (Minneapolis: University of Minnesota Press, 1998).

Regarding Malcolm X and the Nation of Islam as one root of the Black Power movement, Essien Essien-Udom, *Black Nationalism: A Search for Identity in America* (Chicago: University of Chicago Press, 1962) is remarkably fresh. William Strickland, *Malcolm X: Make It Plain* (New York: Penguin, 1994) captures this remarkable personality better than any of the biographical studies, and William Sales, Jr., *From Civil Rights to Black Liberation: Malcolm X and the Organization of Afro-American Unity* (Boston: South End Press, 1994) has important insights about his last year, especially when combined with Jan Carew, *Ghosts in Our Blood: With Malcolm X in Africa, England and the Caribbean* (Chicago: Lawrence Hill, 1994). Otherwise, the narrative of Black Power's origins in this book largely derives from my own research and interviews for a forthcoming book.

Chapter 5

Any study of the peace movement during the Cold War must depart from Lawrence Wittner's impressive scholarship, in *The Struggle Against the Bomb: One World Or None—A History of the World Nuclear Disarmament Movement Through 1953* (Stanford, Calif.: Stanford University Press, 1993) and *The Struggle Against the Bomb: Resisting the Bomb—A History of the World Nuclear Disarmament Movement, 1954–1970* (Stanford, Calif.: Stanford University Press, 1998). Milton S. Katz, *Ban the Bomb: A History of SANE, the Committee for a Sane Nuclear Policy* (New York: Praeger, 1986) opens up the world of liberal peace activism. Amy Swerdlow, *Women Strike for Peace: Traditional Motherhood and Radical Politics in the 1960s* (Chicago: University of Chicago Press, 1993) empathically examines a particular strain within the reviving movement. Again,

Isserman, *If I Had a Hammer*, is important, because of his treatment of *Liberation* and the Committee for Non-Violent Action.

Other than Richard Welch's anecdotal *Response to Revolution: The United States and the Cuban Revolution, 1959–1961* (Chapel Hill: University of North Carolina Press, 1985), no one had studied the Fair Play for Cuba Committee before my *Where the Boys Are: Cuba, Cold War America and the Making of a New Left* (London: Verso, 1993). My study also places considerable emphasis on the popular cultural response in the United States to Castro in 1957–1958 and the longer history of solidarity with Latin American revolution.

Chapter 6

The books already cited by Maurice Isserman, James Miller and Todd Gitlin are all central to understanding the student left, and all depart from Kirkpatrick Sale, *SDS* (New York: Random House, 1973). The volume edited by Paul Buhle, *History and the New Left: Madison, Wisconsin, 1950–1970* (Philadelphia: Temple University Press, 1990) captures much of the distinctive character of the Madison New Left in the 1950s and after. W. J. Rorabaugh, *Berkeley at War: The 1960s* (New York: Oxford University Press, 1989) is a fine, panoramic study linking town and gown in the East Bay. Douglas Rossinow, *The Politics of Authenticity: Liberalism, Christianity and the New Left in America* (New York: Columbia University Press, 1998) is the most in-depth local history, covering all the phases of the white left at the University of Texas in Austin from the late 1950s on. On the Free Speech Movement, see the remarkable collection of analytical essays, mainly by participants, in Robert Cohen and Reginald Zelnik, *The Free Speech Movement: Reflections on Berkeley in the 1960s* (Berkeley: University of California Press, 2002).

Chapter 7

Over the past two decades, beginning with Cynthia Harrison, *On Account of Sex: The Politics of Women's Issues, 1945–1968* (Berkeley: University of California Press, 1988) and Leila J. Rupp and Verta Taylor, *Survival in the Doldrums: The American Women's Rights Movement, 1945 to the 1960s* (Columbus: Ohio State University Press, 1990), there has been an extensive reconstruction of the women's politics in the 1945–1965 decades. More recent works include Susan M. Hartmann, *The Other Feminists: Activists in the Liberal Establishment* (New Haven, Conn.: Yale University Press, 1998) and the wide-ranging studies collected in Joanne Meyerowitz, ed., *Not June Cleaver: Women and Gender in Postwar America, 1945–1960* (Philadelphia: Temple University Press, 1994). Especially important recent works include Daniel Horowitz, *Betty Friedan and the Making of "The Feminine Mystique": The American Left, the Cold War, and Modern Feminism* (Amherst: University of Massachusetts Press, 1998) and Dorothy Sue Cobble, *The Other Women's Movement: Workplace Justice and Social Rights in Modern America* (Princeton: Princeton University Press, 2004), which forces one to move women in the labor movement to the forefront of a narrative formerly focusing on business and professional women.

The scholarship on homophile politics is relatively sparse. D'Emilio's *Sexual Politics, Sexual Communities* remains indispensable, and is ably complimented by Marc Stein's massive community study, *City of Sisterly and Brotherly Loves: Lesbian and Gay Philadelphia, 1945–1972* (Chicago: University of Chicago Press, 2000).

Chapter 8

The only study of the antiwar movement that is both comprehensive and measured is Charles DeBenedetti, with Charles Chatfield, *An American Ordeal: The Antiwar Movement of the Vietnam Era* (Syracuse, NY: Syracuse University Press, 1990). Anyone seeking to understand its Byzantine inner politics should read the narrative of the Socialist Workers Party leader Fred Halstead, *Out Now! A Participant's Account of the American Movement Against the Vietnam War*

(New York: Pathfinder, 1978). Otherwise, I found David Farber, *Chicago '68* (Chicago: University of Chicago Press, 1988) very helpful in getting at how the movement's different wings understood and portrayed themselves at a particularly dramatic moment.

Specific sectors within the antiwar movement have their own historians. The Catholic Left is best approached via Charles Meconis, *With Clumsy Grace: The American Catholic Left, 1961–1975* (New York: Seabury Press, 1979), though much more scholarship is needed. Mitchell K. Hall, *Because of Their Faith: CALCAV and Religious Opposition to the Vietnam War* (New York: Columbia University Press, 1990) examines another form of religious dissent. The movement within the military and among veterans has several effective chroniclers, including Richard Moser, *The New Winter Soldiers: GI and Veteran Dissent During the Vietnam Era* (New Brunswick, NJ: Rutgers University Press, 1996), and Andrew Hunt, *The Turning: A History of Vietnam Veterans Against the War* (New York: New York University Press, 1999). The turn to violent resistance is covered in Ron Jacobs, *The Way the Wind Blew: A History of the Weather Underground* (London: Verso, 1997). More recently, Jeremy Varon has added a useful comparative emphasis, in *Bringing the War Home: the Weather Underground, the Red Army Faction, and Revolutionary Violence in the Sixties and Seventies* (Berkeley: University of California Press, 2004). Most recent and of particular importance is Michael S. Foley, *Confronting the War Machine: Draft Resistance During the Vietnam War* (Chapel Hill: University of North Carolina Press, 2003).

Chapter 9

To a significant extent, this chapter synthesizes my own research. The starting point for understanding the Black Power movement remain the key texts of the time, including Forman's *The Making of Black Revolutionaries*, Stokely Carmichael and Charles V. Hamilton, *Black Power: The Politics of Liberation in America* (New York: Random House, 1967), Harold Cruse, *The Crisis of the Negro Intellectual: A Historical Analysis of the Failure of Black Leadership* (New York: William Morrow, 1967) and *Rebellion or Revolution?* (New York: William Morrow, 1968), and Chuck Stone, *Black Political Power in America* (Indianapolis: Dobbs-Merrill, 1968), as well as the documents in Floyd B. Barbour, *The Black Power Revolt: A Collection of Essay* (Boston: P. Sargent, 1968). A crucial addition is a remarkable piece of contemporary scholarship, Dan Georgakas and Marvin Surkin, *Detroit: I Do Mind Dying, A Study in Urban Revolution* (New York: St. Martin's, 1975), which chronicles the League of Revolutionary Black Workers.

The only comprehensive scholarly work is William L. Van DeBurg, *New Day in Babylon: The Black Power Movement and American Culture, 1965–1975* (Chicago: University of Chicago Press, 1992), which suffers from a lack of historical context, but presents a great deal of useful evidence. Komozi Woodard, *A Nation Within a Nation: Amiri Baraka (LeRoi Jones) and Black Power Politics* (Chapel Hill: University of North Carolina Press, 1999) covers a key individual and a major site of action. Baraka was part of a larger self-conscious "cultural nationalism" defined by Maulana Ron Karenga, and Scot Brown, *Fighting for US: Maulana Karenga, the US Organization, and Black Cultural Nationalism* (New York: New York University Press, 2003) finally brings some balance to our understanding of this important figure. Anyone interested in the Black Arts Movement, a major complement to Black Power, should consult the anthology edited by Baraka and Larry Neal, *Black Fire: An Anthology of Afro-American Writing* (New York: William Morrow, 1968) and James Edward Smethurst, *The Black Arts Movement: Literary Nationalism in the 1960s and 1970s* (Chapel Hill: University of North Carolina Press, 2005).

The Black Panther Party awaits a serious historian. Until then, there are various famous writings from the time by Bobby Seale and Huey P. Newton, and more recent memoirs, by Elaine Brown, *A Taste of Power: A Black Woman's Story* (New York: Pantheon, 1992) and David Hilliard and Lewis Cole, *This Side of Glory: The Autobiography of David Hilliard and the Story of the Black Panther Party* (Boston: Little, Brown, 1993). The collection edited by Charles E. Johnson, *The Black Panther Party Reconsidered* (Baltimore: Black Classic Press, 1998) is remarkably valuable, encompassing scholarly analysis, memoirs, and oral histories.

Chapter 10

On the Native American struggle, there is an excellent and accessible narrative in Paul Chatt Smith and Robert Allen Warrior, *Like a Hurricane: The Indian Movement from Alcatraz to Wounded Knee* (New York: The New Press, 1996). It is fleshed out by the articles and documents in the definitive collection edited by Alvin M. Josephy, Jr., Joane Nagel and Troy Johnson, *Red Power: The American Indians' Fight for Freedom*, 2nd ed. (Lincoln: University of Nebraska Press, 1999). For a contemporary sense of this movement's early days, before AIM, see Stan Steiner, *The New Indians* (New York: Harper and Row, 1967) helpful.

Carlos Munoz, Jr., *Youth, Identity, Power: The Chicano Movement* (London: Verso, 1989) is a politically acute account by a veteran who is also a scholar. More recently,). Ernesto Chavez, *"Mi Raza Primero!" (My People First!): Nationalism, Identity, and Insurgency in the Chicano Movement in Los Angeles, 1966–1978* (Berkeley: University of California Press, 2002) offers the first focused local study of *Chicanismo* from a historian's perspective. Other scholarship, mostly by political scientists, includes Armando Navarro, *La Raza Unida Party: A Chicano Challenge to the U.S. Two-Party Dictatorship* (Philadelphia: Temple University Press, 2000), Ignacio M. Garcia, *Chicanismo: The Forging of a Militant Ethos Among Mexican Americans* (Tucson: University of Arizona Press, 1997), and Juan Gomez-Quinones, *Chicano Politics: Reality and Promise, 1940–1990* (Albuquerque: University of New Mexico Press, 1990).

For the Puerto Rican movement, start with Andres Torres and Jose E. Velazquez, eds., *The Puerto Rican Movement: Voices from the Diaspora* (Philadelphia: Temple University Press, 1998). The arresting photo-diary, Michael Abramson, *Palante, Young Lords Party* (New York: McGraw Hill, 1971) is a great accompaniment, however, to understanding this movement that remains little known outside of the New York area. The major primer to the Asian American movement is a collection of documents and reflections, edited by Steve Louie and Glenn Omatsu, *Asian Americans: The Movement and the Moment* (Los Angeles: UCLA Asian American Studies Center Press, 2001). William Wei, *The Asian American Movement* (Philadelphia: Temple University Press, 1993) is a scholarly summary, though it misses many major developments.

Chapter 11

Besides Evans' *Personal Politics*, another important early study is Jo Freeman, *The Politics of Women's Liberation: A Case Study of an Emerging Social Movement and Its Relation to the Policy Process* (New York: McKay, 1975). Alice Echols, *Daring to Be Bad: Radical Feminism in America, 1967–1975* (Minneapolis: University of Minnesota Press, 1989) is still definitive, though some have noted its geographic focus on the northeast. Flora Davis, *Moving the Mountain: The Women's Movement in America Since 1960* (Urbana: University of Illinois Press, 1999) is lesser-known but especially useful on tracing the broader movement's engagement with conventional politics. The most recent major history, Ruth Rosen, *The World Split Open: How the Modern Women's Movement Changed America* (New York: Viking, 2000) is strong on the cultural milieus of second-wave feminism. All of these are complimented by the enormous range of documents in Rosalyn Baxandall and Linda Gordon, Linda, eds., *Dear Sisters: Dispatches from the Women's Liberation Movement* (New York: Basic Books, 2000). Finally, I relied on Benita Roth, *Separate Roads to Feminism: Black, Chicana, and White Feminist Movements in America's Second Wave* (Cambridge: Cambridge University Press, 2004) to break out of a narrative that centers on the activism of white women.

Chapter 12

Barry D. Adam, *The Rise of the Gay and Lesbian Movement* (Boston: Twayne, 1987) provided the background on homosexual politics in Europe. Stuart Timmons, *The Trouble with Harry Hay: Founder of the Modern Gay Movement* (Boston: Alyson, 1990) compliments D'Emilio's *Sexual Politics, Sexual Communities*. Dudley Clendinen and Adam Nagourney, *Out for Good: The Struggle to Build a Gay Rights Movement in America* (New York: Simon and Schuster, 1999) provides a lively general narrative of how gay liberation turned to gay rights. Donn Teal, *The Gay Militants: How Gay Liberation Began in America, 1969–1971* (New York: Stein and Day, 1971) opens up those early liberatory days with terrific detail, as does Martin Duberman, *Stonewall* (New York: Dutton, 1993). An article by Justin David Suran, "Coming Out Against the War: Antimilitarism and the Politicization of Homosexuality in the Era of Vietnam," *American Quarterly*, 55/3 (2001): 452–488, offers a crucial insight about the relation of gay liberation to the larger left. Finally, all of my understanding of gay and lesbian politics has been shaped by the essays of Jeffrey Escoffier, collected in *American Homo: Community and Perversity* (Berkeley: University of California, 1998) and his essay, "Fabulous Politics: Gay, Lesbian, and Queer Movements, 1969–1999," in the recent collection edited by Richard Moser and myself, *The World the Sixties Made: Politics and Culture in Recent America* (Philadelphia: Temple University Press, 2003), pp. 191–218.

Chapter 13

Books that help one get at the under-studied late years of the New Left include Sandra Levinson and Carol Brightman *Venceremos Brigade: Young Americans Sharing the Life and Work of Revolutionary Cuba* (New York: Simon and Schuster, 1971) and Eric Cummins, *The Rise and Fall of California's Radical Prison Movement* (Stanford, Calif.: Stanford University Press, 1994). Max Elbaum, *Revolution in the Air: Sixties Radicals Turn to Lenin, Mao and Che* (London: Verso, 2002) is a brilliant excavation of a radicalism outside the pale for many radicals. Peter Braunstein and Michael William Doyle, eds., *Imagine Nation: The American Counterculture of the 1960s and '70s* (New York: Routledge, 2002) is the best single volume on that chaotic topic. A recent article by Gael Graham, "Flaunting the Freak Flag: *Karr v. Schmidt* and the Great Hair Debate in American High Schools, 1965–1975, *Journal of American History* (2004): 522–543, is crucial to opening up the larger history of what we mean by the "counter-culture," and its actual relationship to political dissent. In terms of what comes after 1975, and a continuity from the late 1960s stretching into the Reagan years, any serious reader should consult Barbara Epstein, *Political Protest and Cultural Revolution: Nonviolent Direct Action in the 1970s and 1980s* (Berkeley: University of California Press, 1991)

Other than hostile polemics by neoconservative renegades from the New Left, like David Horowitz and Ronald Radosh, or dystopians convinced that the New Left signally failed, like Todd Gitlin, Jim Sleeper, and Michael Tomasky, there is remarkably little actual scholarship that examines the long-term impact of the radical social movements post-1945. Most unfortunate is that the voices of white men have dominated this argument, all arguing from one or another vantage point the failures and excesses of radicalism and "identity politics," so-called. *The World the Sixties Made* is an effort to move beyond diatribes and unquestioned premises about a conservative ascendance. In an introductory essay, "Post-Modern America: A New Democratic Order in a Second Gilded Age," I argue that the unending trench warfare of the past three decades signals both the continuing centrality of the movements of the New Left to our political life. Writing this at a moment when the New Right exercises a sweeping, if to me very precarious, hold over all branches of the federal government, it remains to be seen whether this assessment of the century's last quarter is an exercise in unwarranted optimism, or a more sober assessment than others.

Index

Pritchett, Laurie, 40
Progressive Association of
    Spanish-Speaking Organizations
    (PASSO), 141
Progressive Era, 209
Progressive Labor Party (PLP), 100–1
Progressive Party, 14
Progressive tradition, 66
Protestant churches, 83
PSP, *see Partido Socialista Puertorriqueño*
    (PSP)
psychedelics, 202, 203, *see* LSD
Public Citizen, 201
Public Interest Research Groups, 201
Puerto Rican Independence Party, *see*
    Partido Independentista
    Puertorriqueño (PIP)
Puerto Rican Legal Defense and
    Education Fund, 149
Puerto Rican movement, 148–51
Puerto Rican Nationalist Party, 148, 150
Puerto Rican Revolutionary Workers
    Organization, 149
Puerto Rican Solidarity Committee, 150
Puerto Rican Student Union, 149
Puerto Ricans, 126, 133, 148–9
Puerto Rican Socialist Party, *see*
    Partido Socialista Puertorriqueño
    (PSP)
Puerto Rico, 148
Puzo, Mario, 126

Quakers (Religious Society of Friends),
    27, 136

Radical America, 200
Radical Feminists, The, 159, 160
Radical History Review, 200
Radicalesbians, 172
radical liberalism, 190, 191–4
Radical Teacher, 200
Radio Free Dixie (*see also* Robert F.
    Williams), 50
Rainbow Alliance, 149
Rainbow Coalition, 128, 201
Ramparts, 97
Randall, Dudley, 120
Randolph, A. Philip, 17, 43
Rapid City, South Dakota, 139
Ray, James Earl, 95

Raza Unida Party (United Race Party),
    101, 145–6, 191, 195
Reagan Revolution, 209
Reagan, Ronald, 71, 102, 124, 200, 201, 209
Reconstruction, 20, 46, 118
red diaper babies, 71, 78
Red Guards, 147
Redstockings, 153, 159, 166
Reeb, James, 46
Republican Party (*see also* Dwight
    Eisenhower, George W. Bush, New
    Right, Richard Nixon, Ronald
    Reagan), 5, 12, 13, 32, 34, 37, 45, 74,
    119, 122, 175, 177, 183, 193, 209–10
    African Americans and, 125
    National Convention (1952), 13
    Vietnam and, 88
Republic of New Africa, 122
Reserve Officers Training Corps (ROTC),
    66, 67, 105
Resistance, The, 92, 98, 159
Reuther, Walter, 25
Revolutionary Action Movement, 50, 117
Revolutionary Communist Party, 196
revolutionary nationalism, 121
Revolutionary Peoples Constitutional
    Convention, 127, 189
Revolutionary Union, 196
Revolutionary Union Movements
    (RUMs), 119
Revolutionary Youth Movement, 100
Rhodes, James, 105
Rhodesia, 127
Ribicoff, Abraham, 95
Richardson, Bill, 146
Richardson, Gloria, 50
Ricks, Willie, 116
Rivera, Geraldo, 150
Riverside Church (New York city), 94
Roach, Max, 50, 51
Robeson, Paul, 24, 33, 120
Robinson, Jo Ann Gibson, 33
Robinson, Marty, 177, 178
Robinson, Ruby Doris Smith, 158
Rockefeller, Nelson, 196
Roe v. Wade, 4, 162–3, 182, 201
Rolling Stone, 207
Rolling Stones, 207, 208
Romany (gypsies), 79
Roosevelt, Eleanor, 17, 23, 56, 77